What Are
the Seven Wonders
of the World?

What are the Seven Wonders of the World?

And 60 Other Great Cultural Questions

PETER D'EPIRO AND
MARY DESMOND PINKOWISH

Decorations by Richard Beards

THE FOLIO SOCIETY
London 2005

What Are the Seven Wonders of the World? And 60 Other Great Cultural Questions is an abridgement of the revised United Kingdom edition, first published in 1999 by Metro Books as *What Are the Seven Wonders of the World? And Other Great Cultural Lists — Fully Described.*

This edition is published by arrangement with Peter D'Epiro and Mary Desmond Pinkowish, and Vintage Anchor Publishing, a division of Random House, Inc.

This edition published by The Folio Society Ltd
44 Eagle Street, London WC1R 4FS
www.foliosociety.com

The quotation from *The Cantos* of Ezra Pound is from Canto LXXIV by Ezra Pound. © 1948 Ezra Pound. Reprinted by permission of New Directions Publishing Corp.

The verses from Dante in essay 10 are from Peter D'Epiro's translation of Canto 9 of the *Inferno*, reprinted from *Prairie Schooner* by permission of the University of Nebraska Press. © 1989 University of Nebraska Press.

Set in Joanna at The Folio Society
Printed on Abbey Wove paper by Grafos S. A.,
Barcelona, Spain, and quarter-bound by them in buckram
with paper sides printed with a design by Richard Beards

Tenth printing 2013

To study with the white wings of time passing
is not that our delight?

EZRA POUND, *The Pisan Cantos*

CONTENTS

viii

Which 12 people would the authors like to thank for their gracious help?

Dante D'Epiro
who wrote the essay for Question 23.

Nancy Walsh D'Epiro
who contributed the essays for 20, 27 and 55; made cogent criticisms throughout; and coped with it all.

Edward W. Desmond
who wrote the essay for 60.

Joan Frawley Desmond
who collaborated with us on the essay for 31.

Thomas Matrullo
bos amic, who wrote the essays for 30 and 37 and subjected a goodly number of others to his learned scrutiny.

The commentators on large chunks of the manuscript:

Vladimir Babadzhan, PhD, Vivian Dudro, Richard Jackson, PhD and Morgan Ryan.

Michael Pinkowish
who provided his mother with invaluable late-night commentary on essay 51 (although he should have been in bed).

Peter Pinkowish
for red sauce, black coffee and lots of patience.

And Raphael Sagalyn
our agent, who believed in us from the start.

For our fathers
ANTHONY D'EPIRO
and
JOHN F. DESMOND

How many loved your moments of glad grace.

WILLIAM BUTLER YEATS

INTRODUCTION

A flock of sheep that leisurely pass by,
One after one . . .
I have thought of all by turns and yet do lie
Sleepless!

WILLIAM WORDSWORTH
To Sleep. II, A Flock of Sheep

Wordsworth . . . was a silly old sheep.
EZRA POUND

IF WORDSWORTH could have read this book, he would have counted other things besides sheep. His mind would have been so well stocked with great cultural lists that he could at least have amused and edified himself by recalling the seven wonders of the ancient world (Question 30) or the names and associated arts of the Nine Muses (Question 47), even if he didn't sleep a wink all night. The next day he could have had some fun using these lists to quiz Coleridge and his other Lake District pals.

What Are the Seven Wonders of the World? presents a fund of information that even people who aren't famed poets will enjoy becoming acquainted with, or meeting again after a long estrangement. The book contains sixty-one of the most culturally significant lists that we could devise over several pensive years – our own personal omnium gatherum of high culture as embodied in various canonical listings and numeric groupings.

Each question with its accompanying list is followed by an essay that identifies all the items of the answer and places the list in its larger historical or cultural context. Many readers will heartily disagree with our inclusions and omissions, but our guiding principle has been to choose materials we considered to be fundamental components of educated western awareness. We have excluded pop culture, sports and celebrity trivia, since information in these areas is not lacking elsewhere and only somewhat enhances our ability to lead a more satisfying intellectual life.

The attribution of mystical and sacred properties to numbers and numbered lists has a long history. In early Christianity, the numbers three, seven, ten and twelve were especially venerated because of their associations with the Persons of the Trinity, days of Creation, Commandments and Apostles, respectively (the latter three referred to in Questions 31, 53 and 59). In Jewish tradition, *gematria* was the numerological interpretation of words and phrases in Scripture. And in the ancient Greek world, the Pythagoreans claimed that the entire cosmos was made of numbers. They practically worshipped the *tetractys*, a triangle envisioned with one point at its apex, two beneath it, three beneath those and four at the base, which embraced unity, duality, the mystical number three, and four, the number of justice and of the elements (Question 14) – all adding up to ten, the perfect and sacred number.

Though neither of us is a practising Pythagorean, we thought it would be fun and instructive to compose a challenging question-and-answer book organised around numbered lists that have become 'standard' (the 7 deadly sins, the 12 labours of Heracles) or that otherwise convey significant cultural data via numeric groupings. Whether you read, browse, test yourself or quiz your family and friends, we hope you enjoy this attempt to convey some of the western world's age-old fascination with hierarchies and discernments which is still apparent in all our Top 10s, Top 40s and Fortune 500s.

All sixty-one essays in the Folio Society edition have been carefully reviewed and we have revised a goodly number of details that, after six years, fairly cried out for fine-tuning or updating.

PETER D'EPIRO

MARY DESMOND PINKOWISH

THREE

QUESTION 1

Who were the 3 sons of Adam and Eve?

Cain
Abel
Seth

O F COURSE, you knew Cain and Abel, but what about Seth? If not, consider the fact that the Bible strongly implies that Seth, and not his more illustrious siblings, was the ancestor of us all.

Let's start with **Cain** and **Abel**. In the book of Genesis, Cain is a tiller of the soil whose offering of the fruits of the earth is deemed unacceptable by God. His brother Abel, a keeper of flocks, makes an offering of one of his best firstlings, on which God looks favourably. In a pique of jealousy, Cain lures his brother into a field and kills him. When God asks him the whereabouts of Abel, Cain counters with his famous rhetorical question: 'Am I my brother's keeper?'

Since Cain has desecrated the soil with Abel's blood, which cries out to God for vengeance, the ground will no longer bear fruit for him. When God condemns him to a nomadic existence, Cain fears that his wandering life will make him an easy target for xenophobes: 'Anyone may kill me at sight.' God thus puts a mark on Cain – probably a tattoo – to warn off any potential assailants. And so Cain goes off and settles to the east of Eden in the land of Nod, which merely means 'the land of the nomads' but has given rise to countless jokes about boring sermons and their somnolent effect on churchgoers.

Note that 'the mark of Cain' was not originally meant to brand him as a murderer, as in our usage, but to *protect* him from other murderers.

Yet several questions suggest themselves. If the only people in the world at this time are Adam, Eve and Cain, whom is Cain so afraid of? And when he becomes the father of Enoch (not the better-known Enoch who was the father of Methuselah and was taken up alive into Heaven) – where had Cain found a wife? She must have been one of the unnamed daughters of Adam and Eve who, along with other unnamed sons, are mentioned in Genesis 5:4. But what was she doing in the land of Nod? In any event, among Cain's descendants we meet the world's first bigamist, Lamech; the first musician, Jubal; and the first metalworker, Tubalcain.

Why does God reject Cain's offering? There must be something missing in our biblical text: Cain must have sacrificed in a way that was alien to the ancient Hebrews. Later assertions in the New Testament try to posit a reason: 'By faith Abel offered unto God a more excellent sacrifice than Cain' (Hebrews 11:4). In 1 John 3:12 we read that Cain killed Abel 'because his own works were evil and his brother's righteous'. Or was it simply a case of God's 'election' of Abel – that is, an instance of Calvinist predestination, which assumes that God chooses certain individuals for salvation and condemns others to damnation only because it is his own inscrutable will?

But what about **Seth** (or Sheth)? Adam sires him, at the age of 130, to take the place of Abel. And although Abel was later viewed as a foreshadowing (or 'type') of Christ (because both were good shepherds whose blood was shed unjustly), the genealogy of Christ is none the less traced back to Adam and God through Seth (Luke 3:38). Presumably Abel is killed before he has a chance to propagate – the Bible mentions no descendants – and to trace Christ's descent through the fratricidal Cain (or one of his anonymous brothers) would have been inconceivable. In fact, in one of the authorial strands in Genesis, that of the so-called priestly tradition, Seth is considered the firstborn of Adam and Eve, and Adam's line is followed forward to Noah and the Flood (and presumably to all of us) through Seth (Genesis 5).

It's ironic that, unlike Cain the brother-slayer or Abel the original victim of violent crime, Seth remains a colourless figure, a man without a story, almost a nonentity. His name seems to mean 'granted', because God granted him to Adam and Eve after Abel's death – and we tend to take him a bit for granted, too. Like all the patriarchs, Seth was blessed with great genes: he had a son Enosh (or Enos) at the age of 105 and lived a total of 912 years (just eighteen fewer than Adam). That's it, though. We don't even know what line of work old Seth was in. It's probably enough to have the entire human race trace its descent through him.

Who are the 3 gods of the Hindu Trinity (the Trimurti)?

Brahma
Vishnu
Shiva

THE THREE GODS of the Trimurti (Sanskrit, 'three forms') are really more of a chief triad of Hindu deities (in a pantheon of about thirty million) than a Trinity in the Christian sense. They embody the supreme, impersonal, eternal, universal Spirit or World-Soul, Brahman, in its threefold aspect as creator, preserver and destroyer.

But the creator god **Brahma** must not be confused with Brahman (the absolute World-Spirit mentioned above) or with Brahmans (or Brahmins), the members of the highest Hindu caste. Born from the lotus in Vishnu's navel, Brahma is often portrayed as a four-faced god sitting on a lotus flower. With his own hand, on leaves of gold, he is said to have written the *Rig-Veda*, a collection of 1,028 ancient Sanskrit hymns to the gods.

Worship of Brahma petered out because once his main job of creating the universe was done, the ball was in Vishnu's and Shiva's court. Or perhaps we should say the egg, since some Hindu writings speculate that Brahma laid and hatched the egg of the universe. Hindu tradition also asserts that a day in the life of Brahma lasts one *kalpa*, or 4,320,000,000 years. After each 'day of Brahma', all that exists is destroyed, only to be reborn in the eternal cycle of death and creation.

Vishnu, the preserver god, has had nine major avatars (incarnations) and the tenth and last will be Kalki, the rider on a white horse who, sword blazing in hand, will put an end to all sin and sinners. Among Vishnu's avatars were his seventh, as Ramachandra or Rama, his eighth as Krishna and his ninth as Buddha. Rama is the hero of the Sanskrit epic, the *Ramayana*, in which the young protagonist regains his kingdom and his bride in a mere fifty thousand lines of verse. Later, when a tyrannical demon-king was wreaking havoc in India, Krishna descended to earth after Vishnu plucked a black hair from himself – which became Krishna ('black'), who's often represented in art as black or dark blue. Krishna appears as a mighty warrior in the other great Sanskrit epic, the *Mahabharata*, which, at more than two hundred thousand lines, is the undisputed heavyweight champion of the poetic world.

Vishnu is probably the most popular Hindu god, willingly incarnating himself to save the world and mankind from various giants, demons, tyrants and other calamities. 'When order, justice and mortals are in danger,' said Vishnu, 'I come down to earth.' Many Hindus worship him as the supreme deity. Early in the twentieth century, Indian Christians feared that Christ would also be assimilated into the figure of Vishnu by being considered just one more of his avatars. Vishnu is a god of love through and through, and his greatest avatar, Krishna, is often shown playing a flute to attract the *gopis* (milkmaids he has seduced) to dance with him in the moonlight.

The destroyer god **Shiva** is a composite figure. His fierceness is counterbalanced by kinder, gentler qualities that make him a favourite deity of ascetics and a patron of arts, letters, music and dancing. His most famous representations show him as a white, four-armed figure performing his cosmic dance on the body of a nasty little demon whose back he has broken. The dance of Shiva symbolises the eternal alternation of destruction and creation in the universe since, in Hindu thought, destruction always implies a subsequent restoration.

This idea is responsible for another major aspect of Shiva: his lordship over the powers of fertility and reproduction. As such, his symbol is the lingam, or phallus (as his consort's emblem is the yoni, or vulva). Shiva's phallus is said to be so enormous that even with Brahma travelling up as far as he could and Vishnu journeying down as far as *he* could, neither of them managed to discover where that epic phallus began or ended. Shiva is certainly a god of contradictions: he drinks a narcotic potion made of hemp (and some of his statues show him with 'stoned' eyes), but he also practises yoga. He protects cattle, but he's also the source of the fire that destroys the universe at the appointed end of its aeons. And he has an evil third eye in his forehead that he usually keeps closed because, when he doesn't, it acts much like a flame-thrower.

Unlike Vishnu, Shiva is more esteemed for his consorts than for his avatars. His principal consort Kali ('The Black One') is a bloodthirsty goddess indeed. Our word *thugs* originally referred to her worshippers in northern India who ritually strangled human victims to propitiate her. Kali is usually portrayed as a naked black woman with four arms, a protruding tongue dripping blood, fanglike teeth and red eyes. She wears earrings of corpses and a necklace of skulls and is girdled with snakes. Her face and breasts are smeared with blood. Yet Kali is the goddess of motherhood, too.

The Trimurti, represented in art as a male figure with three heads, is still at least theoretically a feature of contemporary Hinduism, although the worship of the second and third deities of the triad, along with their avatars and consorts, has left the cult of Brahma out in the cold.

Who are the 3 daughters of King Lear?

Goneril

Regan

Cordelia

> FOOL ... I can tell why a snail has a house.
> LEAR Why?
> FOOL Why, to put's head in, not to give it away to his
> daughters and leave his horns without a case.
> SHAKESPEARE, *King Lear*, 1.5.28—32

WILLIAM SHAKESPEARE wrote his tragic masterpiece *King Lear* in about 1605, but the story that begins with a bad daughters/good daughter fairy-tale motif and ends in horror was first recorded in England in the twelfth century by Geoffrey of Monmouth in his unhistorical *History of the Kings of Britain*. It also appeared in various guises in the second edition of Raphael Holinshed's *Chronicles of England, Scotlande and Irelande* (1587) and Edmund Spenser's *The Faerie Queen* (1590). Shakespeare's major source, however, was an anonymous play called *The True Chronicle History of King Leir*, written in about 1590 and published in 1605.

Shakespeare's version of the familiar tale is darker than those he encountered in his sources. In choosing a story set in pagan Celtic times, as many as eight centuries before the birth of Christ, he avoided the thematic limitations that a Christian framework might have imposed. He was thus able to probe more deeply and freely the cosmic questions on Providence, Nature and the meaning (or meaninglessness) of life that so intrigued him.

At the beginning of Shakespeare's play, we meet a vain, self-righteous octogenarian, King Lear, who has decided to divide his kingdom among his three daughters. The portion each receives will be commensurate with the love she expresses for him in a public display of affection. Lear expects each to fawn over him and vie with the others in making the most toadying speech.

The elder sisters don't disappoint. Goneril professes to love her father more than 'eyesight, space and liberty'. Regan claims her sister's sentiments are but a pale shadow of her own and that she abjures all joys except that of basking in her father's love. In reward for their fulsome tributes, Lear bestows choice portions of his kingdom on his two worldly-wise daughters.

Cordelia, the youngest, dumbstruck by the simpering hypocrisy of her sisters and despite her deep love for her foolish old father, can't bring herself to make a *beau geste*. To her father's request of what she can say to earn an even richer share, she replies, 'Nothing, my lord,' explaining that she loves him according to her 'bond' (filial obligation). The enraged king disinherits and banishes his favourite child, dividing her portion between his other two daughters. The King of France, however, more perspicacious than Lear, takes the dowerless Cordelia as his wife: 'She is herself a dowry,' he recognises.

As soon as Goneril and Regan have effective power in the kingdom, they turn on their father, mocking him and stripping him of his retinue of knights. Lear soon learns

> How sharper than a serpent's tooth it is
> To have a thankless child.

The two sisters eventually turn him out of doors on a tempestuous night, in which Lear – now attaining the tragic stature of a Sophoclean Oedipus – braves the elements and sounds the raving depths of despair, regret and madness in the company of the faithful Earl of Kent, his Fool, and an apparent lunatic (whom we know to be the Earl of Gloucester's son Edgar, in disguise).

A parallel subplot, derived from Sir Philip Sidney's *Arcadia* (1590), involves the old Earl of Gloucester, who, like Lear, tragically misjudges his children, the bastard Edmund and his legitimate son Edgar. In an attempt to inherit the earldom despite his illegitimacy, Edmund devises a treacherous scheme to disgrace Edgar in their father's eyes.

Shakespeare links this subplot to the main plot when he makes Edmund join forces with Goneril and Regan to fight the invading French army, which Cordelia has mobilised in her father's defence. Ambitious Edmund, seeing a way to the throne, hands over his father Gloucester to Regan's husband, who gouges out the old man's eyes in retaliation for his support of Lear. Edmund then defeats Cordelia's army, capturing her and Lear.

In the meantime, Goneril and Regan, both infatuated with Edmund, spar over his attentions. Goneril eventually poisons Regan and kills herself. Edmund orders Cordelia hanged. As he lies dying after being defeated in a duel by his valiant brother Edgar, he tries, too late, to countermand the order. In the play's final scene, a broken Lear enters carrying Cordelia's body. 'Thou'lt come no more,' he says to her. 'Never, never, never, never, never.' A moment afterwards, the old man dies of his accumulated griefs.

Generations of scholars have debated which of Lear's elder daughters is the more evil. **Goneril** is certainly the stronger leader. Always clear-eyed (unlike her father), she understands that Lear loves Cordelia best and that his banishment of her is a sign of his deteriorating judgement. She suggests to Regan that they may have to deal harshly with him. When the old King goes to live with her, she gives her servant permission to treat him rudely. On her demand that Lear discharge half of his one hundred knights, Lear angrily departs in expectation of better treatment at Regan's hands. Although Goneril has been compared with Lady Macbeth, she is a less complex character, much too consistently hard-hearted ever to succumb to physical or emotional illness as a result of a guilty conscience.

When Lear flees to his second eldest, **Regan**, she greets him with 'O, sir, you are old,' and continues thus:

> . . . You should be ruled, and led
> By some discretion that discerns your state
> Better than you yourself. Therefore I pray you

That to our sister you do make return,
Say you have wronged her.

(2.4.147−51)

Regan is typically described as a pale version of her elder sister, a woman easily led by both Goneril and her own husband, the monstrous Duke of Cornwall. Actually, she is quite as fierce as her sister, a pit bull with no shortage of evil designs of her own:

CORNWALL The army of France is landed. [*To servants*] Seek out the traitor Gloucester.
REGAN Hang him instantly.

When her husband, in one of the most horrific scenes ever staged, scoops out one of Gloucester's eyes (rather than hanging him), Regan urges him to take both: 'One side will mock another. Th' other too.' When an appalled servant tries to stop Cornwall, she kills him herself, but not before he mortally wounds her husband. Widowed, Regan now plans to make Edmund her husband.

This makes the still-wed Goneril so fiercely jealous that she claims she'd rather lose the battle against Cordelia and the French than lose Edmund to her sister. Already teeming with hate, Goneril becomes even more vicious when her husband, the Duke of Albany, expresses remorse over Lear's plight and his intention to make amends. 'O Goneril!' he says:

You are not worth the dust which the rude wind
Blows in your face.

Albany eventually discovers that scheming Goneril has written to Edmund, declaring her love and begging him to kill her husband. That's when this fine flower of womanhood decides to rid the world of her pestilential self.

The two wicked sisters are variously likened, mostly by Lear, to serpents, sea-monsters, wolves, vultures, foxes, dogs, lionesses, tigresses, degenerate bastards, unnatural hags, hogs, boils, plague-sores and embossed carbuncles (swollen tumours). Goneril is said to have a boar's fangs and she is ultimately the more thoroughly depraved of the two. As the renowned Shakespearean critic A. C. Bradley noted, our disgusted reaction to Regan is somewhat mitigated because, unlike Goneril, she didn't commit adultery, plot to murder her husband, co-sign the order for the death of Lear and Cordelia, or poison her sister.

But who is **Cordelia**? Is she a paragon of virtue whose refusal to stoop to glibness unleashes a tragic chain reaction? Is her murder in prison a Christ-like redemptive act linked to the achievement of greater wisdom and insight on the part of Lear, Edgar, Kent, Albany – and perhaps even Edmund? Or do the tragic life and death of this saintly woman express a nihilistic view of human existence?

Shakespeare probably intended Cordelia to symbolise untainted virtue. She is distant, even from the other decent characters. An unidentified gentleman describes her as one 'who redeems nature from the general curse' (4.6.209). Her tears are 'holy water from her heavenly eyes' (4.3.31).

In an aside, during the public flattery contest in the first scene of the play, Cordelia leaves no doubt of her own sincerity:

> . . . I am sure my love's
> More ponderous than my tongue.

When her turn comes, she declares plainly,

> Unhappy that I am, I cannot heave
> My heart into my mouth. I love your Majesty
> According to my bond, no more nor less.

The stunned Lear exhorts her,

> . . . Mend your speech a little,
> Lest you may mar your fortunes.

Cordelia responds to Lear's attempt to extort love (via an economic threat) with a reminder that she must save half her love for a future husband. She finds it odd that her sisters have husbands, yet have given all their love to their father. When Cordelia emphasises her truthfulness, Lear's rejoinder is 'Thy truth then be thy dower!' once again linking her deficient profession of love to financial loss. Is Cordelia just being stiff-necked? The King of France, who has witnessed the scene, doesn't think so. Interpreting her behaviour as the mark of a sterling character, he takes the disinherited Cordelia as his wife.

Shakespeare's refusal to give his play a poetically just or melodramatic ending, with the innocent Cordelia surviving, was considered so unbearable that for about 150 years English audiences could see only a 1681 version of *King Lear* by Nahum Tate, who rewrote about half of the play. In this version, Lear, Cordelia and Gloucester survive and Cordelia marries Edgar. In 1823, the legendary British actor Edmund Kean finally restored Shakespeare's ending, and by the end of the 1830s the original version of the play was again the standard.

In Tate's happy-ending reworking, the play ends with Edgar's line, 'Truth and Vertue shall at last succeed.' The stern moralist and Shakespearean editor and critic Samuel Johnson (1709–84) preferred Tate's version because Cordelia 'retired with victory and felicity'. This is a far cry indeed from the prevailing tone of the play and from the sentiment Shakespeare put into blind old Gloucester's mouth:

> As flies to wanton boys are we to th' gods,
> They kill us for their sport.

Who are the 3 Musketeers?

Athos
Porthos
Aramis

'ALL FOR ONE, one for all!' You know it even if you haven't read the book – the rallying cry of the Three Musketeers and their protégé, D'Artagnan, as they swashbuckle their way through seventeenth-century France during the reign of Louis XIII.

The plot of Les Trois Mousquetaires, by Alexandre Dumas, goes something like this. In 1625, a poor young man from the countryside, D'Artagnan, arrives in Paris after several adventures along the way, including a scuffle with a scar-faced man who had mocked his yellow pony. Determined to join the Musketeers (who served the King of France as guards), D'Artagnan soon duels with Athos, Porthos and Aramis, the cream of the Musketeers, but wins their admiration when he helps them drive off the guard of the King's scheming enemy, Cardinal Richelieu. Soon admitted to the Musketeers as an apprentice, D'Artagnan learns that **Athos** is gallant, of noble bearing and a bit mysterious about his background and love life. Not so **Porthos**, who is strong, less intellectually inclined and given to bragging about his female conquests. **Aramis** views his tenure in the Guard as just a stop on the way to the cloister.

Bankruptcy looms for the Musketeers, who have spent all the gold given them by the King for their help against the Cardinal. An apparent solution presents itself when D'Artagnan's landlord, Bonacieux, says he will forgive the overdue rent if D'Artagnan and his friends find his wife Constance, who has been abducted by a man whose description reminds D'Artagnan of the man with the scar.

As the Queen's dressmaker and go-between, Constance knows much of her romantic involvement with the English Duke of Buckingham. This information is irresistibly tempting to the Cardinal in his quest to destabilise the royal household and further his own power. Constance frees herself from her abductors and, in the ensuing chase and scuffle, meets D'Artagnan, who falls in love with her on the spot. Constance is too busy to discuss the situation, however, since she must take the disguised Buckingham to meet the Queen, who gives him twelve diamond studs as a token of her love. The ubiquitous Cardinal learns of this gift and, knowing that the diamonds were a present from the King to the Queen, decides to enlighten the monarch as to their current whereabouts.

How lucky the Cardinal is! His good friend, the beautiful and clever Lady de Winter, or simply Milady, happens to be in London at the same time as Buckingham. At his bidding, she clips two of the diamond studs from Buckingham's evening clothes, which the Cardinal can now present to the King as evidence of the Queen's unfaithfulness. D'Artagnan, however, finds out about the plot from Constance and thwarts it.

Soon afterwards, D'Artagnan spots a woman who was with the scar-faced man. What a small world! She is chatting with his friend, Lord de Winter, whose life he had spared in a duel. The lady is Lord de Winter's sister-in-law, and the hormonally enhanced D'Artagnan (probably a self-portrait by Dumas) promptly falls in love with Lady de Winter. She doesn't reciprocate, however, since she is in love with a Monsieur de Wardes, whose recent death has not yet come to her notice. When D'Artagnan disguises himself one night as de Wardes, Milady gives him a substantial sapphire. D'Artagnan shows it to Athos, who recognises it as the one he had given his wife, a beautiful but wicked woman on whose shoulder he noticed a fleur-de-lis criminal brand only after the honeymoon – and whom he thought he had hanged until she was dead.

D'Artagnan learns that when he saved Lord de Winter's life in the duel, he unwittingly derailed a scheme by Milady to have de Winter killed so that she could inherit his money. He also finds out that she is Richelieu's spy and the mastermind behind Constance's second abduction and imprisonment. In a climactic altercation, Milady's dress gets pulled from her shoulder to reveal the tell-tale fleur-de-lis. She's Athos's undead wife!

In the midst of these events, the war between England and France is coming to a head at the siege of La Rochelle, a French town that was allied with the English. The Cardinal tries unsuccessfully to enlist D'Artagnan on his side. Lady de Winter fails in her attempt to have him killed at La Rochelle but succeeds in having hapless Buckingham stabbed to death and Constance poisoned. She is eventually captured and executed. With her death and the fall of La Rochelle to the French, we experience the happy conjuncture of the main strands of the plot. The Cardinal, impressed by D'Artagnan's ability to outwit him, offers him a commission in the Musketeers. Athos returns to his estate, Porthos marries well and Aramis finds his cloister. D'Artagnan is eventually reconciled even to old Scarface, who turns out to be a nobleman.

The Three Musketeers has been enormously popular since its 1844 publication. It's been translated into countless languages and filmed at least five times. The creator of this melodramatic concoction has been called the French Sir Walter Scott – and even more unflattering names.

Alexandre Dumas père (1802–70) was the grandson of a French nobleman who had settled in Hispaniola and a black woman who was a native of the island. His father was a general in Napoleon's army and Alexandre himself had a flashy military career that included participation in Garibaldi's Sicilian campaign of 1860. Dumas called history 'the nail on which I hang my novels', and he and his collaborator, Auguste Maquet, found many of their characters and plots in historical sources. Charles de Baatz D'Artagnan was a historical figure and Dumas says in his preface to the Musketeers that D'Artagnan's memoirs (which were actually written years later by someone else) contain a reference to three characters named Athos, Porthos and Aramis. And apparently Louis XIII's queen really did have an affair with the Duke of Buckingham.

Among the three hundred volumes attributed to the prolific Dumas are The Count of Monte Cristo and The Viscount of Bragelonne – the latter the source of the tragic tale of 'The Man in the Iron Mask'.

Who were the 3 sons of Noah?

Shem
Japheth
Ham

THE HEBREW DELUGE STORY is one of many. The Babylonian flood
myth, glimpsed in *The Epic of Gilgamesh*, features a Noah-figure named
Utnapishtim. The Greek version involves Prometheus' son Deucalion,
and the latter's wife, Pyrrha, who repopulate the world after the flood
by throwing stones behind their backs. The stones Deucalion threw
became men, while Pyrrha's popped up from the ground as women. In
ancient India's flood myth, Manu, the son of the sun, is warned to build
an ark by the god Vishnu (or Brahma) in the form of a fish (see Question 2). After the deluge, Manu becomes the progenitor of the human
race through his daughter.

In the Genesis account, Noah, ninth in descent from Adam (see
Question 1), lived in a time when the whole world had become ineffably wicked, corrupt and violent. At the age of six hundred, Noah is
ordered by God to build an ark with his three one-hundred-year-old
sons, bring male and female of each animal aboard and embark with his
wife, sons and daughters-in-law to escape the universal flood in which
all other humans and animals drown. In this story, the dove, olive leaf
and rainbow first assume their symbolic meanings of peace and the
covenant established between humanity and the incensed deity. After
the waters recede and the ark comes to rest in the Ararat mountains in
eastern Turkey, Noah disembarks and lives another 350 years, dying at
the age of 950.

If you work out the numbers in Genesis, you'll find that Methuselah,
who was Noah's grandfather and survived to be 969 years old, died
in the year of the flood. He's unlikely to have drowned in it, since, as
part of Noah's extended family and as the record-holder for human

longevity, he probably was favoured by God and wasn't one of the wicked. Let's say he succumbed to natural causes just before the deluge. And when was that? In 2348 BC, if you count the years from Adam to the flood in Genesis *and* accept the chronology of the seventeenth-century Irish Anglican archbishop James Ussher, who pinpointed the day of the world's creation as Sunday, 23 October 4004 BC.

But let's get to Noah's sons, whom the biblical narrative identifies as the ancestors of all the main ethnic groups known to the ancient Jews. **Shem**, the eldest son, is the eponymous ancestor of the Semites, including the Jews, Arabs, Assyrians, Elamites and Aramaeans – but not the Canaanites. His great-grandson, Eber, is the eponymous ancestor of the Hebrews. Abram (later Abraham), ninth in descent from Shem, was born 291 years after the flood. Shem himself lived to be six hundred.

One of the narrative strands in Genesis makes **Japheth** the second son of Noah, while another considers him the youngest. As the father of Javan, who was associated with the Ionian Greeks, Japheth was seen as the ancestor of all the Greek tribes in general. In later antiquity he was sometimes identified with the Greek Titan Iapetos, the father of Prometheus. In addition to the Greeks, Japheth's descendants included other Mediterranean and island peoples, the Armenians, the Medes and the inhabitants of Asia Minor (now Turkey).

Ham is said to have been the father of four sons, including Cush (ancestor of the Ethiopians), Mizraim (progenitor of the Egyptians) and Canaan (eponymous ancestor of the original Semitic inhabitants of Palestine). Cush was the father of Nimrod, that 'mighty hunter before the Lord' who was sometimes identified as the frustrated builder of the Tower of Babel (Babylon), where the Confusion of Tongues occurred.

But Ham's story turns tragic, with implications reaching almost to our own times. We are told that Noah was the first to cultivate the fruit of the vine and get drunk on it. When Ham stumbles upon Noah, blind drunk and stark naked in his tent, he goes to call his brothers. The more pious (or merely craftier) Shem and Japheth clothe their substance-abusing father without peeking at his nakedness. When Noah comes to his senses, he curses Ham's son Canaan, and destines him to be the slave of Shem and Japheth.

We can understand why the Hebrew author of this passage makes Noah curse Canaan, since the Hebrews were fierce enemies of the Canaanites and supplanted them in Palestine. But here's the ironic part: Ham's putative connection with Egypt and Ethiopia caused a stigma to attach itself to his African 'descendants'. This means that a biblical passage intended to explain Hebrew animosity against the Canaanites – and indeed the original drunken-Noah episode probably specified Canaan, not Ham, as the unwilling voyeur – was later misinterpreted as a universal condemnation of Africans. The story of Ham the accursed was used by some to justify African slavery well into the period of the American Civil War.

Noah was often a figure of fun in medieval mystery plays, which tended to portray him as an uxorious man driven to drink by a shrewish wife who at first refuses to board the ark. In a more sombre vein is Michelangelo's depiction of the deluge among his frescoes on the ceiling of the Sistine Chapel in Rome (1508–12). His handling of Noah's drunkenness points a moral about the submission of human reason to enslavement by the body. James Joyce, on the other hand, always maintained a healthy respect for the body's demands. In his *Ulysses* (1922), the interior monologue of the book's hero, Leopold Bloom, who is scanning the shelves of a pub trying to decide what to have for lunch, contains a bit of nonsense involving multiple culinary puns: 'Ham and his descendants mustered and bred there.'

What are the 3 ages of Vico's historical cycle?

Theocratic (The Age of Gods)
Aristocratic (The Age of Heroes)
Democratic (The Age of Men)

WHEN GIAMBATTISTA VICO (1668–1744) was seven years old, he took a nasty fall from the top of a ladder, fracturing his skull. He was unconscious for five hours and his surgeon prognosticated that he would either die of his injury or grow up to be an idiot. Instead, he became the greatest Italian philosopher.

Vico's importance rests on his cyclical theory of history, enunciated in *Principles of New Science . . . Concerning the Common Nature of the Nations*, usually referred to as *The New Science*, first published in 1725 and revised for the third and last time in 1744. This immensely pedantic tome, described by nineteenth-century American historian John Fiske as 'the driest, obscurest, metaphysicalest book I ever got hold of', is a seminal work of historical theory. Ignored in its own time and despite Fiske and Vico's surgeon, it went on to influence writers like Goethe, Hegel, Herder, Michelet, Coleridge, Comte, Marx, Carlyle, Croce and Joyce.

The product of a Jesuit education and the early Enlightenment, Vico mingled with the best minds in his native Naples, where he was professor of rhetoric (Latin eloquence) at the university. After the Newtonian revolution in physics and astronomy, some scholars began applying scientific methods – regular laws, constant conjunctions, predictability – to the study of mankind. Vico chose human history as his field of investigation and his 'New Science' claimed an authority that had hitherto been accorded only to the exact sciences. So, what are the laws of history?

This first modern historian begins his quest just after the universal flood has wiped out all but eight humans (see Question 5). A devout (and prudent) Catholic, Vico confines his historical speculations to the postdiluvian gentile nations – the descendants of Ham, Japheth and the non-Hebraic scions of Shem, who, within two hundred years of the deluge, have degenerated into speechless savages roaming the jungles and forests, copulating promiscuously in the open and preying on each other in a Hobbesian state of nature. Vico's theories thus do not apply to Judaeo–Christian sacred history, which he claimed was under the direct influence of Providence.

With the drying out of the sodden earth, the first thunderclap rings out. Picture the terror of these savages, who interpret this as the storm god bellowing down at them: 'Stop copulating like dogs where I can see you! And do something with those dead bodies so I don't have to smell them or watch them rot!' The men flee into caves, each dragging a woman with him. Thus begins **the age of gods**, with the foundation of primitive religion, marriage (and the family) and burial of the dead (which holds out the promise that, if properly done, human souls can attain immortal life). These are the three basic institutions of society, according to Vico. The form of government is a theocracy based on auspices, auguries and divine revelations. The rulers are the patriarchs, who combine the powers of kings, priests, prophets and judges. The form of wisdom is oracular and theological and all physical things are thought to be animated by gods (animism).

In **the age of heroes**, some of the remaining wandering savages weary of fighting off fierce marauders and appeal for protection to the patriarchs, who have made clearings in the forest. The patriarchs kill off as many marauders as they can and, as villages evolve, make agricultural serfs of the helpless suppliants, who lack all rights. Uniting against the serfs, the patriarchs form feudal aristocratic commonwealths in which the serfs are severely oppressed. Gradually, when the serfs begin to rebel, the first agrarian laws are passed. This warlike, valiant and barbaric age is poetic, mythic and imaginative, as in the Homeric poems.

The age of men begins when the serfs become plebeians in newly emerging city-states. They assert their right to the privileges formerly denied them not only by social and political tradition but also by religious taboo – the right to own land, marry according to religious ritual, bequeath property, become citizens, hold political office and even take the auspices. The ethos of this age is rational; legal codes are drawn up and scientific and philosophical thought emerges. This is a more benign and humane age, in which reason applies itself to bettering the lot of all citizens. First, popular republics are established under leaders like Pericles, but soon the mad rush towards equality leads to civil wars, such as those of Rome. More or less enlightened monarchs, such as Alexander the Great or Julius Caesar, assume power to keep order while still loosely preserving the concept of civil rights for all citizens before the law.

But the ease and luxury of the democratic age lead to egoism, bread and circuses, decadence, political corruption à la Caligula and Nero, cynicism, religious scepticism – in short, to the much later Italian concept of *menefreghismo* ('I-don't-give-a-damn-ism'). The society either implodes through internal strife or is conquered by a more vigorous people: 'He who cannot govern himself must let himself be governed by another who can . . . The world is always governed by those who are naturally fittest' – Vico's latter assertion anticipating social Darwinism by a century and a half.

Barbarism now descends on Europe again and the whole cycle recurs (Vico's law of eternal *ricorso*), but on a higher level this time, for the cycles proceed in an upward spiral. Improvement and progress in human dignity and rationality occur because the race retains what it has learned in previous cycles. So, after the Germanic barbarians conquer the Roman Empire, a new theocratic age results, in which the early God-fearing Christians revert to prophecies, miracles, irrationality, revelations, and signs and portents. The crusading and chivalric age is next, the new age of knightly heroes, with its feudalism and martial epics – think of *Beowulf, The Song of Roland, El Cid*. Dante is the new Homer of this aristocratic age. Finally, Vico recognises the return of the new age of men in the natural-law philosophy and age of reason of the seventeenth century. He predicts the rise of democratic republics within a half-century of his time – and is vindicated in 1776.

An important point of Vico's thought is that human nature is not static, but develops in step with changes in religion, law, politics, economic relationships and the arts. The cycles of history represent individual psychological development writ large: nations think childishly at first, then like adolescents and then mature adults, before lapsing into senility. Societies also mirror the stages of biological development. They are born, mature, decline and die – only to be replaced by their offspring, in which the cycle begins again. This organic theory of historical development is driven by class struggle. People with similar rights (or lack thereof) bind together to suppress or overthrow the others.

Vico's cyclical theory supplied James Joyce with the basic organising principle of his polyglot *Finnegans Wake* (1939), in which characters, places and events keep recurring in multifarious guises. This mammoth epic of birth, life, death and resurrection – this collective unconscious of the human race – is thus divided into four parts, in which theocratic, heroic, human and *ricorso* themes predominate, respectively. Joyce's book closes with a sentence fragment ('A way a lone a last a loved a long the') that is completed by the book's opening words: 'riverrun, past Eve and Adam's, from swerve of shore to bend of bay, brings us by a commodius vicus of recirculation back to Howth Castle and Environs.' Who could ask for a better *ricorso* than that? (And *vicus*, which means 'street' in Latin, is also the Latin form of Vico's name.) Like its hero, Humphrey Chimpden Earwicker, *Finnegans Wake* 'moves in vicous cicles yet remews the same'.

With New Ageism, the continuing decline of education, the increasing mistrust of science, spates of near-death-experience memoirs, proliferating cults and the growing influence of religious fundamentalism, are we – like Yeats's rough beast – slouching towards a new theocratic age?

Who were the 3 Magi, and what gifts did they bring?

Melchior: gold
Caspar: frankincense
Balthazar: myrrh

ALTHOUGH ENTRENCHED in Christmas lore, the Magi actually appear only in the Gospel of Matthew. Luke's Gospel, the only other with a Nativity narrative, does not mention them. Furthermore, Matthew specifies no number, saying only that 'some wise men' come to Jerusalem from the East, led by a new star, which traditionally signified the birth of a ruler. They seek the help of King Herod the Great, Roman-appointed King of Judaea (reigned 37–4 BC), in finding the 'infant King of the Jews' to whom they want to pay homage. Herod sends them on to Bethlehem and orders them to return when they find the child, so that he, too, can offer his respects. Continuing on their way, the wise men eventually find the infant in a house (not a manger in Matthew) over which the star has paused. They worship the child and offer their gifts of gold, frankincense and myrrh. When a dream warns them to avoid Herod, who fears the child as a rival, they return home by another route. In describing how Herod plotted to kill the infant, Matthew was probably associating Christ with the infant Moses, whom Pharaoh had tried to kill (along with all other male Hebrew infants) and who went on to deliver Israel from Egypt.

Magi were well-known figures in the ancient world. The word is the plural of Latin *magus*, 'wise man' (from Greek *magos*, from Persian *magush*), designating a member of the priestly caste of several religions, especially the Zoroastrianism of ancient Persia. After the conquest of Babylon by Persia in the sixth century BC, Zoroastrianism was tainted by Babylonian religious practices. Eventually, Persian magi came to be considered the genuine keepers of true and ancient wisdom, while the Babylonian magi – largely sorcerers, magicians and astrologers – were widely regarded as tricksters and charlatans, as our word *magic* still attests. In fact, in the Acts of the Apostles (8:9–24), Simon Magus is a Samaritan sorcerer who tries to buy from St Peter the gift of conferring the Holy Spirit by the laying on of hands. His sacrilegious request gave us the word *simony* for the buying or selling of church offices.

Back to the Matthew narrative. His apparently straightforward, twelve-verse account teems with Jewish and Christian symbolism and is written so that several Old Testament prophecies are fulfilled, notably Isaiah 60:6, 'All they from Saba [Sheba, probably Yemen] shall come, bringing gold and frankincense and showing forth praise to the Lord', and Psalm 72:10–11, 'The kings of Tarshish and the Isles shall offer gifts; the kings of Arabia and Seba shall bring tribute. All kings shall pay him homage, all nations shall serve him.' Apparently because of these passages, early Christian writers transformed the Magi into kings.

In Jewish ritual, only three kinds of people were anointed: kings, priests and prophets. Gold is a gift for a king, frankincense for a priest and pungent myrrh for a sharp-tongued prophet. (Myrrh was used in embalming and its presentation to Christ also portends his death.) The conferring of all three gifts on the infant Jesus means he is triply anointed. Now, 'the anointed one' is a translation both of the Greek *christos* and the Hebrew *mashiach*, and Matthew, writing in about AD 85 for Jewish Christians, was trying to demonstrate that Jesus of Nazareth was the Christ, the Jewish Messiah. The Magi, of course, were gentiles and their veneration of Christ also supports the claim that he came to save all nations.

By the eighth century the Three Kings had acquired names and kingdoms: Melichior (**Melchior**), King of Persia; Gathaspa (Gaspar or **Caspar**), King of India; and Bithisarea (**Balthazar** or Baltasar), King of Arabia. Melchior means 'king of light', Gaspar 'the white one' and Balthazar 'lord of the treasures'. The English historian Bede (c.672–735) opined that Balthazar, the youngest, was black, re-emphasising the idea that Christ had come to save all humankind.

According to a medieval tradition, the Three Magi met to celebrate Christmas in Sewa, a town in Turkey, more than half a century after they followed the Star of Bethlehem to the scene of Christ's birth. Then, in early January, they all died, each well over a hundred years old. The legend adds that their bodies were taken from Sewa to Milan, from where they were filched by the German Emperor Frederick Barbarossa in the twelfth century and brought to Cologne. The Magi were renamed the Kings of Cologne and their remains are still dubiously said to repose in the cathedral.

Marco Polo (1254–1324) probably had a better trail on the Magi. Sojourning in Saveh, south-west of present-day Tehran, he reported seeing their sepulchres in separate, ornate buildings. Their bodies, which he viewed, apparently had undergone only minor decomposition. According to legend still current in this area, the three came, respectively, from Saveh, Hawah and Kashan (all within about a hundred miles of Tehran) and travelled west together to greet the mysterious child. Among the tales Marco heard, one contributed to the theme of 'Christ came for all men': as each King entered separately the house where the infant Jesus lay in Bethlehem, he saw a Christ who bore a great resemblance to himself.

Perhaps the medieval legend places the deaths of the Three Magi in early January because it was on the sixth of this month that the western Church came to celebrate their visit to Christ. The Feast of the Epiphany, one of the Church's oldest liturgical festivals, has its roots in pre-Christian rites. In Latin America and some Mediterranean countries, 6 January, called 'Little Christmas', may be celebrated as lavishly as Christmas itself. In the eastern Church, the Epiphany memorialises not only the visit of the Magi, but also Christ's baptism and the marriage feast at Cana, where Christ performed his first miracle, changing water into wine. This triple commemoration is in keeping with the Greek *epiphaneia*, meaning 'manifestation' – in this case, of divine power or godhead.

The Magi story, beginning with only a dozen verses in Matthew, took on a long, varied life of its own. The Adoration (or Journey) of the Magi became a stock motif in medieval and Renaissance art, partly because it reminded earthly potentates that even they had to submit to

Christ, the King of Kings. The Italian masters Giotto, Sassetta, Gentile da Fabriano, Fra Angelico, Benozzo Gozzoli, Ghirlandaio and Leonardo da Vinci are only a few of the myriad painters who treated this subject. Even in the sceptical twentieth century, T. S. Eliot wrote a devotional poem entitled 'Journey of the Magi'.

What are the 3 components of the Freudian psyche?

Id (*das Es*)
Ego (*das Ich*)
Superego (*das Über-Ich*)

TRIPARTITE DIVISIONS OF the human psyche, soul, or mind long antedate the work of Sigmund Freud (1856–1939), the Austrian psychiatrist who mapped our modern mental topography, pioneered psychoanalysis and became one of the most revolutionary and influential thinkers of the twentieth century. Plato (c.429–347 BC) had divided the individual soul into three faculties, each corresponding to a class of citizens in his ideal *Republic*:

- Appetite, concerned with the pleasures of nutrition and generation, was characteristic of the merchant class.
- High spirit (or angry passions and a thirst for martial glory and fame) was the distinguishing mark of the warrior class.
- Reason, imbuing the souls of the ruling class, delighted in wisdom, learning, philosophy and justice.

Plato's student Aristotle (384–322 BC), in *De Anima* (*On the Soul*), posited the triad of a nutritive or vegetative soul (nutrition, growth, reproduction), a sensitive soul (sensations, emotions, memory) and an intellective or rational soul (thought, judgement, reasoning, contemplation), each coexisting to varying degrees in all humans.

But a more immediate influence on Freud's three psychic faculties may be found in the nineteenth century. In *The Brothers Karamazov*, which Freud called 'the most magnificent novel ever written', Fyodor Dostoyevski (1821–81) created three characters – the three legitimate brothers of the title – who roughly embody Freud's id, ego and superego: the debauched, drunken brawler Dmitri, the atheistic intellectual Ivan and the saintly monk Alyosha.

According to Freud, the **id** (or 'it') is the unconscious seat of sexual and self-preserving instincts, primitive passions and irrational urges. It is the infant howling to be fed – and not only that. In Freud's largely discredited view, little boys develop an Oedipus complex and girls an Electra complex – a libidinous attachment of the id to the parent of the opposite sex and a rivalry with the same-sex parent. When this is seen to be a losing game (especially for boys, with the ever-present threat of castration), the id strategically retreats by shedding the Oedipus complex and identifying with the parent of the same sex.

If allowed free rein, the id, 'this great reservoir of libido', would transport us back to Thomas Hobbes's 'war of all against all' and his vision of life in a state of Nature: 'solitary, poor, nasty, brutish and short' – or to Darwin's Nature, 'red in tooth and claw' (in Tennyson's phrase). This roiling, roistering, old roué of an id understands only the pleasure principle.

But the **ego** ('I'), on the other hand, is concerned with the reality principle. Out of the id's amorphous mass of instincts, a primitive ego develops through increasing contact with the environment. It begins to realise that adapting to its surroundings increases the odds of survival more effectively than the id's in-your-face style. The ego, representing reason and common sense, increasingly brings the reality principle to bear on the id's constant demands for instant gratification and uses repression (the erasing from consciousness of unacceptable impulses) in the attempt to nullify the id's clamourings. Freud once succinctly defined psychoanalysis as 'an instrument to enable the ego to achieve a progressive conquest of the id'. But a weak ego remains prey to anxiety not only from the environment and the id, but also from the superego.

The **superego**, incorporated into a coherent theory with the other two components of the mind in Freud's *The Ego and the Id* (1923), is an outgrowth of the ego that internalises parental and societal values. This 'super-I', or internal cop, holds the ego to strict account for not adhering to the various taboos and moral strictures of home, school, religion, society and the law. Its cruelly punitive weapons are the guilt it induces and the conscience it wields so self-righteously. Like the id, the superego works mainly unconsciously, so that feelings of guilt are often misinterpreted by the person as neurotic or somatic symptoms. Freud believed that the superego's effects could be seen in the development of religions that feature wrathful, vengeful deities.

Freud's division of the psyche emphasises how our thoughts and actions are determined by the unconscious interplay and conflict of our biological drives (id), our adjustment of those drives to external reality (ego) and our reactions to the restrictions of society (superego). Though all his theoretical constructs are metaphorical and based on anecdotal evidence from the couch rather than on verifiable scientific experimentation, Freud profoundly stirred the imagination of healers, artists, writers and thinkers throughout the twentieth century with concepts like infantile sexuality, repression, sublimation, the unconscious and dozens more. An apt comment on Freud's epic saga of the soul may be the Italian saying, '*Se non è vero, è ben trovato*' ('It may not be true, but it's a *great* story').

What 3 beasts confront Dante in Canto 1 of the Inferno?

Leopard
Lion
She-wolf

BEFORE DANTE ALIGHIERI (1265–1321) embarks on the epic journey to the other-worldly realms of the Inferno, Purgatorio and
Paradiso described in the three parts of his *Divine Comedy*, he pictures
himself losing his way in a terrifying forest where he wanders throughout a 'dark night of the soul'. At dawn he finds himself at the foot of a
hill whose sun-clad summit encourages him to leave behind the gloomy
forest, which symbolises the sin, ignorance and spiritual death that
threaten to engulf him.

Just as he starts climbing the hill, Dante sees a nimble **leopard** in his
path – and then a ferocious **lion** and a famished **she-wolf**. There is a
crescendo of fearsomeness in the three mysterious beasts, which seem
to materialise out of thin air. After the menacing she-wolf appears,
Dante turns tail and starts dashing for cover in the dark forest.

But now there's another apparition – the spirit of the long-dead
Roman poet Virgil (70–19 BC), author of the greatest Latin epic, the
Aeneid, and Dante's literary idol and poetic model. Virgil checks Dante's
headlong retreat, explaining that he was sent by the heavenly spirit of
Beatrice, Dante's dead love, to rescue him from the perils of sinfulness
that might land him in Hell. But Virgil, who is a soul in Limbo, where
virtuous heathens go after death, also informs Dante that he can't escape
the forest by climbing the hill. He assures him that the beasts barring his
path – especially the she-wolf – won't let him through alive.

Where did the beasts come from? On a literary level, from the Bible:

> And this is why a lion from the forest strikes them down,
> a desert wolf makes havoc of them,
> a leopard lurks around their towns:

whoever goes out is torn to pieces –
because of their countless crimes,
their ever-increasing apostasies.

This is Jeremiah (5:6) launching a jeremiad against the corrupt kingdom of Judah. But what do the three beasts mean in Dante's poem? Most scholars agree that they represent either the sins of lust, pride and avarice, respectively, or the three major degrees of sin: (1) incontinence (lack of self-control), resulting in sins such as lust, gluttony and anger; (2) violence; and (3) fraud (or malice). Compare 1 John 2:16: 'For all that is in the world, the lust of the flesh [the leopard] and the lust of the eyes [the she-wolf] and the pride of life [the lion], is not of the Father, but is of the world.'

Because of these evil propensities of ours, we need divine grace to attain eternal salvation. Thus, in the fiction of the poem, Beatrice, symbol of divinely revealed Truth, sends Virgil to guide Dante through Hell (so that he can see first-hand the wretched effects of sin on the human soul) and Purgatory (so that he can witness the long, laborious, painful process of the soul's repentance). Beatrice herself will then appear to Dante at the summit of Mount Purgatory and lead him through the ten heavens of Paradise, so that he can experience the ineffable joy of the saints, who have managed to overcome the sinfulness of our fallen nature and achieve the goal for which humans were created: the Beatific Vision of God in a perpetual peace 'which passeth all understanding'.

Only after completing this cosmic journey (in 14,233 lines of sublime verse) does Dante merit the vision of God vouchsafed at the end of the *Paradiso*. There are no short-cuts to salvation. Like Dante, we all must take the long way home, through knowledge and purgation, instead of trying to sneak past the barriers symbolised by the three beasts of our evil nature.

Was Dante personally assailed by the leopard with the pretty pelt (lust), the fierce lion (pride) and the starving she-wolf (avarice)? We glean from his own poems that, after the death of his beloved Beatrice in 1290, he was attracted to various other women and in the *Purgatorio*

(Canto 27) Dante depicts himself crossing the wall of flame that is the punishment of the lustful souls he encounters there. As for pride, there never lived a prouder human being than Dante Alighieri, the embittered and scornful political exile who boasted in the *Paradiso* that he had formed a party of himself alone, since his political enemies in Florence and his fellow exiles were equally reprehensible. Avarice he would have denied – though it was precisely for the (trumped-up) charge of graft and embezzlement of government funds that Dante was exiled and, subsequently, condemned to death by burning in 1302. (He wisely never returned to face charges.)

No matter what sinful qualities the three beasts of Canto 1 of the *Inferno* symbolise, Dante receives the counterbalancing intercession of three blessed ladies in the very next canto. There, Virgil informs him of how the Virgin Mary summoned St Lucy, who then appealed to Beatrice, who in turn descended to Limbo to send Virgil on his rescue mission for Dante's imperilled soul. This threefold chain of grace on the part of sainted women in Heaven more than tips the scale against the three beasts that bar Dante's path. In Dante's view, God gives all of us more than a fair crack at working out our salvation, if only we can get beyond the beast in us.

Who were the 3 Furies?

Alecto
Megaera
Tisiphone

IN CANTO 9 of the *Inferno*, Dante approaches the walls of lower Hell,

> Where I beheld three hellish Furies rise
> Erect at once, with clotted blood embrowned:
> Women they seemed in body and in guise,
> But greenest hydras girded them around,
> And hornèd snakes they had instead of hair;
> With vipers were their savage temples bound.

These fierce apparitions, who proceed to terrify Dante by shrieking while clawing their breasts and striking themselves with their hands, had their literary origins more than two millennia earlier in the Erinyes of Homer, who were as yet nameless and of undetermined number. In Homer and later Greek myth, they were the embodiments of curses – dread ministers of vengeance whose bailiwick was murder (especially of blood relatives), crimes against parents or the elderly, perjury and violations of the customs protecting guests or beggars. The Erinyes, who sprang from the blood of Uranus when his son Cronus castrated him with a sickle (see Question 57), came to symbolise the remorse of conscience. The Furies, or *Dirae*, are their Latin equivalents.

As avenging goddesses of the underworld who pursue those guilty of heinous crimes, these snaky-haired crones with blood oozing from their eyes figure prominently in *The Eumenides* of Aeschylus (c. 525–456 BC). This is the concluding play of *The Oresteia*, the tragic trilogy that won first prize in the Athenian dramatic festival in 458 BC. Aeschylus' greatest work – and the only Greek dramatic trilogy that has survived complete – *The Oresteia* also includes *Agamemnon* and *The Libation Bearers* (*Choephoroe*).

In the first play of the trilogy, Clytemnestra, wife of the returning commander-in-chief of the Greek forces in the Trojan War, King Agamemnon of Argos, treacherously stabs him to death in his bath. The lonely Queen, sister to another *femme fatale*, Helen of Troy, had taken a lover during Agamemnon's ten-year absence – his cousin, Aegisthus. The chorus of the play provides some exposition: we are told how Agamemnon's father Atreus had been cuckolded by his brother Thyestes and thus had butchered two of Thyestes' young sons and served them up cooked to their father, who unknowingly fed on their flesh. When informed of the nature of his meal, Thyestes quite understandably cursed Atreus and his descendants. But Thyestes' son Aegisthus escaped and vowed revenge. Apart from this crime of his father's, Agamemnon had made a human sacrifice of his daughter Iphigenia to obtain a fair wind to sail to Troy. To cap things off, the proud conqueror of Troy returns home with a young mistress, the Trojan princess and prophetess Cassandra, who is also duly murdered by Clytemnestra.

At the command of Apollo, however, and with his sister Electra's enthusiastic support, Agamemnon's son Orestes avenges his father's murder by cutting his mother's throat with a sword. Of course, he also despatches Aegisthus. For the sacrilege of matricide, Orestes is immediately haunted by the Erinyes, who, at the end of *The Libation Bearers*, chase him from Argos and hound him to the edge of insanity. Orestes flees to the oracle of Apollo at Delphi and is absolved of his crime – but the relentless Erinyes refuse to abandon their pursuit. Apollo bids him flee to Athens, where Athene will protect him.

The third play, *The Eumenides*, is the story of a clash between, on the one hand, Apollo and Athene (and the civilised, enlightened values of the Olympian gods) and, on the other, the Erinyes, who embody the primitive, barbarous, pre-rational *lex talionis* – the law of an eye for an eye and of 'cruel and unusual punishments'. The Erinyes are draconian literalists, considering neither the motivation of the accused nor any extenuating circumstances in their blind pursuit of revenge. Supposedly this play's chorus of wildly dancing Erinyes – probably twelve of them – was so horrific with their long black robes and red tongues that pregnant women in the original audience had miscarriages and children went into convulsions.

A murder trial ends the play. Athene appoints twelve Athenian jurors to try the vexed case of Orestes, who pleads the equivalent of 'guilty with an explanation' – namely, that Apollo himself had commanded him to kill Clytemnestra and that he was now cleansed of guilt through his sufferings. Apollo, Orestes' defence lawyer and a formidable shyster, argues that only fathers are true parents of their children, since a mother serves only to nurture the husband's seed. Thus, he concludes, Orestes is innocent of any blood guilt. When the jury becomes deadlocked at six ballots for each side, Athene casts the deciding vote in favour of acquittal, putting an end to the three-generational curse on the House of Atreus.

The Erinyes are furious, but Athene's blandishments soon prove too much for them. They accept an honoured shrine and worship at Athens as the Eumenides ('The Kindly Ones') – gentle chthonic fertility goddesses with whom they now become identified. Aeschylus thus provides a mythic explanation both for the origin of the Eumenides cult and for the divine foundation of the Athenian Court of the Areopagus, the revered council that tried cases of homicide, arson, treason and offences against religion. The reconciliation at the end of the play stands for the mitigation of the instinctual rights of older folk customs by the intellectual virtues of reason and moderation. As such, The Eumenides celebrates the establishment of the rule of law in place of the crude justice of tribal vendettas and blood feuds.

Euripides (c.484–406 BC), in his play Orestes, is the earliest author to refer to the Erinyes as a group of three, and later Alexandrian Greek writers named them. Virgil (70–19 BC) used these names in his Aeneid, where the Furies are depicted either as monstrous dispensers of torment in the underworld or as inspirers of terror, strife and warfare on earth. **Alecto** means 'she who does not rest' (in her pursuit); **Megaera** is 'the envious one'; and **Tisiphone** is 'the avenger of murder'. Greek vases often represent them as dog-headed and bat-winged.

St Paul preached before the Areopagus, some of whose members burst into incredulous laughter when he claimed that God had raised Christ from the dead (Acts 17:19–34). John Milton's impassioned plea for non-licensing of the English press is named *Areopagitica* in honour of that ancient council and the Erinyes make a cameo appearance in the Hell of his *Paradise Lost* as the 'harpy-footed Furies'.

What are Newton's 3 laws of motion?

1. An object moves at a constant velocity — which may include zero velocity — unless an outside force intervenes. (Or: An object in motion tends to stay in motion and an object at rest tends to stay at rest, unless compelled to change that state by forces impressed upon it.)
2. The change of motion is proportional to the motive force impressed and is made in the direction of the straight line in which that force is impressed.
3. For every action, there is an equal and opposite reaction.

REFERRING TO HIS PREDECESSORS, including Galileo and Kepler, English mathematician and physicist Isaac Newton (1642–1727) wrote to fellow scientist Robert Hooke, 'If I have seen further it is by standing on the shoulders of Giants.' Newton's graciousness did not extend to his contemporaries, however. The man who explained the rainbow, invented calculus, provided the foundation for modern optics, devised the three laws of motion and formulated the law of universal gravitation was bellicose, absent-minded, insecure and suspicious. He was nearly constantly embroiled in rancorous disputes with some of the finest minds of his time, most notably Hooke and German philosopher and mathematician Gottfried Leibniz. Probably rivalled only by Einstein for scientific achievement, Newton wrote more about theology than about mathematics or physics and he interpreted the Bible literally, especially the books of Daniel and Revelation. He was also devoted to the study of astrology.

Tiny, sickly Isaac Newton was born in Woolsthorpe, Lincolnshire, on Christmas Day in 1642, a few months after the death of his father (and Galileo). His mother married a wealthy minister two years later and moved to a nearby hamlet, leaving Isaac with his grandmother. He lived apart from his mother for nearly a decade and later wrote that the trauma of this separation made him consider burning down the house in which she lived with his stepfather.

After an unremarkable performance in grammar school, Newton entered Trinity College, Cambridge, in 1661. Although the curriculum was still Aristotelian, Newton soon immersed himself in the work of French mathematician and philosopher René Descartes and English chemist Robert Boyle. In a notebook he kept at this time he wrote, 'Plato is my friend, Aristotle is my friend, but my best friend is truth.' He insisted that he did not invent hypotheses, meaning that he chose to provide observations, not explanations, and strove to describe his observations mathematically.

Shortly after he received his baccalaureate in 1665, the university was closed because of the advancing plague and Newton remained at home for the next two years – perhaps the most significant two years in the history of science. Working in solitude, Newton devised calculus, revolutionised optics and formulated the laws of motion and of universal gravitation.

Newton returned to Cambridge in 1667, circulated his manuscript on 'fluxions', or calculus, and became Lucasian Professor of Mathematics. His initial lecture series covered most of the material later included in Book One of his *Opticks*. A major contribution was his observation that white light could be separated by a prism into its rainbow components – red, orange, yellow, green, blue, indigo and violet – and reassembled into white light when passed through another prism. This elucidation of the composition of light had vast consequences in astronomy and physical optics.

It wasn't until 1687 that Newton published *Philosophiae Naturalis Principia Mathematica*, in which he expounded his three laws of motion and the law of universal gravitation. The *Principia*, probably the greatest scientific book ever written, brought international acclaim to its author.

The laws of motion are axiomatic, that is, they can't be proven. **The first law** seems logical enough and Galileo had proposed it a half-century earlier: an object at rest wants to stay at rest and an object in motion wants to stay in motion, unless an outside force acts on it. A force is nothing more than a tug or push in one direction or another. Couch potatoes will understand why the first law is also called the law of inertia.

The trick with the first law is that it specifies a constant velocity. Velocity is not the same as speed because the velocity of an object changes if the direction of the object changes. Thus, a race car travelling around a track at a constant speed is travelling at a constantly changing velocity.

The second law implies that the force (F) of an object is the product of the object's mass (M) and its acceleration (A), often expressed as $F = MA$. The law confirms our intuition: the greater an object's mass, the more force will be required to get it moving up a ramp or across a floor. Conversely, the greater its mass and acceleration, the greater will be the force of the impact if it collides with something. Applying the second law becomes more difficult when the mass of an object changes during acceleration, an unusual complication best exemplified by the launch of a spacecraft, when boosters and rocket stages drop off as the craft accelerates spaceward.

The third law specifies that if an object acts with a given force on a second object, the second object reacts with an equal, but opposite, force. Imagine yourself standing on ice in leather-soled shoes trying to liberate your car from a snow rut. Lean over and give that bumper a push – the car goes nowhere, but you fly backward.

Just warming up, Newton applied the laws of motion to the study of circular motion, since he hoped to determine the nature and strength of a force that could persuade an object such as a planet moving in a straight line to adopt a circular course. The result was Newton's law of universal gravitation, which states that two bodies (such as the earth and sun) attract each other with a force that is proportional to their masses and inversely proportional to the square of the distance that separates them. If the mass of one object is doubled, the attractive force between the objects is also doubled. On the other hand, as the distance between the objects grows, the force between them diminishes by the inverse of the square of the distance between them. So, if the distance between two objects is quadrupled, the force between them is now only $1/16$ what it was. The law may be expressed algebraically as

$$F = \frac{G \times m_1 \times m_2}{d^2}$$

Here, F is the force of gravitational attraction between any two objects, the two ms stand for their respective masses, d is the distance between them and G is a constant called the constant of gravitation.

When Newton proposed his law of gravitation, critics noted his failure to provide a description of the nature of gravity. Much later, Albert Einstein hypothesised that it was due to the warpage of space-time in the vicinity of massive objects. Newton himself was content to explain how gravity worked rather than what it was. And yes, he did claim that the idea of gravitation was 'occasioned by the fall of an apple'.

After publication of the Principia, Newton became the acknowledged dean of British science and this was the peak of his career. Over the next several years he suffered at least one mental breakdown and became increasingly involved in theological and astrological studies. His quarrels with his scientific contemporaries continued. He moved to London, where he was appointed Warden of the Royal Mint. During his tenure there, he became obsessed with counterfeiting and, applying himself to that problem with the same assiduity he had shown in mathematics and physics, he sent several men to the gallows for transgressions against the Crown's coinage. Newton was appointed president of the Royal Society in 1703 (a post he held until his death), and when Queen Anne knighted him at Cambridge in 1705 he became the first person so recognised for his scientific achievements.

Throughout his later years, Sir Isaac continued to revise his major works and publish Latin and English editions of them. He sharply challenged Leibniz over which of them had first established the methods of calculus (Newton had) and he continued his vicious attacks long after his rival had gone to his grave.

It's difficult to reconcile this Newton with the man who wrote in his memoirs, 'I do not know what I may appear to the world; but to myself I seem to have been only like a boy playing on the seashore and diverting myself in now and then finding a smoother pebble or a prettier shell than ordinary, whilst the great ocean of truth lay all undiscovered before me.'

What were the 3 temptations of Christ?

To turn stones into loaves of bread with which to feed
   himself
To throw himself down from the parapet of the Temple to
   prove he was the Son of God
To worship Satan in return for all the kingdoms of the world

IN MATTHEW'S GOSPEL, when Jesus is baptised by John the Baptist in the River Jordan, the voice of God proclaims Christ to be his Son. Jesus then goes into the wilderness to fast and be tempted by Satan for forty days (Matthew 4:1–11). When the Devil tempts him **to turn stones into bread**, the famished Christ replies by quoting Scripture: 'Man does not live on bread alone but on every word that comes from the mouth of God' (Deuteronomy 8:3). This may be interpreted as a refusal to distrust God's providence and a rejection of a mission dedicated to satisfying merely physical and material needs.

Since 'the Devil can cite Scripture for his purpose', Satan now whisks Christ away, dares him **to throw himself down from the parapet of the Temple at Jerusalem to prove he is the Son of God** and reminds him of the words of Psalm 91 (11–12): 'He will put angels in charge of you and they will support you in their arms, for fear you should strike your foot against a stone.' But Christ refuses to be the type of miracle-worker who gains converts with 'magic tricks' to win over an incredulous populace. Fighting Scripture with Scripture, Christ rejects Satan's proposal by citing Deuteronomy 6:16: 'You must not put the Lord your God to the test.'

In the third temptation, Christ is taken to a very high mountain and asked **to fall at Satan's feet and worship him in return for all the kingdoms of the world**, which are visible from that eminence. Christ now chases the pest away ('Get thee behind me, Satan!'), quoting Deuteronomy for the third time – 'You must worship the Lord your God and serve him alone' (6:13) – thus flatly rejecting any bargain with the Devil. After Satan's departure, angels come and minister to Christ, who, on leaving the wilderness, returns to Galilee and calls his first four disciples (see Question 59).

Matthew, writing for Jewish Christians, draws parallels between the experiences of Christ and of Moses in the wilderness. The forty days that Christ spends in the desert, subjected to Satanic temptations before embarking on his public ministry, recall the forty years that the Jews wander in the desert before their entry into the Holy Land. The temptation to turn stones into bread mirrors the Jews' longing for 'the fleshpots of Egypt' and their being fed with breadlike manna (and quails) in Exodus 16. Christ's refusal to perform a miracle to prove that he is the Son of God is reminiscent of the Jews' clamouring for Moses to give them water to drink, to which he replied, 'Why do you put Yahweh to the test?' (Exodus 17). And Christ's refusal to worship Satan contrasts with the Jews' idolatrous worship of the golden calf (Exodus 32).

Medieval exegetes saw an instructive contrast between the failure of the first man, Adam, to withstand Satan's temptation and the exemplary triumph of Christ, the second Adam, over the Adversary. Thus, Adam's tasting of the forbidden fruit in the Garden of Eden was paralleled by Christ's refusal to change stones into bread and succumb to the sin of gluttony. The Devil's appeal to vainglory took the form of 'You shall be as gods' in Genesis and 'If you are the Son of God, throw yourself down' in the New Testament. Finally, Satan's promises that Adam and Eve will know good and evil and that Christ will receive all the kingdoms of the world were both temptations of avarice. These two sets of temptations were said to be recalled in 1 John 2:16.

John's Gospel does not mention the temptations of Christ, Mark's does so very cursorily (1:12–13) and Luke gives a version similar to Matthew's but switches the order of the second and third temptations (4:1–13). This is the order that John Milton (1608–74) followed in his brief epic, *Paradise Regained* (1671). After his full-length epic poem, *Paradise Lost* (1667), which deals with the consequences of Adam's disobedience of God, Milton decided to celebrate in verse the perfect obedience and trust in God of the second Adam at the outset of his ministry.

The climax of *Paradise Regained* occurs when Satan cruelly and cynically places Christ on the needlepoint pinnacle of the Temple, bidding him either stand there or else cast himself down and presumptuously rely on God's providence. Miraculously, Christ continues to stand, thus fully recognising his own divinity and, at the same time, manifesting it to Satan, who falls from the heights, vanquished. Milton implies that, like Christ, each human must withstand the snares of Satan and the world to regain the paradise lost by Adam. This is not a mere place (the Garden of Eden), nor only a moral state (the 'paradise within . . . happier far' of *Paradise Lost*), but eternal salvation in Heaven, whose gates Christ re-opened by his sacrificial death on the cross and final rout of Satan.

In 1951, the Greek writer Nikos Kazantzakis (1883–1957), author of *Zorba the Greek*, caused a furore with his novel *The Last Temptation of Christ*, mainly for a long dream sequence that takes place during a split second when Christ faints while on the cross. This last and most powerful of Satan's temptations makes Christ believe he has only dreamed that he was crucified. The vision entices him with the lure of the flesh and the delights of this world in the form of a sex scene with the prostitute Mary Magdalene in an Edenic garden and, after her death, a *ménage à trois* with Martha and Mary of Bethany, who bear his children. But Christ soon wakes in agony on the cross, rejects the seductive vision sent by Satan and fulfils his redemptive mission by dying for mankind.

Martin Scorsese's 1988 film version of the novel adheres to it closely. As a result, on the day before it opened, twenty-five thousand protestors demonstrated against it at Universal Pictures in Los Angeles.

Norman Mailer's 1997 novel, *The Gospel According to the Son*, is a first-person narrative of Christ's life. The book contains an expanded version of the temptations of Christ in which Satan claims to share power with God – a tempting theodicy that absolves God of blame for the evil in the world by ascribing it to a wicked Other, as did the Albigensians, Manicheans and Zoroastrians long before Mailer.

Who were the 3 Fates?

Clotho
Lachesis
Atropos

DAUGHTERS OF THE NIGHT. Weavers of destiny. Distributors of good and evil, prosperity and suffering. They are the Three Fates, or *Moirai*, the awe-inspiring goddesses whom the ancient Greeks considered the dispensers of all good luck and ill fortune. Because of their prominent role at the very beginning of human life, they were sometimes viewed as goddesses of childbirth. But since the Fates dash human aspirations more often than they abet them, these three sisters were nearly always depicted as jealous, capricious and malevolent creatures. No guardian angels or merry midwives here.

In his *Theogony*, the Greek poet Hesiod (fl. c.700 BC) was apparently the first to enumerate three of these charming ladies, as opposed to the earlier abstract concept of Fate. **Clotho**, 'the spinner', is said to be the youngest of the sisters. She forms the child in the womb and, distaff in hand, spins out the thread of the newborn's life. **Lachesis**, 'the measurer', determines the length of the thread of life spun by Clotho and assigns a destiny to the newborn. **Atropos**, 'the relentless one', is the eldest of the sisters. With her 'abhorred shears' (as John Milton called them), Atropos cuts the thread of life at the point determined by Lachesis. Our word *atropine* (for a drug of the belladonna or deadly nightshade family) is derived from her name.

Greek mythology contains various accounts of the origin of the Fates and the extent of their dominion. According to Hesiod, Zeus fathered the Fates on Themis, the goddess of justice and right. Other poets identified them as the daughters of Erebus (Hell) and Nyx (Night) or as the parthenogenetic offspring of the grim goddess Ananke (Necessity).

Aeschylus insisted that not even Zeus himself stood above the Fates' decrees, 'For he, too, cannot escape what is fated.' Other poets claimed Zeus maintained veto power over what the Fates ordained, while some sanguine thinkers believed it was possible to lengthen Lachesis' thread by behaving judiciously – the ancient equivalent of wearing a seat belt or giving up smoking. On one occasion the god Apollo got the Fates drunk to save the life of his doomed friend Admetus. Even so, the Three Tipplers drove a hard bargain: Admetus had to find someone willing to die in his place. His young wife Alcestis agreed, but the play of Euripides named for her has a happy ending after Heracles descends into the underworld and brings the heroic woman back.

Not surprisingly, the Fates are usually represented in art as ugly, deformed old women. Occasionally they are given a statelier, more classical look, with Clotho holding a spindle, Lachesis a scroll (probably a book of fate) and Atropos a blade for cutting the thread of life.

To the Romans, the Fates were the *Parcae* or the *Fata*. The origin of the word *parcae* is *parere*, 'to bring forth', in an allusion to the Fates' connection with childbirth. The Latin word *Fata* comes from *fatum* – something spoken or decreed. At the end of a newborn's first week of life, the *Fata Scribunda* were called down to inscribe the child's fate in life. The Roman names for the individual Fates were Nona, Decuma and Morta, which again were references to childbirth: a nine-months' birth (Nona), a ten-months' birth (Decuma), or a stillborn child (Morta).

In Norse mythology, the function of the Fates was assumed by the Norns – Urth, Verthandi and Skuld, meaning past, present and future, respectively. They, too, were said to haunt the cradles of newborns. The Norns also guarded the well that fed Yggdrasil, the great ash tree that supports the universe. They put in an appearance in the first scene of Richard Wagner's opera *Götterdämmerung* to determine the fate of the universe (it's bad news for everyone). The three witches or 'Weird Sisters' in Shakespeare's *Macbeth* are probably British descendants of the Norns.

The Three Fates have even managed to survive in contemporary Greek consciousness. The *Moirai* are still said to appear on the third night after a baby's birth to lay out the course of its life.

FOUR

What were the 4 elements and their associated humours?

Earth: melancholic   Air: sanguine
Water: phlegmatic   Fire: choleric

WHAT ARE THINGS MADE OF? Various pre-Socratic philosophers of ancient Greece speculated about which material substance was the ultimate building block of the universe. Thales considered water the origin of all things (see Question 37). For Anaximenes, it was air. Heraclitus opted for fire, Pherecydes for earth. The Sicilian Greek philosopher Empedocles (fifth century BC) claimed that all four of these substances might be the primal 'elements' of things. Although he considered the elements permanent and unchangeable in themselves, he thought they could be divided, combined and rearranged in various proportions through the actions of Love and Strife, the constructive and destructive forces in the world. This perpetual intermixture generated all things in nature – including ourselves.

Aristotle (384–322 BC), who later articulated the theory of the four elements into an influential philosophical system, believed that the elements could even be changed into one another. For example, cold and moisture produced water, but if heat were then applied, the result would be air (steam). He also taught that each of the four elements had its proper 'sphere' or habitation: earth and water here on the earth, air above us and fire above the sphere of air, but below that of the moon. Stars were accordingly thought to be tiny holes in the sphere of air that revealed glimpses of the fire blazing in the sphere above it.

Medieval and Renaissance medicine and psychology, taking their cue from the Greek physician Galen (c.129–c.200), often associated the four elements with four bodily fluids and four temperaments. Imbalances of these fluids produced the temperaments (or personality types) called 'humours'.

Earth corresponded to black bile (or gall) and too much of this fluid, secreted from the kidneys and spleen, caused a person to be melancholic (Greek, 'black bile'). Hamlet, 'the melancholy Dane', is Shakespeare's most famous study of this temperament, which was marked by introspection, *Weltschmerz*, depression, affectation and reclusiveness. The melancholic intellectual, like Hamlet, was only one type. The melancholic lover, furiously scribbling love sonnets, was a staple of Elizabethan comedy. There was also the melancholic malcontent, like the spiteful and slanderous Thersites in *Troilus and Cressida* and the malicious Don John of *Much Ado About Nothing*. And nobody knows why Antonio, the merchant of Venice, was melancholic. He himself was clueless: 'In sooth, I know not why I am so sad.' The seventeenth-century English author Robert Burton wrote his interminable treatise *The Anatomy of Melancholy* (1621) as a therapeutic attempt to alleviate his own melancholic depression.

Water was linked to phlegm, the body's watery substances. An excess of these resulted in phlegmatic characters, who were cowardly, dull, sluggish and apathetic – in short, cold fish. The puritanical killjoy Malvolio in *Twelfth Night* – who has to be reminded by Sir Toby Belch, 'Dost thou think because thou art virtuous, there shall be no more cakes and ale?' – might serve as an example of the phlegmatic humour.

The element of **air** was associated with blood (Latin, *sanguis*) and too much blood produced someone like Falstaff, a larger-than-life embodiment of the sanguine humour – lusty, cheerful, good-natured, optimistic, carefree.

Fire corresponded to yellow bile (Greek, *chole*), secreted from the liver, and produced a choleric man like King Lear or the young Henry Percy (Hotspur) in *Henry the Fourth, Part 1* – easily angered, stubborn, vindictive and impatient.

Shakespeare's friend Ben Jonson elaborated his own version of these notions in his 'comedies of humours', in which the main characters of

47

plays such as *Every Man in His Humour*, *Every Man out of His Humour* and *Volpone* all have a dominant 'humour' – a character trait, whim or quirky obsession. It's a short step from this sense of 'humorous' characters in comedy to our own meaning of 'funny' or 'amusing'.

The psychology and physiology of the humours died hard. In the eighteenth century, the noted botanist and taxonomist Linnaeus absurdly tried to associate the four humours with four main ethnic groups:

Africans: phlegmatic
American Indians: choleric
Asians: melancholic
Europeans: sanguine

And well into the nineteenth century, some physicians tried to restore the balance of their patients' humours by bleeding them or making them sweat, vomit or purge their bowels.

But Aristotle had suspected that, beyond the four material (or sublunary) elements, there was the mysterious quintessence ('fifth essence or element') – the pure, immaterial, unchangeable substance of the heavenly bodies. In a different vein, Pope Boniface VIII in 1300 identified the fifth element with the wealthy and ambitious Florentines, who, like the other four elements, 'seem to rule the world'. And much later, Napoleon, bogged down in the nightmarish fiasco of his invasion of Russia, disgustedly asserted that the fifth element was none other than mud.

What are the 4 voyages of Lemuel Gulliver?

1. To Lilliput
2. To Brobdingnag
3. To Laputa, Balnibarbi, Glubbdubdrib, Luggnagg and Japan
4. To the country of the Houyhnhnms

GULLIVER'S TRAVELS (1726), the masterpiece of Jonathan Swift (1667–1745), an Anglican churchman born of English parents in Dublin, was published anonymously as *Travels into Several Remote Nations of the World. In Four Parts. By Lemuel Gulliver, First a Surgeon and then a Captain of Several Ships.* The book is a satire of travel narratives, utopian literature, contemporary England and Europe – and one of the most trenchant excoriations of the vices, stupidities and pretensions of our species.

After serving the Tory government in London as a political journalist, Swift hoped to be rewarded with an English bishopric. His satire on religious factions, however, *A Tale of a Tub* (1704), had offended the Archbishop of York by its coarseness, and his caustic wit had alienated at least one duchess, so in 1713 Queen Anne made Swift the Dean of St Patrick's Cathedral in Dublin instead. Soured by the ingratitude of the high-and-mighty, he viewed his appointment as a sentence of exile.

Is it accidental that *Gulliver's Travels* chronicles the change of the narrator – an honest, reasonably well-educated (though naïve) ship's surgeon – from a kindly man into a misanthrope? The four voyages represent the successive stages of the gullible Gulliver's education on the nature of the human race: its petty political and personal malice, physical and moral grossness, intellectual aberrations and quintessential bestiality. Gulliver becomes progressively more disgusted with humans – corrupt in soul, body and mind – finally identifying them with the repulsive Yahoos.

Book I is mainly a satire on court life and its sycophancy, vindictiveness, treachery and cruelty. Gulliver, shipwrecked on **Lilliput** (presumably an island south-west of Sumatra), finds himself among the six-inch Lilliputians, in whose country everything is one-twelfth the size of ours. In the political allegory, the Emperor of Lilliput represents King George I (reigned 1714–27) and the Empress is based on his predecessor Queen Anne (1702–14). The neighbouring island of Blefuscu (France) is also populated with tiny inhabitants and the age-old conflict between it and Lilliput had originated in the division between Big-Endians and Little-Endians (Catholics and Protestants) over the momentous question of which end to crack their eggs on. After Gulliver ends the current war between them (the War of the Spanish Succession, 1701–14) by capturing the entire Blefuscudian fleet, he becomes the Lilliputians' man-mountain of the hour.

But when the Empress's apartments catch fire and Gulliver urinates on part of the palace to quench the flames, she conceives a deep enmity for him. Soon other court intrigues and ministerial jealousies seal his fate. When the fickle Lilliputians sentence him to be starved to death, Gulliver escapes to Blefuscu, whence he returns to England.

On his second voyage, Gulliver ends up in **Brobdingnag** (somewhere near Alaska), whose gigantic denizens enjoy an exemplary political system. Gulliver now looks out the other end of the telescope to discover that he is one-tenth the size of the sixty-foot Brobdingnagians. On this voyage he realises that concepts such as human beauty and power are highly relative. Because his senses are exquisitely acute in this gargantuan land, the body odour and skin blemishes of the saucy maids of honour at the royal court, who strip him naked and place him on their breasts or nipples, arouse his unspeakable disgust. But when Gulliver proudly recounts the fierce wars and political machinations of Europeans, the humane King of Brobdingnag concludes that Gulliver and his kind are 'the most pernicious Race of little odious Vermin that Nature ever suffered to crawl upon the Surface of the Earth'. Now it's Gulliver's turn to feel like an insectile Lilliputian as the moral and physical puniness of his species is revealed.

After returning home and embarking again, Gulliver encounters various corruptions of the intellect in Book III, which describes unknown islands located east of Japan. Swift's close friend Alexander Pope

(1688–1744) wrote that 'the proper study of mankind is Man', and the useless speculation and scientific research ridiculed in this book are absurdly irrelevant to human well-being and moral wisdom. In Swift's view, the adherents of abstract science, abstruse mathematics and musical theory in **Laputa** (Spanish, *la puta*, 'the whore') have prostituted their reason to the service of a barren intellectualism. They might as well live in the Cloud-Cuckoo-Land of Socrates as depicted by Aristophanes – and, indeed, their Flying Island of Laputa is literally in the clouds.

The Laputans, absent-minded professors *par excellence*, need 'flappers' to smack them with a balloon-like device on the mouth when they're expected to speak, on the ears when they should listen and on the head before they cross the street. They're so constantly engrossed with their cogitations and calculations that their wives can cuckold them in front of their eyes, provided the husbands are furnished with pencil and paper.

Balnibarbi, the island beneath Laputa, contains the city of Lagado, with its Grand Academy (read the Royal Society of London), where 'projectors' spend years engaged in experiments such as trying to extract sunbeams from cucumbers, change human excrement back into food, develop sheep without wool, build houses from the roof downward and write books with the aid of a protocomputer that spits out random words. Others substitute things for words in a 'language' that requires people to carry huge sacks of objects for whatever they might want to say. On the neighbouring island of **Glubbdubdrib**, where magicians summon up the spirits of the dead, Gulliver learns that many of the movers and shakers of the past hundred years were 'bawds, whores, pimps, parasites and buffoons'. In the island of **Luggnagg**, the ghastly death-in-life of the immortal Struldbruggs conveys a warning to those who hope that science might someday conquer death. From Luggnagg, Gulliver sails to **Japan** before proceeding to Amsterdam and England.

After five months at home, Gulliver's wanderlust gets the better of him again. This time he sets out as a ship's captain, but his men mutiny and abandon him on an unknown island, **the country of the**

Houyhnhnms. In Book IV, the futile attempt to transcend human limitations is portrayed in the dull, functional, sovietised, spartan, stoical, impersonal society of the equine Houyhnhnms, whose name is meant to suggest a horse's whinnying. These parodic equivalents of the citizens of Plato's Republic or Thomas More's Utopia lack all emotion, good or bad, and face the myriad vicissitudes of life with the sangfroid of well-programmed robots. The choice of horses as the epitome of reason is ironic: in his *Phaedrus*, Plato had used the image of a charioteer reining in his horses to represent reason controlling the excesses of passion, and the half-man, half-horse centaurs of Greek myth were, except for wise Chiron, a lusty, brawling, drunken crew.

Counterbalancing the Houyhnhnms are their slaves − the obscene, filthy, malicious Yahoos, who seem to be swinishly savage naked humans on all fours. Gulliver is astonished to learn that his beloved Houyhnhnms, with whom he has lived three years, after hearing his account of European events, consider his people to be Yahoos with 'some small Pittance of Reason' that makes them even more dangerous. In the end, despite Gulliver's fervent wish to remain with them and advance in virtue, they send him away to protect themselves from his corrupting influence. Gulliver sadly reflects, 'I thought it might consist with Reason to have been less rigorous.'

How far does Gulliver speak for Swift in idolising the Houyhnhnms and equating the loathsome Yahoos with humans? This is the main scholarly crux of *Gulliver's Travels*. Let's examine the book's ending.

Gulliver relates that, after returning to England, he faints in horror when his wife kisses him on his arrival: 'My Wife and Family received me with great Surprize and Joy . . . but I must freely confess, the Sight of them filled me only with Hatred, Disgust and Contempt.' When he's told that he still walks and whinnies much like a horse, he takes this to be a great compliment. Finding the smell of his family intolerable, he buys a pair of stallions and talks with them for at least four hours a day in the barn.

True, the author shared Gulliver's obsession with bodily functions and human smells, which has been called Swift's 'excremental vision' and is also evident in some of his humorously scatological poems, such as 'The Lady's Dressing Room' and 'A Beautiful Young Nymph Going to Bed'. But Gulliver, who considers his wife and children to be Yahoos, is ludicrously deranged by the end of the book, his long gaze into the abyss of human nature on his four voyages having driven him hopelessly insane.

In Book IV, Swift has separated humans into two parts, rationality and bestiality. While humans are capable of subordinating their irrational passions to their reason, they cannot banish the emotions that result from their corporeality and fallen natures. Swift's deeply conservative view of the limited potential of mankind, ultimately rooted in his Christianity, led him to claim that man was not a rational animal, but an 'animal rationis capax' – one only capable of reason. While habitual irrationality is self-destructive, any attempt to live unwaveringly by the dictates of reason is doomed to failure and highly presumptuous. The corollary of Gulliver's modelling himself on the prelapsarian Houyhnhnms is his ridiculous blindness to anything but bestiality in his fellow humans. A cynic is often a disillusioned idealist.

The Houyhnhnms love their species but are indifferent to individuals; Swift claimed that he loved individuals but hated the human species in the abstract. Perhaps both viewpoints are forms of misanthropy: in the Latin epitaph he wrote for himself, Swift tells us he has departed to where 'fierce indignation [saeva indignatio] can lacerate his heart no more'.

One thing is clear: Gulliver's Travels is anything but 'a children's book'. The usually astute Samuel Johnson (1709–84) was wrong to say of it, 'When once you have thought of big men and little men, it is very easy to do all the rest.'

What were the 4 chief winds in ancient Greece?

Boreas: the North Wind   Notus: the South Wind
Zephyrus: the West Wind   Eurus: the East Wind

THE ANCIENT GREEKS saw gods and goddesses everywhere, even in the wind. Although most of their many wind gods, including **Notus** and **Eurus**, remained mere names or abstractions, two of them – Boreas and Zephyrus – were often personified.

Boreas, the North Wind, had two winged sons, Calais and Zetes, who accompanied Jason on his quest for the Golden Fleece. Armed with swords, they used their power of flight to drive off the bird-women Harpies, who were starving the blind old prophet King Phineus by either snatching his food or defecating on it whenever he tucked into a meal. In historical times, the Athenians built a shrine for Boreas because a nor'easter had shattered part of King Xerxes' invading Persian fleet (480 BC).

Zephyrus, the West Wind (compare our word *zephyr* for a gentle breeze), once fell in love with a beautiful young Spartan prince named Hyacinthus. He became so jealous of Apollo, though, who was also courting Hyacinthus, that when the god and the boy were throwing the discus one day, Zephyrus caused Apollo's cast to come crashing down on to Hyacinthus' skull, killing him. The hyacinth sprang from the young prince's blood.

Since horses that were 'as swift as the wind' were often said to be the offspring of a wind god, the two immortal horses of Achilles in Homer's *Iliad* were thought to have been sired by Zephyrus. One of them, Xanthus, had the power of speech (several millennia before Jonathan Swift's Houyhnhnms (see Question 15) and prophesied Achilles' death to him in one of the more moving episodes of the poem. Similarly, the twelve fillies born from the mating of Boreas with twelve Trojan mares could skim over the waves of the sea and race over the tops of standing grain without bending the crops.

The Greeks also believed that mares could conceive merely by lifting their tails and turning their hindquarters to the caresses of the lascivious winds. In more primitive times, it was believed that even women could be impregnated by gusts of wind, which represented the spirits of dead ancestors. And the Roman polymath Pliny the Elder (AD 23–79), who believed just about anything, assures us in his encyclopaedic *Natural History* that if a menstruating woman is exposed to the wind with her belly naked, all hailstorms, whirlwinds and lightning will be promptly scared off.

In Graeco-Roman myth, the ruler of all the winds was Aeolus. When Odysseus and his men land at Aeolus' island kingdom while trying to sail to Ithaca on their way back from the Trojan War, Aeolus traps all the winds in an ox-skin bag – except the West Wind, which the wanderers will need to waft them gently home. But Odysseus' men think that the bulging bag stowed in the ship's hold contains a gift of gold and silver that their captain has neglected to share with them. Already in sight of their homeland (and with Odysseus safely asleep), they open the bag: the howling winds rush out and blow them all the way back to Aeolus' island. Convinced that the gods must be angry with a shipload of such bunglers, Aeolus sends them packing without the benefit of a new ox-skin bag. This adds years to Odysseus' odyssey and thousands of verses to Homer's *Odyssey*.

In Virgil's *Aeneid*, the goddess Juno decides to postpone Aeneas' destined founding of the Roman people, who will one day conquer her beloved Greece. As he and his men sail towards Italy, fleeing their devastated homeland after the Trojan War, the goddess bribes Aeolus with a lovely nymph to grace his marriage bed if he will unleash the fury of the winds that he normally keeps pent up in a cavern. Aeolus complies and the shrieking winds stir up a seastorm that blows the ships of the Trojan refugees off course to Carthage on the north African coast. There Aeneas dallies with Queen Dido until the gods order him to get on with his heroic mission in Italy and Dido is left to her suicidal rage.

Aeolus lent his name to the aeolian (or wind) harp, which produces musical chords when breezes play over its strings. The aeolian harp became a favourite Romantic image of the poet's mind, which is receptive to the 'intellectual breeze' of inspiration and pours forth the music of verse in response. Famous examples of this image occur in Samuel Taylor Coleridge's lyrics 'The Eolian Harp' and 'Dejection: An Ode'.

Which 4 US Presidents were assassinated, and who were their killers?

Abraham Lincoln: John Wilkes Booth
James Garfield: Charles J. Guiteau
William McKinley: Leon Czolgosz
John F. Kennedy: Lee Harvey Oswald

THOUGH I MAY BE EXECUTED for what I have done, I do not care. I shall become the most celebrated man in modern history.' Which presidential assassin said this? You're right if you guessed Charles J. Guiteau, though he was quite wrong about his great fame. Yet the world will long remember the names of Oswald and Booth.

John Wilkes Booth (1838–65), his brother Edwin and their father, Junius Brutus Booth, would still be recognised as eminent Shakespearean actors and the foremost theatrical family in American history even if John Wilkes had not assassinated Abraham Lincoln only five days after Robert E. Lee surrendered at Appomattox Court House, Virginia. Junius, born in London, was considered the peer of the great actor Edmund Kean before moving to America in 1821. Of his ten children, only John Wilkes and Edwin followed him into serious acting.

Despite the acclaim John Wilkes Booth garnered for his performances in the South during the Civil War, his attentions were not focused entirely on his thespian career. He was a staunch Confederate and a member of the militia that hanged John Brown. By 1864, he had conspired with a Washingtonian named John Surratt and several others to kidnap the President. When these plans failed and the Confederacy lurched to defeat, Booth and his co-conspirators decided to kill Lincoln, Vice President Andrew Johnson and Secretary of State William H. Seward.

Booth was a familiar face at Ford's Theater in Washington, where

President and Mrs Lincoln and another couple went on 14 April 1865 (Good Friday) to see the frivolous play *Our American Cousin*. Easily gaining access to the presidential box during the third act, Booth shot Lincoln from about two feet away. He then jumped from the box to the stage, breaking his leg in the process and shouting '*Sic semper tyrannis!*' ('Thus always to tyrants!') – the state motto of Virginia. He escaped through an alley. Lincoln died the following morning.

Booth's accomplice, Lewis Payne, managed to wound Seward and his son at their home, but both survived. The plot against Vice President Johnson failed. Federal troops tracked Booth and a companion to a tobacco farm in Bowling Green, Virginia, where Booth was shot or shot himself, it's unclear which. Four co-conspirators, including John Surratt's mother Mary, who was probably innocent, were hanged in July after a trial by a military commission.

Charles J. Guiteau (1841–82), certainly not the most celebrated man in modern history, but quite probably a schizophrenic, was born in Freeport, Illinois. He was a hyperactive child and his father beat him to help rid him of a speech impediment. As a disciple of Perfectionism and the writings of John Humphrey Noyes, the elder Guiteau believed that death could be defeated and sin was irrelevant. This last bit came in handy at the cult's community in Oneida, New York, where members lived in so-called complex marriages.

Young Charles Guiteau also became a follower of Noyes and moved to the Oneida compound when he was in his early twenties. There, he remained friendless – and celibate – after sharing the news that he was destined to be President of the United States and, eventually, ruler of the world. In addition to free love, the Oneida group also had frequent free-criticism sessions. Subjected to far too much free criticism, Guiteau moved to New York City, where his mental health deteriorated and his various careers flopped.

In 1880, Guiteau distributed numerous copies of a jumbled speech he had written for the presidential campaign of liberal Republican James A. Garfield and his running mate, Chester A. Arthur. Guiteau became a joke in the campaign with his delusional beliefs that he was an intimate of Garfield and that his hard work would be rewarded with a high-level diplomatic post in Paris or Vienna. After the election, the joke became a pest, visiting the White House and State Department to demand his European appointment. Once he actually made it into Garfield's office before being whisked away.

Garfield and Arthur represented different factions of the Republican party whose major differences centred on the issue of federal patronage jobs. Once elected, Garfield ignored Arthur and other members of the so-called Stalwart faction when filling top government positions. News coverage of this political infighting inflamed Guiteau, who, frustrated with his inability to land a federal job, sided with the Stalwarts. He decided that Garfield was destroying the Republican party and must die.

Guiteau spent June 1881 stalking the President, who walked around Washington openly and sometimes alone. On 2 July, at the Baltimore & Potomac Station, as the President was preparing to go on holiday, Guiteau came up behind him and shot him twice. Garfield had been in office for only four months. When he was caught by a police officer, Guiteau explained, 'I am a Stalwart. Arthur is now President of the United States.'

One of the first people to arrive at the station after the shooting was a distraught Robert Todd Lincoln, Abraham Lincoln's son and a member of Garfield's cabinet. Only sixteen years had passed since his father's assassination.

Garfield lingered painfully for seventy-nine days, finally succumbing on 19 September 1881, at a seaside home in Elberon, New Jersey, where he had been moved. Guiteau was hanged in June 1882, while singing an original ditty, 'I am going to the Lordy'.

Some consider the assassination of President William McKinley by **Leon Czolgosz** (1873–1901) the last gasp of the violent anarchist movement in the United States. Czolgosz, born in Detroit to Polish parents, is said, like Guiteau, to have had a history of mental problems. As a young wire-mill worker in Cleveland, he was exposed to anarchist doctrines and came to believe that the US government and economy were the natural enemies of all workers. He thus decided to make the ultimate anarchist gesture and kill McKinley, a Republican who had defeated Democrat William Jennings Bryan for the presidency in 1896 and 1900.

McKinley was a rather spineless president. Although aware that Spain was willing to make concessions after the American battleship *Maine* was blown up in Havana Harbour on 15 February 1898, he kow-towed to the warhawks in Congress, who rallied the press and spoke for big business in declaring war – 'Remember the *Maine!*' As a result of the four-month Spanish–American War, the United States gained Puerto Rico, Guam and the Philippines.

Early in his second term, on 6 September 1901, the President appeared at a Pan-American trade exposition in Buffalo, New York, during which he greeted the public in a receiving line at the exposition's Temple of Music. This aspect of the trip in particular worried some of his staff because the 1900 presidential campaign had been marred by anonymous threatening letters. McKinley would tolerate no increased security measures, however. While a Bach sonata was played, the President reached out to welcome Czolgosz, who fired two shots from a gun hidden in a handkerchief. McKinley collapsed, saying of the angry bystanders, 'Don't let them hurt him.' The President died in Buffalo on 14 September 1901, after his wound became gangrenous. Theodore Roosevelt succeeded him, the youngest man (aged forty-two) to become President. Czolgosz was electrocuted in the prison at Auburn, New York, on 29 October 1901. In 1903, Congress passed laws facilitating the exclusion and deportation of foreign anarchists.

Norman Mailer asks, 'Can there be an American of our century who, having failed to gain stature while he was alive, now haunts us more?' He's speaking, of course, about **Lee Harvey Oswald** (1939–63), the enigmatic figure who shot and killed President John F. Kennedy and wounded Texas Governor John B. Connally in Dallas on 22 November 1963. Two days later, while being transferred to another jail, Oswald himself was shot dead by Jack Ruby, a Dallas nightclub owner – on live, nationwide television.

That's where the facts end and conjectures begin. Did Oswald act alone, as the Warren Commission (1963–4) concluded? Or was he one of two or three gunmen involved in a conspiracy, a possibility left open by a special US House of Representatives Assassinations Committee in 1979? If he acted with others, who were his co-conspirators? Cubans? Soviets? Oswald had moved to the Soviet Union in 1959, married a Russian and tried to renounce his American citizenship. Repatriated in 1962, he then tried to travel to Cuba. Why? Did he have links to the FBI or CIA? Jack Ruby, who claimed he acted as an enraged citizen and died of cancer before his trial, had deep ties to the underworld, raising questions about possible Mob involvement. So much time has now passed that any secrets will probably remain in Oswald's Texas grave.

Who are the 4 Horsemen of the Apocalypse?

War (or Conquest or Christ) on a white horse
Slaughter (or War or Violence) on a red horse
Famine (or Pestilence or Poverty) on a black horse
Death on a pale horse

WHEN THE LAMB (Christ) breaks the first four of seven seals from the scroll in the sixth chapter of the book of Revelation (also called by its Greek-derived title, the Apocalypse), four horrific horsemen materialise, one for each seal, and set out on their task of destruction. The vision of which they're part bodes ill to the Romans, who at the time of this work (c. AD 95) were massacring Christians under the Emperor Domitian (reigned 81 –96).

The Book of Revelation, written by an unknown 'I, John', is traditionally ascribed to St John the Evangelist (see Question 21) in exile on the island of Patmos. This last book of the New Testament, which had a hard time making it into the accepted scriptural canon, comprises a series of visions that Christ vouchsafed to the writer. Its purpose was to strengthen Christians in their resolve to die, if need be, rather than worship the Roman gods and deified emperors during a time of persecution.

Just before the vision of the horsemen, God is pictured on his throne holding a scroll with seven seals that contains a prophecy of what must come to pass (Revelation 4). The source of this scroll is Ezekiel 2:9–10, where 'dirges and laments and words of woe' aimed at Jerusalem are written all over another scroll that Ezekiel, like the author of Revelation, is ordered to eat. God speaks of four dreadful scourges that he will send against Jerusalem as 'sword and famine, wild beasts and pestilence' in Ezekiel 14:21 – pretty close to what the Four Horsemen serve up. In any event, these riders stand for war and its consequences, which will precede the end of the world and destroy the rulers and the rich, while sparing God's servants and martyrs – but judge for yourself (Revelation 6:1–8):

Then I watched as the Lamb broke the first of the seven seals . . . And there before my eyes was **a white horse**, and its rider held a bow. He was given a crown and he rode forth, conquering and to conquer.

When the Lamb broke the second seal . . . out came **another horse, all red**. To its rider was given power to take peace from the earth and make men slaughter one another; and he was given a great sword.

When he broke the third seal . . . there, as I looked, was **a black horse**; and its rider held in his hand a pair of scales. And I heard what sounded like a voice from the midst of the living creatures, which said, 'A whole day's wage for a quart of flour, a whole day's wage for three quarts of barley-meal! But spare the olive and vine.'

When he broke the fourth seal . . . there, as I looked, was **another horse, sickly pale**; and its rider's name was Death, and Hades came close behind. To him was given power over a quarter of the earth, with the right to kill by sword and by famine, by pestilence and wild beasts.

Albrecht Dürer (1471–1528), greatest of German artists, carved a series of fifteen large woodcuts illustrating the Apocalypse (1498). His depiction of the Four Horsemen is justly famous for its Gothic terror. Various well-fed figures are prostrated beneath the horses' hooves, and the riders include a grinning, emaciated Death on an emaciated, grinning horse.

In 1916, the Spanish writer Vicente Blasco Ibáñez (1867–1928) published an international blockbuster novel entitled *The Four Horsemen of the Apocalypse* (*Los cuatro jinetes del Apocalipsis*), contrasting French and German attitudes towards World War I and advocating the Allied cause. In it, Tchernoff, a bearded Russian socialist revolutionary intellectual wino living in Paris at the outbreak of hostilities, conjures up for the young protagonist and another friend the four biblical horsemen, which here stand for conquest (or plague), war, famine and death. The American edition of the 1918 English translation of the book went through fifty-six printings in six months. Film versions of the novel include a 1921 silent classic starring Rudolph Valentino and a 1962 box-office bomb featuring Glenn Ford.

The Ingmar Bergman film *The Seventh Seal* (*Det Sjunde Inseglet*, 1956) evokes the stark, doomsday atmosphere of Revelation, from which it derives its title. The protagonist is a knight (Max von Sydow), home from the Crusades, who plays a game of chess with the hooded figure of Death in a time of plague. At stake is the knight's life. The film is sometimes considered the Swedish director's masterpiece and firmly established his worldwide reputation.

The events foreseen in Revelation were supposed to be imminent – the end of the world, the defeat of the seven-headed dragon Satan by Michael the Archangel, the reign of the beast (thought to be Antichrist), the destruction of the Whore of Babylon (the Roman Empire), the Millennium, the battle of Armageddon, the Last Judgement, the establishment of the New Jerusalem. When these events were delayed, Christian exegetes began allegorising them in thousands of ways, some of them dangerous.

Of the Book of Revelation itself, Harold Bloom has written:

> The influence of Revelation always has been out of all proportion to its literary strength or spiritual value. Though it has affected the strongest poets, from Dante and Spenser through Milton on to Blake and Shelley, it also has enthralled the quacks and cranks of all ages down to the present moment in America. A lurid and inhumane work . . . it is a nightmare of a book: without wisdom, goodness, kindness, or affection of any kind. D. H. Lawrence judged it pungently: 'The Apocalypse does not worship power. It wants to murder the powerful, to seize power itself, the weakling.'*

* Harold Bloom, *The American Religion: The Emergence of the Post-Christian Nation* (New York: Simon & Schuster, 1992), pp. 162–3.

When will the Four Horsemen ride? The American religious leader William Miller (1782–1849) predicted the end of the world would occur 'about the year 1843', and then, more precisely, on 22 October 1844. When nothing happened, the non-event was dubbed the Great Disappointment. None the less, the Millerite movement gave rise to such thriving millenarian sects as the Seventh-Day Adventists and, less directly, Jehovah's Witnesses.

Predictions of the Apocalypse abound. Some saw it in World War I, others in the first Persian Gulf War. One of the more curious identifications of the beast that rises from the sea – whose number is 666 – was that it stood for Ronald Wilson Reagan, each of whose three names contains six letters. Biblical scholars have applied the number, somewhat more appropriately, to another chief executive, the Christian-slaughtering Emperor Nero. In the continuing saga of Revelation and its vicissitudes, the Branch Davidian cult, expecting Armageddon, instead met an apocalyptic death in 1993 at the hands of the Bureau of Alcohol, Tobacco and Firearms at Waco, Texas. And still this 4.5-billion-year-old 'pragmatical, preposterous pig of a world', as Yeats called it, just keeps schlepping along.

Who were the Big Four, and what nations did they represent at the Paris Peace Conference (1919)?

Woodrow Wilson: United States
David Lloyd George: Great Britain
Georges Clemenceau: France
Vittorio Emanuele Orlando: Italy

O N 18 JANUARY 1919, the representatives of twenty-seven nations that had been the principal Allied and Associated Powers in World War I assembled in Paris to impose a peace treaty on the vanquished Central Powers. The plenary sessions, however, were just window dressing; the important decisions were made by the Big Four – or, as Orlando quickly realised, the Big Three. The American President and the three European prime ministers did not make a happy mix: Wilson was idealistic, stubborn, Calvinistically smug and dour, and lacking in diplomatic tact; Lloyd George was fickle, opportunistic and irascible; Clemenceau, nicknamed 'The Tiger' because of his ruthless toppling of French ministries, was a cynical seventy-seven-year-old fiercely nationalistic Germanophobe and duellist (with sword or pistol); and Orlando was a Sicilian law professor and feckless Italian politico.

Thomas Woodrow Wilson (1856–1924) had been president of Princeton University and governor of New Jersey before serving as Democratic president of the United States (1913–21). On 22 January 1917, before America entered the war, he gave his 'Peace Without Victory' speech, which envisioned an eventual settlement that would eschew vengefulness, minimise enmity and incorporate his idea for a League of Nations. But when Germany's unrestricted submarine warfare had exhausted his country's patience, Wilson asked Congress to declare war on 2 April 1917, claiming that 'the world must be made safe for democracy'.

While American doughboys and industrial wealth were helping to put an end to the Great War, Wilson urged Germany in October 1918 to accept an armistice based on the Fourteen Points he had enunciated on 8 January – and which Germany now recognised as the best deal it could hope to get. The shooting stopped on 11 November and at the peace conference Wilson put his plan for a peacekeeping League of Nations ahead of all other considerations. In return for concessions to the Allies that compromised the liberal sentiments of his Fourteen Points – and enraged helpless Germany, which felt betrayed – the covenant of the League was written into the peace treaty with Germany, the Treaty of Versailles (1919). The US Senate demurred at certain provisions of the League of Nations, but Wilson's stiff-necked refusal to have the treaty significantly amended inspired him to undertake a speaking tour of the nation to defend the League. The result was physical collapse, two incapacitating strokes and a slow decline towards death. Wilson's League was established at Geneva in 1920 – the year he won the Nobel Peace Prize – but his country never joined it. The Senate refused to ratify the Treaty of Versailles, and separate peace treaties were negotiated with Germany, Austria and Hungary in August 1921, under Republican President Warren G. Harding.

In Paris, Wilson had generally tried to follow criteria of language, nationality and self-determination in reshaping the boundaries of Europe, but the mind-numbing complexities of this problem were bound to anger and 'betray' some group in just about every instance. Old majorities became new minorities and vice versa, and Wilson did not appreciate the myriad intricacies and acrimonies of European nationalistic micropolitics.

David Lloyd George (1863–1945) was the Liberal Prime Minister of Great Britain (1916–22) who, as chancellor of the exchequer, had presided over the introduction of old-age pensions and national health insurance. His successful political campaign in December 1918 had featured the altruistic slogans 'Hang the Kaiser!' and 'Make Germany pay!' At the peace conference his main goal was to preserve or, better yet, expand the British Empire – which he certainly did, in both the Middle

East and Africa. He generally tried to mediate between Clemenceau's vindictiveness and Wilson's crusading idealism. Lloyd George feared, rightly, that the redistribution of 13 per cent of Germany's 1914 territory and France's demand for excessive reparations could only lead to German revanchism and another European war.

Georges Clemenceau (1841–1929) was a man of intellectual tastes. In his youth he had translated Goethe's *Faust* into French verse. He also founded the journal *L'Aurore*, in which he defended Alfred Dreyfus, publishing (and entitling) Émile Zola's open letter, 'J'accuse', in 1899. Twice premier of France (1906–9 and 1917–20), Clemenceau headed a dictatorial 'victory cabinet' during the war and rallied France to absolute victory and a fight to the death.

Clemenceau found that peacemaking was also a tough business, sitting, as he claimed, between a man who thought himself Napoleon Bonaparte (Lloyd George) and another who fancied himself the Messiah (Wilson). His main concerns at the peace conference were to provide for the security of France against another German invasion and to exact reparation from Germany for all expenses and damage incurred during the war, including the cost of war pensions. Wilson and Lloyd George thought his reparation claims much too extravagant and bitterly contested French claims on German territories. Yet the Tiger – who was shot and wounded during the conference – fell from power in 1920 for supposedly having let Germany off too lightly.

A close friend of Claude Monet, Clemenceau wrote a monograph on him, as well as a book of philosophy and one on the Greek orator Demosthenes, in his mid-eighties. He certainly made the most of his sunset years.

Vittorio Emanuele Orlando (1860–1952) wasted everybody's time at the conference by demanding Fiume (later Rijeka), a small Croatian seaport city on the Adriatic that was home to twenty-five thousand Italians. This particular bubble was burst, mostly by Woodrow Wilson. According to the secret Treaty of London (26 April 1915), England and France pledged to award Italy substantial territories of its age-old enemy, the Austrian Empire, if Italy entered the war on the Allied side.

Although Italy received Trieste and large Austrian possessions in northern Italy after the war, it didn't get the Dalmatian coast of future (now former) Yugoslavia and other cities and islands in the Adriatic – not to mention Fiume, which the Treaty of London had stipulated should remain Croatian. Orlando stormed out of the conference over the Fiume issue but returned two weeks later when he realised his tantrum hadn't changed anyone's mind. He resigned the premiership in June 1919, after serving for less than two years.

In September 1919, the flamboyant Italian poet, war hero and proto-fascist Gabriele D'Annunzio (1863–1938) seized Fiume bloodlessly with about three hundred disgruntled military men and held it for fifteen months. By declaring Fiume a separate state, with himself as leader, D'Annunzio thumbed his nose at 'cowardly Italy' (on which he declared 'war') while retroactively bearding the detested Woodrow Wilson. Discontents – and malcontents – such as these contributed to Mussolini's accession to power in October 1922. Soon after that, Italy did get Fiume, only to lose it again permanently in the chaos of World War II.

When the two-hundred-page peace treaty was presented to the Germans in May 1919, they indignantly refused to sign it. Germany was to assume responsibility for the war in the infamous 'war-guilt clause'. It was to hand over its fleet (which it scuttled at Scapa Flow in the Orkneys – seventy-four warships in five hours – rather than comply with this stipulation). It was to have no air force, tanks or submarines, and an army limited to a hundred thousand men. Alsace-Lorraine, seized in the Franco-Prussian War of 1870–1, was to be returned to France. Germany was to lose all its colonies, which were assigned to various Allies as mandates under the League of Nations covenant. Poland was to be an independent state and enlarged at Germany's expense, with the 'Polish corridor' splitting East Prussia from the rest of Germany. Reparation was to be paid (the amount fixed at thirty-three billion dollars in 1921).

Since the Allied naval blockade would continue to starve Germany until it signed the treaty, two German nobodies were despatched to append their signatures to the shameful document of 'dictated peace' on 28 June 1919. This was the fifth anniversary of the assassination of Archduke Francis Ferdinand of Austria, and the signing took place in the Hall of Mirrors at Versailles – where Germany had proclaimed itself an empire in 1871 after thrashing France in the Franco-Prussian War.

By the Treaty of St Germain (10 September 1919), Austria was shorn of its empire, which became independent states such as Hungary and Czechoslovakia, part of new composite countries such as Yugoslavia and Poland, or territories ceded to Italy. By the Treaty of Sèvres (10 August 1920), the former Middle East empire of the Ottoman Turks was distributed as mandates to Great Britain (Palestine, Jordan and Iraq) and France (Syria, including Lebanon), while Arabia became independent.

The Treaty of Versailles that the Allies forced on Germany – which had no part in the negotiations – pleased few. The Germans saw it as so humiliating that it paved the way for Adolf Hitler's repudiation of everything it stood for. The French judged it far too lenient. The American Senate refused to ratify the treaty, mainly because of its inclusion of the League of Nations covenant. The Italians were disgusted that they got no major colonial plums (or Fiume). The Chinese walked out of the conference. The Russians, still consolidating their Bolshevik revolution, did not attend this conference of capitalistic imperialists and deplored its outcomes.

Centuries earlier, Machiavelli said that the Prince's personal enemies 'must either be coddled or crushed'. As it was, the territorial losses and reparations imposed on Germany were harsh enough to inflame but not to utterly prostrate the country. The treaty caused enormous rancour without attaining its primary objective of rendering Germany incapable of waging aggressive warfare. Worst of all, the Allies did not enforce the treaty rigorously in later years and modified it too casually.

Paris, venue of the Big Four's failure to take the long view of things, found itself in Nazi hands less than twenty-one years after the signing of the Treaty of Versailles, when, in May and June 1940, the German blitzkrieg resulted in French capitulation within five weeks.

Who were the 4 Brontë siblings?

Charlotte	Anne
Emily	Branwell

THE TINY VILLAGE of Haworth in the West Riding district of York-shire was home to a remarkable and reclusive family from 1820 to the 1850s. The story of the Brontës began in September 1802, when a young Irishman named Patrick Brunty left the wild and rough Mountains of Mourne in County Down. He sailed for England and modified his surname in honour of Lord Nelson, who had been created Duke of Brontë (in Sicily) by the King of Naples in 1800. Patrick studied theology at St John's College, Cambridge, began his Yorkshire ministry, married, and fathered six children. In 1820 the family took up residence in the Haworth Parsonage. Although Haworth was hardly a destitute village, conditions were primitive. Amenities such as sewers were lacking, and the drinking water was frequently contaminated. The average age at death was twenty-five.

Not long after the Brontë family settled in at the parsonage, Maria, the frail mother, died and left her young brood to her dour, scholarly husband. He determined that their well-being would best be served by residence at the Clergy Daughters' School in Cowan Bridge, Lancashire. In 1824 the two eldest children, Maria and Elizabeth, departed for the boarding-school that would later be immortalised as the ghastly Lowood School in Charlotte's *Jane Eyre*, where young girls had their characters improved with scant heat and food and much harshness. While their souls were carefully tended with interminable sermons, the girls themselves sat shivering in chapel in rain-soaked clothes. Both Maria and Elizabeth promptly contracted tuberculosis and died in 1825 within a month of each other at ages eleven and ten, respectively.

Charlotte and Emily also attended Cowan Bridge briefly until the elder girls became ill. The surviving children remained at the parsonage for the next five years, receiving their education from an aunt and one another, and creating the two imaginary worlds of Angria and Gondal. The hundred tiny notebooks of the chronicles of Angria (the work of Charlotte and Branwell) still survive and tell of the exotic, and often erotic, adventures of the men and women of a vast African empire. In the kingdom of Gondal (brainchild of Emily and Anne), factions of Royalists and Republicans warred and intrigued against each other. Nothing has survived of this saga except the poems Emily wrote for it.

Much of what is known about the reticent Brontës stems from **Charlotte** (1816–55), the oldest surviving sibling. More willing than the others to venture beyond the gates of the parsonage, Charlotte attended school in Roe Head, Yorkshire, and then in Brussels (1842–4) in the school of Constantine Héger. She chronicled her experiences in the Belgian capital – and disguised her frustrated love for the married Héger – in her first novel, The Professor (published posthumously in 1857), and in her last, Villette (1853), in which the imaginary city of Villette, based on Brussels, is the backdrop for the loneliness and unhappiness of Lucy Snowe. Charlotte's extensive correspondence provided much of the information for her friend Elizabeth Gaskell's Life of Charlotte Brontë (1857), a detailed depiction of the Brontë world.

Charlotte's masterpiece, Jane Eyre, was published in October 1847. The novel follows the orphaned heroine as she endures years of misery at Lowood School and the death by consumption of her childhood friend. Jane later accepts a post as governess at Thornfield Hall, where she meets and falls in love with her Byronic employer, Edward Rochester. After considerable effort, he persuades her to marry him, but Jane learns just before the wedding that he is already married – to Bertha, a mad Creole woman who has long been kept in the attic. Jane and Rochester are unhappily separated for many years and through numerous vicissitudes. Only towards the end of the novel are they reunited, Rochester now blind and maimed from an unsuccessful attempt to save his wife from a fire that ravaged Thornfield Hall. Jane Eyre was an immediate popular and critical success, and such it remains both in print and on film.

Charlotte's novel *Shirley* (1849), set in the latter part of the Napoleonic Wars, features an independent-minded heroine, Shirley Keeldar (based on her sister Emily). At this time the mill towns in northern England were suffering because of war restrictions and the agitation of the Luddites, who expressed their reservations about the mechanisation of the textile industry by smashing machinery. In part a plea for greater freedom of employment choices for women, the book was intended by its author to be 'as unromantic as Monday morning'.

Charlotte, the only Brontë sibling to marry, was wed to Arthur Bell Nicholls, her father's curate, in 1854. She died the following year, of pregnancy toxaemia complicated by tuberculosis, a few weeks before her thirty-ninth birthday.

Her sister **Emily** (1818–48) remains a more evasive and enigmatic figure. The obsessive intensity, darkness and flouting of convention in *Wuthering Heights* (1847) caused the novel to be greeted with considerable incomprehension and disapprobation. Today it stands as the greatest of the Brontë achievements. The tragedy of Heathcliff and Catherine Earnshaw – their shared wild childhood contrasting with their misery-plagued, 'civilised' adult existences lived out in separation – is the romantic story of two characters so intimately fused ('I *am* Heathcliff,' Cathy realises) that their being kept apart, by circumstance and convention, destroys them. Without the primeval, demonic life force of Heathcliff, Cathy is as shallow, foolish and banal as Emily considered society to be. But without Cathy's civilising influence, tempestuous Heathcliff devolves into a monster of icy cruelty and violence. (The Earnshaw home into which he was adopted becomes truly *wuthering*, a Yorkshire term for 'tempest-tossed'.) Their tragedy is resolved only when order is restored to the universe of their bleak Yorkshire moors by the union of their children.

Before dying of tuberculosis in 1848 at the age of thirty, Emily also composed an impressive body of poetry. Charlotte described her younger sister's verse as 'wild, melancholy and elevating'.

Anne (1820–49) briefly attended school with Emily at Roe Head but was educated largely at home. She worked in two households as governess of spoiled, ill-behaved children and recorded her experiences in her first novel, *Agnes Grey* (1847).

Anne's better-known work is *The Tenant of Wildfell Hall* (1848), the story of a mysterious widow, Helen Graham, who, with her small son, moves into a large, dilapidated house near the residence of Gilbert Markham, the book's narrator. Gilbert falls in love with Helen, defending her against the vicious gossip of neighbours who believe she is sexually involved with the owner of Wildfell Hall. In fact, the owner is her brother, who has provided her with a refuge from her violent, debauched husband, Arthur Huntingdon. Helen returns to him, however, on learning of his protracted fatal illness, which he exacerbates by ongoing dissipation. After his death, the two principals are united.

In a biographical notice about Anne after her death from tuberculosis at the age of twenty-nine, Charlotte suggested that the awful Huntingdon was modelled on none other than brother **Branwell** (1817–48), whose childhood promise in the arts remained unfulfilled. He failed as a portrait painter and as a tutor (after a romantic involvement with his employer's wife), and he got fired from a railway job. He spent his last years at Haworth solacing himself with alcohol and opium, much to the grief of his sisters. He died at the age of thirty-one.

Biographers and critics continue to be fascinated with all the Brontës, and periodic attempts are made at rehabilitating poor Branwell. These foredoomed efforts are hilariously satirised in a subplot of Stella Gibbons's 1932 novel, *Cold Comfort Farm*, in which the ludicrous Mr Mybug is busy writing a 'Life of Branwell Brontë', setting forth the hypothesis that the latter actually wrote all the Brontë books. (After all, the sisters had published their poems and novels under the male pseudonyms of Currer Bell, Ellis Bell and Acton Bell. Startled disbelief ensued when the sex of the authors was revealed.) In Mr Mybug's view, the sisters, 'devoured by jealousy of their brilliant brother', engaged in the game of 'passing his manuscripts off as their own . . . They wanted to have him under their noses so that they could steal his work and sell it to buy more drink . . . for themselves. They were all drunkards, but Anne was the worst of the lot.'

A minority view, to be sure. Today the Brontë reputation rests solidly on Charlotte, Emily and Anne, and the astonishing novels and poems they created out of a cloistered world but a seemingly boundless imaginative faculty. In Branwell's haunting oil portrait of them, the Brontë sisters still gaze into mystery like three doomed young Fates.

Who were the 4 Evangelists, and what were their symbols?

Matthew: a man (or angel)   Luke: an ox
Mark: a lion   John: an eagle

THE EVANGELISTS are the traditional authors of the four canonical Gospels (*godspel* means 'good news' in Anglo-Saxon, a literal translation of the Latin *evangelium* and Greek *euangelion* – the opening word of Mark). These accounts of the life, sayings and teachings of Jesus, proclaiming the good news that the Messiah had come and the kingdom of God was at hand, were written in Koine ('common') Greek, the lingua franca of the eastern Mediterranean at the time of Christ. In Gothic and later art, Matthew was often depicted as writing his Gospel while looking over his shoulder at an angel; Mark while in the company of a reclining winged lion; Luke while an ox placidly chews the cud of rumination; and John the Divine as an epicene young man with an eagle in the background. Sometimes, especially in earlier art of the Romanesque period, an angel (or man), winged lion, winged ox and eagle were used to represent the Evangelists themselves.

These icons all derive from the four 'living creatures', or angels, in Revelation 4:7 and, ultimately, from the four-faced cherubim of Ezekiel 1 and 10. The second-century Church Father Irenaeus first used the creatures of Revelation to symbolise the four Evangelists, claiming that the man's face stands for Christ's Incarnation, the lion for his royalty, the ox (or calf) for his priestly (sacrificial) office, and the eagle for the grace of the Holy Spirit. Other interpretations based on the characteristics of the four Gospels are mentioned below.

Matthew was one of the Twelve Apostles (see Question 59), but the attribution to him of the first Gospel, written *c.* AD 85, after the fall of Jerusalem, is traditional rather than historical. This Gospel, which may have been composed in Antioch, Syria, is addressed to Jewish Christians and often quotes from the Old Testament to prove that Christ is the

Messiah and that his life fulfilled many prophecies of the Hebrew scriptures. Matthew accordingly begins with the genealogy of Jesus, a descendant of David and Abraham (through his foster-father, St Joseph). This emphasis on Christ's humanity helps explain Matthew's symbol in art as a man. The stories of Christ's infancy in Matthew are meant to draw parallels between him and Moses, just as the Sermon on the Mount is the 'New Law' of perfection that transcends the Mosaic Law.

The Gospel of **Mark** is the shortest and most primitive of the four canonical Gospels, and also the earliest (c. AD 65–70), though orthodox tradition placed it second. It was probably composed at Rome and addressed to Christians who were suffering persecution there. Its author was said to have been either an associate of St Peter or the John Mark who travelled with St Paul and St Barnabas.

Mark's symbol of the lion is sometimes explained by his beginning his Gospel with John the Baptist and Jesus in the wilderness. Since the lion was supposed to sleep with its eyes open, and its cubs were thought to be born dead until their sire roared three days later, it also symbolised Christ's Resurrection after three days in the tomb.

In the ninth century, some Venetian merchants smuggled Mark's body out of Alexandria, Egypt – assuring the Muslim customs inspector that their casket was full of pork – and brought it to Venice. Thus, Mark became Venice's patron saint, and the magnificent cathedral and square dedicated to him are the pride of that city.

The third Gospel, of **Luke**, probably written between AD 80 and 90, and its sequel, the Acts of the Apostles (the fifth book of the New Testament), may be the work of a non-Jewish Christian. The author was traditionally identified with the Luke who was a companion of St Paul – 'the beloved physician' of Colossians 4:14. In some works of art, Luke is shown painting a picture because of the legend that he once painted a portrait of the Virgin Mary. In medieval guilds, both painters and apothecaries belonged to the guild of St Luke.

The Gospel begins with the Jewish priest Zechariah, soon to be the father of John the Baptist, sacrificing in the Temple at Jerusalem. The ox, symbol of sacrifice, was thus seen to be a fitting emblem of Luke and of

Christ's Passion. Luke's is the only Gospel that contains the parables of the Good Samaritan and the Prodigal Son. Like Matthew's, Luke's Gospel provides an account of the birth of Jesus. The splendid hymns usually referred to as the 'Magnificat' (of Mary) and the 'Nunc Dimittis' (of Simeon) also have their origin in Luke. This Gospel is notable for its humane concern with the poor, the oppressed, the outcast. Ernest Renan, the French author of a highly controversial and rationalistic *Life of Jesus* (1863), considered Luke's Gospel the most beautiful book ever written.

Matthew and Luke both used the Gospel of Mark as a source. They also relied heavily on a hypothetical Greek document called 'Q' (for German *Quelle*, 'source'), which apparently consisted mostly of Christ's sayings, such as the Lord's Prayer, the Sermon on the Mount, and the Eight Beatitudes (see Question 45), but also contained some narratives such as the preaching of John the Baptist and the temptation of Christ (see Question 12). The text of Q has been reconstructed by biblical scholars.

The first three Gospels are called synoptic (Greek, 'viewed together') because they have many parallel passages (including much exact wording) that can be compared side by side. The relationship between them seems to be roughly as follows: both Matthew and Luke used Mark and Q as sources; in addition, Matthew used a separate hypothetical source (referred to as 'M'), whereas Luke used another ('L') – both of which may have been oral traditions. Of the 661 verses in the Gospel of Mark, only thirty-one are totally unrepresented in either Matthew or Luke. Because Matthew reproduces more than six hundred of Mark's verses, his Gospel has been referred to as 'the second edition of Mark, revised and expanded'. In addition, the Gospels of Matthew and Luke have about 235 verses that are parallel and seem to derive from the Q source. And did Matthew or Luke know the other's Gospel? Hard to say.

The soaring eagle, symbol of **John**, denotes the sublimity of his Gospel, which begins with a prologue identifying Christ with both God and the *Logos* (Divine Reason or Wisdom, the Word) of Greek philosophy. St John, the Galilean fisherman who was one of the Twelve Apostles, was not the author of the fourth Gospel, the three epistles of

John, and Revelation (see Question 18). A disciple of St John at Ephesus, John the Elder, may have been the author of the Gospel.

Throughout, John's highly spiritual Gospel stresses the mystery of the Incarnation – 'the Word became flesh and dwelt among us' – and the divinity of Jesus much more insistently than the synoptic Gospels. The eagle was supposedly the only creature capable of gazing directly at the sun, which was a symbol of divinity. Christ's Ascension into Heaven is also figured forth by the lofty flight of John's eagle.

John's Gospel, the latest, while having some affinities with the three synoptics, is largely an independent text probably written in Asia Minor between AD 95 and 100. It describes Christ's ministry as taking place mostly in Judaea and mentions three Passovers, whereas the synoptics concentrate on Christ's teaching in Galilee and on only one Passover. From John's Gospel we thus deduce that Christ's ministry lasted three years. Unlike the synoptics, this Gospel is characterised by long discourses, few parables and no exorcisms. Its tone is austere, august and majestic; knowledge of God and Christ is emphasised over good works.

The influence the Gospels have exerted on western theology, philosophy, literature, art, music and everyday life is incalculable. As the authorised 'biographies' of Christ, providing accounts of his words and teachings, they were regarded with infinite awe and veneration. Here, from four different angles, Christian readers could ponder the earthly existence and cosmic significance of their God and Redeemer. In the eighteenth century, however, a few scholars began pointing out irreconcilable contradictions between the four Gospels and expressing some doubt about the authenticity of the miracles recounted therein. By the twentieth century, scepticism regarding the Gospels had become the norm for much of the intelligentsia.

The Evangelists are recalled in Samuel Beckett's play *Waiting for Godot* (1952) by Vladimir ('Didi') for the unwilling edification of Estragon ('Gogo'). Didi's point is that only one of the Evangelists (Luke) assures us that one of the thieves crucified with Christ was saved ('Today shalt thou be with me in paradise'). 'One out of four' is Didi's sombre comment on the thief's chances of attaining salvation – and maybe ours.

FIVE

What are the 5 pillars of Islam?

Witnessing that God is one and Mohammed is his prophet
Praying five times daily
Giving a portion of one's wealth to charity yearly
Fasting during daylight hours in the holy month of Ramadan
Making the pilgrimage to Mecca at least once

ISLAM WAS FOUNDED in Arabia between 610 and 632 by Mohammed (570–632), an inhabitant of Mecca. Derived from the Arabic root *salaama* ('peace', 'purity'), *Islam* means 'submission' to the will of God; one who has made this submission is called by the related word *Muslim*.

It's said that while meditating in the desert, Mohammed (or Muhammad) received a number of revelations enjoining him to lead the idolatrous Arabs to a knowledge of the one true God, Allah. The angel Gabriel brought down to him the Koran (Qur'an), the eternal, uncreated Word of Allah. The 114 suras (chapters) of this sacred book of Islam and the *sunna*, made up of collections of traditions (*hadith*) of the deeds and sayings of Mohammed, are the sources of the Islamic creed.

Mohammed saw himself as the culminating prophet in a series of at least twenty-five Old and New Testament figures, including Adam, Noah, Abraham, Ishmael, Isaac, Moses, David and Jesus. He was the Seal of the Prophets, that is, the last and most important. Mohammed had to flee from Mecca to Medina, where his prophetic mission was well received. This event, which occurred on Friday 16 July AD 622, is known as the hegira (*hijrah*, 'migration') and marks the beginning of the Muslim era – Anno Hegirae (or AH) 1. In 630 Mohammed entered Mecca as a conqueror, and he died two years later at Medina. From Arabia, his followers propagated their faith by the sword in a wide swath stretching from Morocco and Spain in the West to Indonesia in the East.

The edifice of Islam is supported by five pillars that represent the basic duties of those who wish to be considered part of the Islamic community. The first is a statement of faith, and the other four are manifestations of it. **Witnessing** (*shahada*) **that Allah is one and Mohammed is his prophet** must be done publicly at least once in a lifetime. It involves a fervent recitation of the following words, with full acceptance and understanding of all the main articles of Islamic belief: *Ashhadu alla ilaha illa Allah wa ashhadu anna Muhammad rasulu Allah* ('I bear witness that there is no God but Allah, and I bear witness that Muhammad is His messenger'). Here the uncompromising monotheism of Islam and its teaching that Mohammed is the final fulfilment of all prophecy are affirmed.

Praying (*salat*) **five times daily** is incumbent on every Muslim past puberty. The prayers, prefaced by ablution (*wudu*) of face, hands (to the elbow) and feet, are always the same, containing verses from the Koran recited in Arabic while the Muslim faces in the direction of Mecca. Muslims say these prayers while bowing and prostrating themselves on a carpet with shoes removed and head covered. Each day, from the minaret of a mosque, a muezzin, or crier, calls Muslims to their obligatory prayers at early morning, noon, mid-afternoon, sunset and evening.

Any delayed obligatory prayers must be made up. While these daily prayers can be said almost anywhere, Muslims are required to offer their Friday noon prayer in a mosque together with its congregation. The prayers, led by an imam, are supplemented by readings from the Koran and a sermon.

Obligatory almsgiving (*zakat*) involves a donation of 2.5 per cent that Muslims must pay each year on their net assets, given in kind or coin, if their net worth is above a certain level. The recipients are mainly the poor, needy, wayfaring and debt-ridden. Any voluntary charity over and above the *zakat* is called *sadaqat*.

Fasting (*sawm*) **between dawn and sunset during Ramadan**, the Islamic year's ninth month (which migrates throughout the seasons because of the Muslims' uncorrected lunar calendar), involves complete abstinence from eating, drinking, sexual relations and smoking. It was during this month that the Koran was sent down by Allah from the seventh heaven to Gabriel in the first heaven that it might be revealed to Mohammed. All adult Muslims are required to keep the fast, except those who are mentally or physically unfit, elderly, on a journey, serving in the armed forces, working as manual labourers, or, in the case of women, menstruating, pregnant or nursing a child. The end of Ramadan is celebrated with a festival called Id al-Fitr.

The pilgrimage (*hajj*) **to the holy Arabian city of Mecca at least once in a lifetime** is required of all Muslims who are mentally, physically and financially sound. Each year, several million Muslims journey from all quarters of the globe during the twelfth month of the Islamic year to take part in the world's largest religious convention. Pilgrims, wearing simple garments, commemorate the rituals observed by Abraham and his son Ishmael, father of the Arabs. These two were believed to have built the Kaaba (*ka'bah*, 'square building'), a small stone edifice located in the court of the Great Mosque (*al-Haram*) at Mecca. The Kaaba is considered the house of Allah on earth, although it had earlier contained the idols of the pagan Meccans. It enshrines a sacred black stone, apparently of volcanic or meteoric origin, thought by Muslims to be one of the stones of Paradise given by the angel Gabriel to Abraham. Pilgrims circle the Kaaba seven times (three times running, four times slowly, in memory of Adam's imitation of the circling of the angels around the throne of Allah), kiss the black stone, run seven times between the hills of Safa and Marwa, as Hagar did during her frantic search for water for her son Ishmael, and stand together and pray in the broad plain of Mount Arafat in anticipation of the Day of Judgement.

An important duty during the *hajj* is that of sacrificing a ram in the valley of Mina on the tenth day of the pilgrimage month. This is now usually done by an official proxy, and the sacrificed animals are donated as food for the poor. A visit to the tomb of Mohammed in Medina is recommended but not obligatory. The close of the annual period of the *hajj* is marked by the great festival of *Id al-Adha*, celebrated with prayers and the exchange of gifts in Muslim communities all over the world.

Jihad ('striving') is sometimes seen as an additional duty imposed on Muslims, but interpretations of it range from 'holy war' to a personal striving for adherence to the ethical norms of the Koran.

What were the 5 events of the ancient Olympic pentathlon?

Footrace	Long jump
Discus throw	Wrestling
Javelin throw	

THE FIRST OLYMPIAN GAMES, held in Olympia in western Greece, are said to have been celebrated in 776 BC, the year when the first champion was listed in their records. They were inaugurated as a religious festival – some said by Heracles – in honour of the chief god, Zeus. But to the Greeks, the games were not only a religious ceremony and a sporting event but an art form in which the beauty, gracefulness and strength of the human body were displayed to full advantage in the context of friendly competition. So important were these games to the Greeks that the four-year intervals between them were called Olympiads. Not only were the dates of events kept with reference to the Olympiads, but the Greek calendar itself began in 776 BC.

The games were held during the second or third full moon after the summer solstice, usually between 6 August and 19 September. Foreigners and married women were not allowed to compete. (Young and unmarried girls, however, had their own games, the Heraia, in honour of Zeus's queen, Hera, which took place at Olympia, probably just before the men's games, and consisted only of a footrace.) Any man could compete in the Olympian Games, provided he was of pure Hellenic blood, free of any legal infraction, and clear of any penalty owed to Zeus.

Although these were the only requirements, the standard training procedure for the games usually necessitated some funding. Despite the existence of government-subsidised gymnasiums in the city-states of ancient Greece, proper training could involve considerable time, money and instruction. By the sixth century BC, athletes began training in specialised areas under expert coaches. Many subjected themselves to regimens regarding diet, exercise and sex, although some of these were idiosyncratic by modern standards. For example, Milo of Croton in southern Italy (late sixth century BC), the greatest Olympian wrestler, allegedly consumed forty pounds of meat and bread at one sitting, washing it down with two gallons of wine. Families usually absorbed the bulk of the expenses, although at least one trainer requested government subsidies by about 300 BC. Two centuries later, professional athletes with memberships in young men's organisations began to surface.

Athletes trained for ten months before the games with great intensity and focus. Their last month of training, the most strenuous, was spent under the guidance of Olympian judges called *Hellanodicae*, who had completed ten months of training themselves. During this last harrowing month, these judges weeded out the weaker competitors.

The remaining qualifiers had to take an oath administered by the *Hellanodicae* and attesting to their worthiness: 'If you have exercised yourself in a manner worthy of the Olympian Games, if you have been guilty of no slothful or ignoble act, go on with a good courage. You who have not so practised, go wherever you wish.' After swearing this oath, the athletes formed a religious procession. Before a statue of Zeus, the contestants offered a boar as sacrifice. They then placed their hands on the beast's entrails and swore they had trained faithfully for ten months and would treat the other competitors fairly and honestly. The judges swore they would render fair and honest decisions without accepting any bribes.

Because the ancient Greeks considered the human body to be pure and beautiful, male athletes competed naked. (In fact, it is from the Greek *gymnos*, 'naked', that we derive *gymnast* and *gymnasium*.) In the *Republic*, Plato claims that one of the differences between barbarians and Greeks was that the latter weren't ashamed to compete in the nude.

Admission to the games was free. Except for the judges and officials, most spectators sat on the ground. A capacity crowd may have been about ten thousand. The only married woman allowed to attend was the priestess of Demeter, all others being barred on pain of being hurled off a nearby mountain. Unmarried girls were free to come and watch, presumably in lieu of anatomy class.

The only known attempt of an adult woman to circumvent the rules occurred when the aristocratic Callipatira disguised herself in a unisex robe as the trainer of her son, who was competing in the boys' boxing match. When he won, she was so excited that she leaped over the barricade to congratulate him – and her robe flew open. The *Hellanodicae* pardoned her but ruled that, in the future, trainers had to appear naked.

Initially, there was only one Olympian event, a **footrace** that covered one length of track. This measured about 650 feet, a distance referred to as a stade, which gave rise to our word *stadium*. More events were gradually added, including the two-stade race in 724 BC and the long-distance race (probably about three miles) in 720 BC. By 708 BC, the complete pentathlon ('five contests') was in place.

The **discus throw** involved hurling a flat piece of stone or metal that was hardly standardised. The few discuses that have been dug up range in weight (three to twelve pounds), diameter (seven to thirteen inches) and material. By comparison, the modern discus weighs slightly less than four and a half pounds. Although the exact ancient method of throwing the discus remains unknown, Roman copies of the *Discus Thrower* (*Discobolus*) of the Greek sculptor Myron (fifth century BC) suggest it did not differ significantly from modern techniques. In the only surviving description of the distance of a toss, the mighty athlete Phayllus of Croton managed one of about one hundred feet.

The **javelin throw** was judged for distance or, in later times, accuracy. The javelin itself was a light, six-foot wooden pole that was blunt at both ends. Ancient Greeks threw it in much the same way that modern athletes do, with a running start to the throwing line. By the end of the fifth century BC, the goal of the event shifted from the distance to the accuracy of the toss. The pole was replaced by a spear that was hurled towards a target both from on foot and from horseback.

The **long jump** involved getting a running start, jumping as far as possible, and landing with the feet together. The Greeks also used two jumping weights (something like dumb-bells) to help them put greater momentum behind their leaps. The distance of the jump seems to have included the hop and skip, too, as opposed to only the jump itself. This helps explain the fifty-five-foot jump recorded of Phayllus of Croton.

The final event of the pentathlon was **wrestling**, in which the two top overall competitors from the previous events battled each other. Ancient Greek wrestlers took certain liberties – choking, shoving, finger-twisting – that are now frowned upon. The winner was the first to bring his opponent down with three separate clean throws.

Historians still debate how the pentathlon was scored. Some form of progressive elimination, down to the final wrestling event, must have been used. Although victors in the Olympian Games received only a wreath of wild olive, this was just the beginning. On returning to their home towns, they were often honoured with statues bearing their likeness, as well as significant monetary awards – none more generous than the equivalent of about £150,000 that Athens granted its Olympian winners in the time of Solon (early sixth century BC). A few lucky winners in the first half of the fifth century BC were presented with splendid epinician ('victory') odes by the Greek lyric poet Pindar (see Question 50). Although most of his odes were written for victories in chariot racing, Pindar celebrates one winner of a pentathlon at the Olympian Games of 464 BC, Xenophon of Corinth (*Odes*, 'Olympian 13'). It's far from his best poem.

After Rome had consolidated its conquest of Greece in 146 BC, participation in the games at Olympia (and the rest of Greece) dwindled as the city of Rome gradually became the centre of athletic competition in the empire. The Olympian Games continued, however, until growing Christian influence on the government prompted Emperor Theodosius I to abolish them as pagan practices in AD 393.

It was only in 1896 that these games were revived in Athens as the Olympics. Since then, they have been held in different venues every four years, except for 1916, 1940 and 1944, when they were suspended for the grimmer competition of war. (In ancient times, it was often the other way around, wars being suspended because of the games.) The chasm dividing the original five competitions of the pentathlon and the constantly proliferating summer and winter Olympic events is just one indication of the vastly broadened conception of 'athletics' over the past twenty-eight centuries.

What are the 5 classical architectural orders?

Doric   Composite
Ionic   Tuscan
Corinthian

THE MONUMENTAL ACHIEVEMENTS of Graeco-Roman architecture
are epitomised in their architectural orders. An order is a discrete,
standard style unit consisting of a column, base and entablature (see
illustration on p. 90). Three orders – the Doric, Ionic and Corinthian –
were Greek creations; the Composite and Tuscan were Roman deriva-
tives. The orders are perhaps the best-known elements of the western
architectural vocabulary – consider the columns of the Parthenon and
(to compare great things with small) those of the White House or even
a Depression-era US post-office building.

The earliest Greek temples were built of wood. Eventually, limestone
was used and, when funds were available, marble. Regardless of the
order used or the temple's size, the basic plan and function remained
the same. In the centre of these open, usually rectangular structures was
the *cella*, or *naos*. Here was kept an image of the deity to whom the temple
was dedicated. In the simplest temples only a porch with two columns
was added, whereas larger, grander temples had a second porch or even
a colonnade (peristyle). All were constructed with lintels (rarely, if ever,
an arch) and sloping roofs. The temple was meant to be admired from
the outside, since access to the interior was somewhat restricted, and
public religious ceremonies were conducted just outside the temple.

The orders share several features. Starting at the bottom, the unit rests
on the stereobate and stylobate. Except for Doric constructions, the column itself rests on a base, which is more or less decorative depending
on the order. The column shaft is composed of a series of drums stacked
on one another and secured with bronze or wooden pivots running
through the centre of each. No mortar was used, attesting to the Greeks'

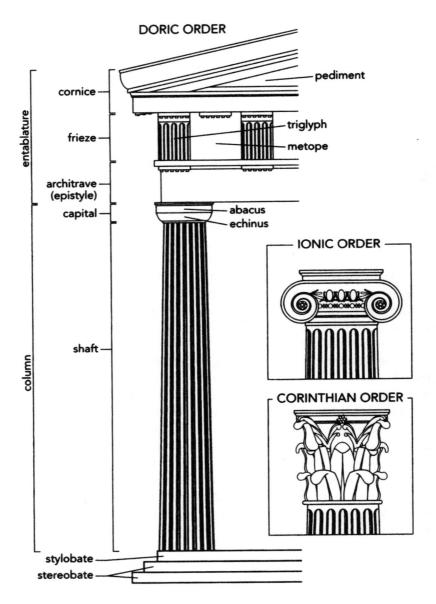

DORIC ORDER

pediment

cornice

entablature

frieze

triglyph

metope

architrave
(epistyle)

capital

abacus
echinus

IONIC ORDER

shaft

column

CORINTHIAN ORDER

stylobate

stereobate

The Elements of Classical Architecture

skill and precision in cutting stone. The vertical flutes, which were incised into the stone after the column had been assembled, contribute a visual dynamism while disguising the drum joints. The height of a column was defined in terms of its diameter at the base. For example, builders were given directions to make the columns eight or nine diameters high.

At the top of the column shaft, the neck marks the transition to the capital, comprising the echinus and abacus. The capital most readily displays the distinguishing characteristics of each order. The section above the capital, the entablature, includes in ascending order the architrave (which bears and distributes the weight above), the frieze, pediment and cornice. The architrave, often left unadorned, might also contain panels called fasciae. Above this, the frieze might be bare or decorated with triglyphs and metopes, carvings in relief, or other elements. The remainder consists of the cornice and the pediment (which might also have been decorated). The cornice encloses the triangular form of the pediment.

The **Doric**, the oldest order, was developed in mainland Greece. What is known of one of the most ancient examples of a Doric edifice, the temple of Artemis at Corcyra (modern Corfu), suggests that the order had been codified by about 600 BC. Although the source of their inspiration remains unclear, the architects were no doubt influenced by Greek pre-Archaic wood-and-mud-based structures, as well as by Mycenaean and Egyptian models. Compared with the other orders, the Doric seems plain, massive and stolid, an impression confirmed by its ancient designation as a 'masculine order'.

Doric columns rested directly on the stylobate without a base. They tapered towards the top in a slight curve, or entasis, creating a feeling of lightness to offset the order's solidity. Conventional Doric columns contain exactly twenty flutes. In the most ancient examples, like the so-called Basilica at Paestum in southern Italy (c.530 BC), the echinus portion of the Doric capital resembles a pillow or giant marshmallow bulging from beneath the weight of an even massier abacus.

In these old exemplars, the columns were placed quite close

together, prompting the Roman architect Vitruvius (first century BC) to comment that their narrow spaces created problems for groups of matrons who wished to enter the temple with their arms around each other but who instead had to form a single file. In fact, these squat, closely set columns suggest that early architects were a bit unsure about how their designs would hold up – literally. Over time, the proportions of the Doric order became more visually pleasing, as the architects became more confident of the structural integrity of their design. The capitals, in particular, assumed a more refined look, and the narrower, more graceful columns were spaced more widely. This transition occurred on the Greek mainland by about 500 BC. The outstanding example of the Doric is the Parthenon on the Athenian Acropolis, the most revered of surviving Greek temples.

The **Ionic** order was developed in Asia Minor and the Aegean Islands only shortly after the Doric, probably by about 560 BC. Designated a 'feminine order' by the manly Greeks, the Ionic features a column that is more slender and less tapering than the Doric, has a decorated base and twenty-four flutes, and is eight diameters high. Its most distinguishing feature is the scroll, or volute, that subsumes the echinus and is typically carved with a motif termed 'egg and dart'. As with the Doric Parthenon, the finest examples of the Ionic order are also on the Athenian Acropolis: the Erechtheum and the Temple of Athene Nike.

The highly decorative **Corinthian** order evolved by about 425 BC. Vitruvius repeats a fanciful tale about the origins of this order, which he compares to the figure of a young girl, 'for the outlines and limbs of maidens, being more slender on account of their tender years, admit of prettier effects in the way of adornment'.

The story goes that the Athenian sculptor Callimachus passed by the tomb of a recently deceased Corinthian girl. Her nurse had placed a basket of her favourite possessions on top of the tomb and covered it with a tile. Beneath the basket was an acanthus plant, which sent its shoots up and through the sides of the basket. According to Vitruvius, Callimachus was so smitten with the sight of the interwoven basket and tendrils that he was inspired to design the Corinthian capital.

Unlike the Ionic capital, meant to be viewed from only two sides, the Corinthian, usually perched atop a column ten diameters high, may be admired from all four angles. At first, Corinthian capitals, which include staggered rows of elaborately carved acanthus leaves below the abacus, were used only in the interior of edifices. After a century of indoor use, they began to be erected on the exteriors of structures. The oldest surviving example is the Monument of Lysicrates in Athens (334 BC). Later, the Romans used the elegant, sumptuous Corinthian more widely than any other order.

Favouring more elaborate decoration than the Greeks, the Romans were somewhat less concerned with geometric perfection. They felt free to replace lintels with arches, and their entablatures were often more highly decorated. In their **Composite** order, they combined the scroll of the Ionic capital with the acanthus leaves of the Corinthian. The columns were often ten diameters in height.

The Romans also devised the **Tuscan** order, a simplification of the Doric. Tuscan columns have the characteristic Doric capital but, unlike Doric columns, rest on a base. They also lack fluting and are typically only seven diameters high.

Further variations on these themes include the Superposed and Colossal orders. The Superposed, a Roman invention, was used when columns were erected on several storeys of a building. By convention, Doric columns adorned the first storey, Ionic the second, and Corinthian the third, resulting in a visual epitome of the three ancient Greek orders, as in Rome's Colosseum. During the Renaissance, architects sometimes worked two- or three-storey columns (or half-pillars) of a single order into their edifices – examples of the aptly named Colossal order.

Who were the Russian composers known as the Mighty Five?

Mili Balakirev	Modest Mussorgsky
Nikolai Rimsky-Korsakov	César Cui
Aleksandr Borodin	

THE HISTORY OF DISTINCTLY RUSSIAN MUSIC — other than folk tunes — has been said to date from the first performance, in 1836, of the opera *A Life for the Czar* (also called *Ivan Susanin* by the Soviets) by Mikhail Glinka (1804–57). Glinka followed with another opera, *Russlan and Ludmilla*, in 1842, and portions of both were performed in Paris under the direction of Hector Berlioz — the first time that Russian orchestral music was played outside of Russia. Glinka's importance lies not only in the merits of his work but also in his role as father of the Russian nationalist movement in music. This movement peaked with the accomplishments of the Mighty Five, or Mighty Handful (*Moguchaya Kuchka*), as music critic Vladimir Stassov, later a close friend and promoter of the group, dubbed them in 1857.

Until the mid-nineteenth century, the composers most influential in Russia, as throughout Europe, were German, Italian and French. The establishment of a consciously Russian nationalist movement in music by Glinka and his followers was a reaction to this foreign influence. Because the German musical orthodoxy was considered the most over-bearing, the Mighty Five were dedicated to founding a native Russian school of music to rival Germany's.

Although the Five were near-amateurs, some music critics have asserted that this lack of formal training in theory and composition worked to their advantage. Had they been more familiar with conventional harmony and counterpoint, they might not have sought inspiration in Russian folk-song idioms.

Mili Balakirev (1837–1910) spent most of his early life in the company of eminent musicians. He studied mathematics and musical composition at the University of Kazan and by the mid-1850s had become a prominent concert pianist. He eventually became the concert conductor at the St Petersburg Conservatory. During his early years in St Petersburg, Balakirev met Glinka, who bestowed the nationalist mantle on him, modestly calling him 'a second Glinka'. The state of Russian musical sophistication at this time may be gauged from the fact that there were no Russian-language textbooks on composition, and since Balakirev could read little German, Glinka tutored him privately.

In 1866, Balakirev published an authoritative collection of Russian folk tunes. Traces of them are heard in his best-known compositions, *Islamey* (one of the most difficult piano pieces ever written) and the symphonic poem *Tamara*. He also became the musical mentor of Borodin and Rimsky-Korsakov.

Balakirev's later life was plagued by mental illness. Although his pupils recognised the privilege of studying with him, he apparently had always been unpleasant and almost unbearably rigid and dogmatic. Rimsky-Korsakov wrote that Balakirev the teacher was 'so despotic that he insisted we remodel our music exactly according to his prescriptions'. He added that entire segments of compositions ostensibly written by younger students were actually composed by Balakirev. Several bouts of severe depression took their toll on Balakirev's art. He is now remembered more for his influence on the rest of the Five and later composers than for his own compositions.

While studying at the naval academy of St Petersburg, **Nikolai Rimsky-Korsakov** (1844–1908) met Balakirev, who urged him to broaden his earlier training in music and composition and write a symphony. His association with Balakirev was interrupted when he sailed to America after graduating, spending time in several East Coast ports during the Civil War. Reminiscences of his long sea voyages reappear throughout his works. On returning to Russia, he finished his first symphony, performed in 1865 when he was only twenty-one. This was the first 'real' symphony composed by a Russian. Shortly afterwards, Rimsky-Korsakov wrote *Fantasy on Serbian Themes*. His fame and reputation grew, and he found himself teaching composition at the St Petersburg Conservatory despite his scanty musical education, limited primarily to some work with Balakirev.

His début as a conductor took place at the first performance of his third symphony in 1874, at the start of a successful conducting career that continued into the early years of the twentieth century. He also was editor of a publishing company dedicated to the publication and preservation of Russian music.

Rimsky-Korsakov wrote quite a few operas, but the one performed most often in the West is *Le Coq d'or* (*The Golden Cockerel*) (1909), which was banned in Russia during his lifetime because the court of its king, Dodon, bore too close a resemblance to that of Czar Nicholas II. His most widely known orchestral works are *Capriccio espagnol* (1887), *Scheherazade* (1888), and *The Flight of the Bumble Bee*, from the opera *The Tale of Czar Saltan* (1900).

Rimsky-Korsakov's long career as a teacher spanned two generations of Russian composers. His students included Igor Stravinsky, Sergei Prokofiev and Aleksandr Glazunov, as well as Italian composer Ottorino Respighi, and his influence lives on in the music of Debussy and Ravel, among others.

The charming and urbane **Aleksandr Borodin** (1833–87) was the illegitimate son of an elderly Georgian prince and a twenty-four-year-old woman who later married a doctor. Although his musical talent surfaced early in his privileged childhood, he became a surgeon and later a professor of chemistry and was known in scientific circles for his work on aldehydes. Also gifted in languages, Borodin wrote some of his scientific papers in Italian. Music never left him, however, and he wrote his first symphony soon after meeting Balakirev, who conducted at its première in 1869. His most celebrated work is the opera *Prince Igor*, first performed in an unfinished version in 1879 and conducted by Rimsky-Korsakov. This masterpiece, which Rimsky-Korsakov and Glazunov completed after Borodin's sudden death, includes the familiar *Polovtsian Dances*. (Parts of *Prince Igor* were also reworked decades later for the Broadway play *Kismet*.) Borodin's other important works include the symphonic sketch In the Steppes of Central Asia (1880), the Second Symphony in B minor (1885) and many well-regarded songs.

Because Borodin's instrument was the cello, he was inspired to compose several chamber works, an endeavour that his friend Mussorgsky initially discouraged for being overly German and therefore politically incorrect. His second string quartet, his best-known chamber work, evokes his courtship and marriage on the Italian Riviera.

Borodin is still regarded as an outstanding Russian composer. He is particularly renowned for his dual facility with lyrical and heroic subjects — and especially for exotic harmonies derived partly from Russian folk tunes that set them distinctly apart from European music of the time. In fact, his works incorporate many Russian musical elements, including abundant syncopation and dissonance. Yet he considered himself primarily a scientist and was a pioneer in organising a medical-school curriculum for women. In view of his musical achievements, it is astounding that composition was relegated to his spare time.

Modest Mussorgsky (1839–81) is acknowledged as the most naturally gifted of the Mighty Five, although his deficiencies in musical education were the most glaring. In his autobiography, Mussorgsky credited his nurse for his early exposure to Russian fairy tales. This gave him a 'familiarity with the spirit of the people . . . [and] lent the first and greatest impetus to my musical improvisations'.

Although his mother taught him to play the piano at an early age, his musical studies were postponed when his father enrolled him in a military academy. Mussorgsky eventually became a member of an elite guard unit, all the while composing music. During this period he met fellow Five members Borodin and Balakirev and first heard the music of Glinka. Galvanised by the nationalist movement, he quit the military to pursue music full time — a decision that had serious financial consequences when the serfs were freed in 1861 and he lost his inheritance.

Balakirev taught Mussorgsky most of what he knew about composition. Mussorgsky's early success with songs began in the 1860s. His most familiar work may be A Night on the Bare Mountain (1867), which is included in the soundtrack of Walt Disney's 1937 animated feature, Fantasia. In

97

1869, he completed his masterpiece, the frenzied, brooding, sombre and flamboyant opera *Boris Godunov*, based on the play by Aleksandr Pushkin. The opera did not début until 1874, however, because it lacked a romantic subplot, which Mussorgsky went on to provide. Since there were rumours that the imperial family resented the opera's revolutionary themes, *Boris* was soon pulled from the Imperial Opera's repertoire.

This unfortunate event was compounded by what Mussorgsky considered César Cui's betrayal in panning *Boris*. Mussorgsky tired of Balakirev, and he believed Rimsky-Korsakov and Borodin had lost their artistic identities by writing overly polished music and indulging in art for art's sake. Adding to Mussorgsky's social isolation was Rimsky-Korsakov's moving out of the apartment they shared to get married while *Boris* was being revised.

Mussorgsky's piano suite *Pictures at an Exhibition* (1874), later orchestrated by Ravel, was inspired by the death of a painter friend at the age of thirty-nine. During this time he worked on his opera *Khovanshchina*, which the ever-helpful Rimsky-Korsakov finished after Mussorgsky's death. Near the end of his short life, his friends spent little time with him, and Mussorgsky succumbed to alcohol-related illness at the age of forty-two.

If Mussorgsky was one of the least productive of the Five, he was certainly the boldest and most original, especially in his use of harmony and unconventional tonalities. His works were so idiosyncratic that Rimsky-Korsakov decided to edit nearly all of them after his friend's death to rid them of what he considered eccentricities. Fortunately, the original versions of many of his works, including *Boris*, were restored in the first half of the twentieth century. For Mussorgsky, music was a path to truth – in his case, to a full revelation of the character of the Russian people. Some of his pieces actually seem to imitate Russian speech.

César Cui (1835–1918) was the son of a Lithuanian woman and a French naval officer under Napoleon's command who remained in Russia after his capture in the campaign of 1812. Although his childhood training in music and composition seemed to be directing Cui to a musical career, he took a university degree in military engineering instead. He became a professor of this discipline, and Czar Nicholas II was one of his students. Cui's friendship with Balakirev eventually led him back to music, and he wrote ten operas, including *The Prisoner of the Caucasus* (1883), *Feast in the Time of the Plague* (1901) and *The Captain's Daughter* (1911), which were based on works by Pushkin. His orchestration, however, was glaringly weak, and Balakirev and Rimsky-Korsakov rewrote much of these works. His songs and piano pieces are more highly regarded.

Cui was probably more important in his roles as music critic and journalist, which he used to boost the Russian nationalist movement in music. His extreme devotion to the nationalist cause apparently blinded him to the merits of composers outside the circle of the Mighty Five. Yet, maybe because of his non-Russian lineage, Cui's works have little of the Russian flavour so characteristic of the Five, and he himself turned to French and German sources for the majority of his operas.

What were the 5 rivers of the classical underworld?

Acheron   Cocytus
Styx   Lethe
Phlegethon

WE BLASÉ POSTMODERNISTS don't think about Hell much, but when we do, we tend to associate it with fire. For the ancient Greeks, who lived when bodies of water were much more formidable obstacles than now, rivers were the most salient features of the underworld, specifically the five rivers separating the land of the living from the dead.

In Homer's *Odyssey*, the goddess Circe informs Odysseus that he must sail to the land of the dead to consult with the shade of the Theban prophet Tiresias. In the process, she reveals that four of the infernal rivers are geographically linked: 'There Pyriphlegethon and Cocytus, a branch of the waters of Styx, flow into Acheron.'

Issuing from a gloomy gorge, the **Acheron** ('river of woe') in Epirus in north-western Greece was thought to be the entrance to the underworld realm of Hades, god of the dead, and his queen Persephone. The kingdom of Hades, guarded by the three-headed watch-dog Cerberus, was imagined to be in the far west and, later, underground. Three judges decided the soul's fate (Minos, Rhadamanthys and Aeacus); heroes and virtuous souls went to the Elysian Fields, a place of bliss, but the wicked were condemned to Tartarus, where they paid the penalty for their offences. Those neither particularly good nor bad went to the shadowy Meadows of Asphodel.

The waters of the **Styx** ('hated'), a small stream in Arcadia in the Peloponnese that fell from a cliff six hundred feet sheer down into a ravine, were said to be highly toxic. The nymph of the River Styx had four children – Zeal, Victory, Force and Strength – who came to the help of the Olympian gods when they were fighting against the Titans (see

Question 57). In recognition of this assistance, Zeus decreed that the gods must swear their sacred oaths by the Styx – 'the fearful oath-river' in Homer's *Iliad*. When a god wished to make a solemn vow, Iris, the messenger of the gods, brought back water in a golden cup from the Styx, which the god then poured out while reciting the words of the oath. Any god who swore falsely by the Styx had to lie speechless and breathless for a year and endure banishment from the banqueting of the gods for nine years. The great majority kept their word.

The irascible and squalid old boatman Charon ferried the souls of the dead across the Styx, but only if they had been properly buried. To be left exposed without burial was a cruel fate because the soul of such a corpse could not cross the Styx to join the rest of the dead. Instead, according to Virgil (70–19 BC), the piteous soul was forced to wander on the near shore of that Stygian stream for a hundred years.

In Book 6 of Virgil's *Aeneid*, Charon at first demurs from conveying the living Aeneas across the Styx but immediately changes his tune when Aeneas' guide through the underworld, the Cumaean Sibyl, Deiphobe, draws a golden bough from beneath her robe. In *The Golden Bough*, the Scottish anthropologist Sir James George Frazer claimed that Aeneas' talisman was really mistletoe, considered to be protective against witches and trolls. (Remember that next Christmas-time.)

Less prominent in myth than Acheron or Styx were Phlegethon and Cocytus. **Phlegethon**, or Pyriphlegethon ('flaming'), was thought to be a river of liquid fire, and **Cocytus** was 'the river of lamentation'. The **Lethe** ('oblivion') became popular in Roman literature. Virgil, imitating in the *Aeneid* what Plato had written in 'The Myth of Er' at the end of the *Republic*, claims that the souls of the dead who are about to be reincarnated drink of the Lethean waters to forget their previous existence.

Entire books have been written on the complex 'hydraulic system' of Dante's *Inferno*. All four rivers of his Hell – which are actually huge pools of still water – are interconnected. They all arise from the tears, stained with blood, of a mysteriously symbolical Old Man of Crete, a colossal statue that represents all the woes of the human race.

In Canto 3 of the *Inferno*, the souls of the recently dead who are Hell-bound gather on the shores of Acheron. This river separates the incontinent sinners of upper Hell from the scorned fence-sitters, who weren't even committed enough to evil to be allowed into Hell proper after death (see Question 52). Charon is here the foul-tempered boatman of the Acheron rather than of the Styx. When he tries to prevent Dante – a living man destined for Purgatory – from climbing aboard, Dante's guide Virgil silences Charon's opposition by citing heavenly sanction for the epic journey to Hell and parts beyond. Charon has no choice but to acquiesce and redirect his anger towards some of the terrified newly dead:

> Charon the demon, with eyes like glowing coal,
> Beckons the souls to board from all around,
> Striking whoever lingers with his pole.
> (*Inferno*, 3.109–11)

Further down the slopes of Dante's Hell, those who were wrathful beat and tear one another apart in the muddy waters of the Styx, river of hate. In addition, the shades of the sullen are totally submerged in the ooze, which they choke on, as in life they choked on their own venom. Here Dante again lets Virgil pacify Phlegyas, the furious boatman of the Styx, which is imagined as a swampy circular moat around the walled city of Dis (lower Hell). While in the boat, Dante has a run-in with the muddy shade of an arrogant Florentine knight, Filippo Argenti, who hopes Dante doesn't recognise him. They exchange some verbal rapiers, culminating in Dante's nasty rejoinder, 'although you're filthy, I still know your face':

> At that, he grabbed the skiff; without delay,
> My wary master pushed him off and cried:
> 'Get down there with the other dogs! Away!'
> (*Inferno*, 8.40–2)

Virgil then congratulates Dante on being so righteously indignant by kissing his cheek. Dante expresses the wish to see Argenti 'dunked into this soup', and soon afterwards the other shades of the wrathful attack Argenti while he turns his own teeth against himself in impotent rage.

All those who were violent against others – tyrants, murderers, highwaymen – are punished in Dante's Phlegethon, a river of boiling blood, guarded by centaurs armed with bows and arrows. The depth to which the sinners are immersed in the searing blood varies with the gravity of their crimes. Tyrants like Attila are sunk in the blood up to their brows, whereas the least violent of those violent souls have only their feet scorched in the liquid they loved to spill. Virgil tells Dante of the centaurs' role in making sure the sinners remain at their allotted depth:

> In troops of many thousands they invest
> The moat, and shoot whichever souls withdraw
> More of themselves than is their guilt's bequest.
> (Inferno, 12.73–5)

Dante crosses the boiling Phlegethon by riding on the back of a centaur.

At the bottom of Dante's Hell, four kinds of traitors (to kin, country, guests or friends, and benefactors) are imprisoned in the frozen pool of Cocytus, some with their heads sticking out of the ice, others entirely submerged in it, like flies inside an ice cube. The Cocytus is frozen by the flapping wings of gigantic Lucifer, who is punished in the deepest pit of Hell. (For Dante, the sin of treachery is cold, not fiery.)

Dante does not situate Lethe in his underworld but at the summit of Mount Purgatory, in what used to be the Garden of Eden. The Lethe is a blessed river that, when tasted by souls bound for Paradise, washes away all memory of their sins. Drinking from the nearby River Eunoe (Greek, 'well-minded'; Dante's own invention) restores the memory of all their good deeds to these same Heaven-aspiring souls who have completed their purgation.

In John Milton's epic, *Paradise Lost* (1667), we find the same five serviceable infernal rivers. After the devils fall into Hell, they fly off to explore their prison. They come upon the 'baleful streams' of

> Abhorred *Styx* the flood of deadly hate,
> Sad *Acheron* of sorrow, black and deep;
> *Cocytus*, nam'd of lamentation loud
> Heard on the rueful stream; fierce *Phlegeton*
> Whose waves of torrent fire inflame with rage.
>
> (2.577−81)

Far from these four is 'Lethe the River of Oblivion', which the souls of the damned are prevented from ever tasting.

SIX

QUESTION 27

What are the 6 flavours of quarks?

Up	Charmed
Down	Bottom (or Beauty)
Strange	Top (or Truth)

ATOMS ARE COMPOSED OF PROTONS, neutrons and electrons. For a long time, these subatomic particles were considered the irreducible building-blocks of all matter. And then came quarks.

Apparently at first just a nonsense word coined at their discovery, *quarks* was later found in James Joyce's *Finnegans Wake* – 'Three quarks for Muster Mark!' Usually pronounced to rhyme with corks, quarks differ from previously known particles in that each has only a partial (1/3 or 2/3) positive or negative electrical charge (see table on p. 107). Quarks are bound in families of three to form protons and neutrons; these triplets are called hadrons. The pairing of a quark with its antiquark of the same 'colour' is known as a meson.

The indivisible constituents of matter now appear to be the six flavours of quarks and six other kinds of particles known as leptons: the electron, muon and tau particle, each with its own neutrino. Furthermore, according to quantum field theory, all the forces *between* particles of matter are mediated by force-carrying particles called gauge bosons. One of these, the gluon – as in glue – is responsible for holding quarks together. Other gauge bosons include the photon, associated with electromagnetic forces such as light, and the graviton, the postulated messenger particle of gravity.

Quarks are part of an evolving system known as the Standard Model that has been proposed as an explanation of the fundamental forces of nature. Their existence was first postulated in 1963 by Murray Gell-Mann, a physicist at the California Institute of Technology whose work on these subatomic particles secured him the Nobel Prize in Physics in 1969. Besides naming the particles, Gell-Mann whimsically described them as coming in flavours and colours, but these reflect his imaginativeness rather than any actual physical properties. Quarks are far smaller than any particle that can be detected with visible light and have no empiric, sensory-derived qualities.

Each flavour of quark comes in three colours (red, green and blue); each hadron, or grouping of three quarks, has one of each colour. The flavours were originally classified as up, down and strange; subsequent work established the existence of others, dubbed charmed, bottom and top. Only the **up** and **down** flavours are believed to exist in nature today.

Protons, for example, have two up quarks and one down quark, whose electrical charges combine as follows: $2/3 + 2/3 - 1/3 = 1$. Thus, protons end up with a +1 charge. Neutrons are made of one up quark and two down quarks. The electrical charge is thus $2/3 - 1/3 - 1/3 = 0$, which accords with the neutral charge of the neutron.

The other four flavours of quarks – **strange, charmed, bottom** and **top** – were theoretically present only for an infinitesimal fraction of a second during the Big Bang about thirteen billion years ago and can now be 'observed' only from the self-annihilating collisions that occur when protons and antiprotons are accelerated at speeds approaching that of light in particle accelerators. The particles that result from these high-speed collisions exist for too short a time to actually be seen – roughly a hundredth of a billionth of a billionth of a second – before starting to decay into other types of particles. But since these decay products leave 'footprints' that can be detected and measured, the existence of the original particle can be inferred and its mass determined.

Only in March 1995 was the top quark finally identified amid intense rivalry between two groups of physicists at the Fermi National Accelerator Laboratory (Fermilab) in Batavia, Illinois. The top quark turns out to be a real heavyweight. Compare its mass with that of its fellows:

Flavour	Charge	Mass (billions of electron volts)
Up	+2/3	0.38
Down	−1/3	0.34
Strange	−1/3	0.54
Charmed	+2/3	1.50
Bottom	−1/3	4.72
Top	+2/3	175.60

The mass of the top quark is about the same as that of an atom of gold – which has a total of nearly two hundred protons and neutrons.

Who were the 6 wives of Henry VIII?

Catherine of Aragon	Anne of Cleves
Anne Boleyn	Catherine Howard
Jane Seymour	Catherine Parr

THE MARITAL HISTORY of King Henry VIII (1491–1547) makes more sense if you consider that his father, Henry Tudor, Earl of Richmond, who wrenched the English crown from Richard III at the battle of Bosworth Field in 1485, had only a weak claim to the throne. Thus, as King Henry VII, he wisely negotiated an excellent match between his elder son, Arthur, and the infanta **Catherine of Aragon** (1485–1536), daughter of Columbus's powerful patrons, Ferdinand and Isabella of Spain. The ultimate goal of this union, as in royal marriages down to our day, was a male heir.

Catherine arrived in England in 1501, after marrying Prince Arthur twice by proxy, with the Spanish ambassador standing in for her. She and Arthur wed a third time, in person, in November 1501 in St Paul's Cathedral, London. Until the day she died, Catherine insisted this marriage was never consummated. In fact, Arthur, who was fifteen and ill, died four months after the wedding.

Catherine remained in England and became a wretched pawn of power politics. Although young Prince Henry obtained a papal dispensation to marry his dead brother's wife, negotiations with Spain got bogged down in wrangling over the dowry and various dynastic machinations. Seven years after she was widowed, Catherine married Henry on 11 June 1509, seven weeks after his succession to the throne.

During her marriage to Henry VIII, Catherine gave birth to six children. A daughter, Mary, went on to become queen (1553–8). The rest died young. Henry was genuinely fond of his wife, but her failure to produce a male heir who survived infancy was a potentially lethal blow to the House of Tudor.

Henry now claimed he was troubled by his marriage to his brother's widow, despite the Pope's dispensation. By February of 1526, it became clear to members of the court that the King was smitten with **Anne Boleyn** (1500/1-36), a maid of honour to Catherine and sister of the notorious Mary Boleyn, who had had a four-year affair with Henry. In 1527, Henry announced plans to seek an annulment of his marriage to Catherine, but the Pope, largely at the behest of the Queen's nephew, all-powerful Holy Roman Emperor Charles V, deferred his decision for years. By 1531, Henry had pressed the English bishops to recognise him as 'Protector and Supreme Head of the Church of England', a title confirmed in 1534 by Parliament's passage of the Act of Supremacy. All ties with Rome were severed.

Henry and Anne Boleyn were secretly married on 25 January 1533, several months before the King's appointee, Thomas Cranmer, Archbishop of Canterbury, annulled his marriage with Catherine on 23 May. In the same year, a baby girl, destined to reign from 1558 to 1603 as the incomparable Elizabeth I, was born to Henry and Anne, but she was followed by three stillborn infants. Again, Henry saw the House of Tudor threatened by a queen's inability to bear a healthy son. In addition, Anne turned out to be a highly unpopular queen who had proposed murdering Catherine and her daughter Mary at a time when they were being particularly vexatious. And Henry had a chance of gaining a much-needed alliance with Charles V – but only without Anne. Chancellor Thomas Cromwell charged her with adultery, incest with her brother George, and high treason – fabrications all. Anne Boleyn was beheaded on 19 May 1536. Just for good measure, Henry had had their marriage annulled a few days earlier.

Wasting no time, the King was betrothed to **Jane Seymour** (1507/8-37) the next day, marrying her ten days later. Jane had been lady-in-waiting to both Catherine and Anne, and Henry had courted her for at least six months before Anne's death. Throughout his life Henry claimed he loved her best of all his wives. His feelings for her were undoubtedly enhanced by the birth of a male heir, Edward (1537-53), a sickly boy who succeeded Henry in 1547 but died in his teens. Jane died twelve days after Edward's birth.

Two years passed before Henry, increasingly portly and plagued by a chronically infected, foul-smelling leg, married the German princess **Anne of Cleves** (1515–57). This political marriage, engineered by Cromwell, took place on 6 January 1540. Henry, however, found Anne so repugnant – he'd only seen a Holbein portrait of her – that they never bedded down. But Anne of Cleves was the most fortunate of Henry's wives. The marriage was annulled after seven months, and Henry paid Anne four thousand pounds a year, gave her two manors and Anne Boleyn's castle, and made her his honorary sister. Matchmaker Cromwell was executed nine days after the annulment.

On the day Cromwell died in 1540, Henry married Anne Boleyn's fifteen-year-old cousin, **Catherine Howard** (c. 1525–42), a favourite of the Catholic faction. Four months later, the Archbishop of Canterbury informed Henry that Catherine had had several lovers before her marriage, as well as an engagement that might invalidate the royal union. Serious allegations of adultery also emerged. Henry, who was probably impotent by this time, was regarded as a cuckold, and Francis I of France said of Catherine, 'She hath done wondrous naughty!' Catherine got the axe, literally, on 13 February 1542 – a low blow, since even her cousin Anne had merited a more refined decapitation by sword.

Twice-widowed **Catherine Parr** (1512–48) was in love with Thomas Seymour, Jane Seymour's brother, when Henry set his sights on her and had his rival posted overseas. The King married his last wife on 12 July 1543, with Anne of Cleves as a witness. This third Catherine, warm, amiable and acutely intelligent, was a caring stepmother to Henry's daughters and young son, and an effective regent while Henry campaigned. She was renowned for her learning, and her home was a haven for young female scholars.

Henry died on 28 January 1547. And, in a finale worthy of daytime TV, Catherine Parr died the next year, after giving birth to a daughter by her new husband, Thomas Seymour.

Who were the 6 French composers known as Les Six?

Darius Milhaud   Louis Durey
Francis Poulenc   Georges Auric
Arthur Honegger   Germaine Tailleferre

Wagner . . . was an idiot [for claiming all art springs from suffering].

DARIUS MILHAUD

THE DESIGNATION LES SIX was coined in 1920 by a French music critic, Henri Collet, when he compared this group of six neoclassical musicians living in France with the Russian Mighty Five composers (see Question 25). Profoundly influenced by composer and eccentric Erik Satie (1866–1925) and by poet, essayist and dramatist Jean Cocteau (1889–1963), the Six reacted against the Romantic excesses of Richard Wagner and Richard Strauss and the Impressionism of Claude Debussy and Maurice Ravel. That's about where their similarities end. Les Six, who rarely met, composed in quite distinct styles, so their grouping is somewhat artificial.

The music of Les Six has been called une musique de tous les jours, everyday music. This was the legacy of Satie, who eschewed musical heroics in favour of small, precise, almost surreal pieces spiced with humour and parody. The Six felt that sentimentalism and Romanticism had gone too far in the music of the nineteenth century and that, in the works of the Impressionists, the intensely personal had been allowed to outweigh clarity, precision, objectivity and crispness. As Milhaud said, 'I am left helpless in the presence of rhapsodic works devoid of structure or overladen with endless developments of unnecessary complexity.' Like their great contemporary Igor Stravinsky (1882–1971), they sought to balance emotion with form and order.

Darius Milhaud (1892–1974) was born into a Jewish family in Aix-en-Provence in southern France. As a student in Paris, he met the poet and dramatist Paul Claudel (1868–1955), with whom he went to Brazil when Claudel was appointed ambassador in 1917. At the end of World War I, they spent time in New York City before returning to France. During this brief period of travel, Milhaud was deeply influenced by American jazz and Brazilian music, especially samba and tango, as witnessed by the twelve dance tunes for piano he composed under the title of *Saudades do Brasil* (*Souvenirs of Brazil*, 1921).

Milhaud championed polytonality (the use of two or three musical keys simultaneously), a technique pioneered by Stravinsky. In some of Milhaud's pieces, such as *Les Choëphores*, the men and women of a chorus sing in different keys. (The resulting dissonance is, admittedly, an acquired taste.) Milhaud was also one of the first composers to use whips, hammers and other noisemakers in his music.

In the early part of the twentieth century, these musical innovations shocked some of Milhaud's listeners. This, coupled with his reputation as one of the most radical and antagonistic of Cocteau's circle, ensured that his music received mixed or hostile reviews. Several decades passed before he was recognised as one of the foremost composers of the century. His musical moods vary from highly dramatic and austere to folklike and charming. In keeping with neoclassical restraint, his musical ideas are expressed succinctly and in a disciplined, logical fashion – characteristics generally revered by *Les Six*.

Milhaud's early compositions were based on texts by Claudel. During the 1920s and '30s, he travelled in Russia, Spain and the Middle East. When France fell to the Nazis in 1940, Milhaud fled Europe, taking a position on the faculty of Mills College in Oakland, California. After the war, he continued his association with Mills and the Aspen Music School, splitting his time among Europe, California and Colorado. His affection for America and other places he visited is reflected in the number of pieces he wrote in honour of various cities, including Boston, San Francisco, Lisbon and Prague, and in his send-up of George Gershwin – *A Frenchman in New York*.

In fact, Milhaud and Gershwin were introducing jazz idioms into concert-hall music at roughly the same time, Milhaud with the ballet *La*

Création du monde (1923), music laced with French elegance, yet deeply influenced by his 1922 visit to Harlem and the jazz he heard there. 'An authentic small masterpiece', Aaron Copland called this work, which evokes the creation of the world according to African folklore. Milhaud also wrote the music for *Le Boeuf sur le toit* (*The Bull on the Roof*, 1919), sometimes translated as *The Do-Nothing Bar*, a comically bizarre pantomime-cum-ballet choreographed by Cocteau and set in a bar in Prohibition-era America.

Milhaud's operas include *Christophe Colomb* (1930), with libretto by Claudel, *Médée* (1939), *Bolivar* (1943) and *David* (1954). He also wrote three miniature operas based on classical myths dealing with Theseus, Ariadne and Europa that take less than ten minutes each to perform. Some critics consider his opera *Les Euménides*, the last in a trilogy based on Aeschylus as translated by Claudel, one of the finest musical works of the century, on a par with Stravinsky's *Le Sacre du printemps*.

With more than four hundred works to his credit, including eighteen string quartets, Milhaud was one of the most prolific twentieth-century composers, and he was considered France's most eminent living composer after the death of Ravel in 1937. In addition to his work in opera, ballet and chamber music – indeed, in every branch of composition – Milhaud wrote thirteen symphonies.

Of all the Six, the music of self-taught **Francis Poulenc** (1899–1963) is most like that of Satie, with influences from Stravinsky and even Ravel. The musical idiom of Poulenc is often marked by warmth, lucidity and a personal quality. A master of twentieth-century song, he wrote more than a hundred polished, melodic songs based on poems by Guillaume Apollinaire and Paul Éluard, among others. His early experience as a piano accompanist enhanced his proficiency in this musical form. His best-known piano music, *Trois mouvements perpétuels*, was composed when he was nineteen, about the time he was linked with *Les Six*. His chamber music, heavily influenced by jazz during the 1920s, became somewhat more sombre during the war years. His later chamber pieces included two written as memorials to Arthur Honegger and Sergei Prokofiev.

By the 1930s, Poulenc was writing chiefly religious works marked by fervour, simplicity and serenity, including *Litanies à la Vierge Noire de Rocamadour* (1936) for women's voices and organ, the *Mass in G major* (1937) and *Stabat Mater* (1951). Other prominent works are *Les Biches* (*The House Party*, 1923), a ballet produced by the great impresario Sergei Diaghilev; *La Voix humaine*, a one-act, forty-minute opera with libretto by Cocteau; and *Concerto in G minor* for organ, strings and percussion.

Poulenc served in the French underground during World War II, and one of his cantatas, the subversive *Figure humaine*, was printed under the noses of the Nazis. Poulenc's masterpiece, *Les Dialogues des Carmélites*, set in the French Revolution and first performed at Milan's La Scala in 1957, is considered one of the outstanding operas of the twentieth century.

Poulenc's serious, sensitive side was complemented by a witty, surreal, good-humoured and ironic one. His burlesque opera *Les Mamelles de Tirésias* (*The Breasts of Tiresias*, 1947), based on a 1903 play by Apollinaire, features a woman who becomes a man when her breasts (balloons) explode, while her husband becomes a woman and spawns forty thousand babies. In 1945, Poulenc wrote incidental music for *Babar the Elephant*, in part to amuse some young relatives.

Of the Six, the music of Swiss–French composer **Arthur Honegger** (1892–1955), who studied in Zurich, was the least like Satie's. With time, some listeners have come to call his music conventional. Honegger couldn't quite separate himself from grandiose musical ideas, especially in his operas. His first and perhaps most lasting success was an oratorio, *Le Roi David* (*King David*, 1921), which was followed by the operas *Judith* (1926) and *Antigone* (1927), the latter with libretto by Cocteau. Like Milhaud, he set texts by Paul Claudel, including the oratorios *Jeanne d'Arc au bûcher* (*Joan of Arc at the Stake*) and *La Danse des morts* (*The Dance of Death*).

When *Pacific 231* was first performed in 1924, the cacophony of this orchestral tone poem imitating a locomotive stunned and amused audiences. Another programme piece, *Rugby* (1928), called to mind rough-and-tumble sports. Honegger was now far removed in many ways from the ideals of Satie and Stravinsky. He also wrote music for movies and radio plays. Other works include the *Piano Concertino, Concerto da camera* for flute and strings, and the chamber orchestra piece *Pastorale d'été* (*Summer Pastoral*).

The music of Milhaud, Poulenc and Honegger still lives, long after the heady, avant-garde days of the early twentieth century. The other three of the original Six are all but forgotten as serious composers.

Louis Durey (1888–1979), though he lived long, had an abbreviated musical career, apparently preferring politics. He joined the French Communist Party in 1936 and, like Poulenc, was a member of the Resistance during World War II, composing songs for the movement. In deference to Communist thought, Durey wrote music that was supposed to appeal to 'the people'. Beginning in 1950, he was music critic for the Communist newspaper *Humanité*. None the less, his musical achievements were sufficiently impressive to garner the Grand Prix de la Musique in 1961.

Georges Auric (1899–1983) was best known as a composer of scores for stage productions and ballets. Three of his ballets, *Les Fâcheux* (1924), *Les Matelots* (1925) and *La Pastorale* (1926), were produced by Diaghilev. Auric wrote music for more than sixty films, including *Moulin Rouge* (1952). In the early 1960s, he was appointed general manager of both the Paris Opéra and the Opéra-Comique. For more than twenty years, until 1977, Auric was president of the French Union of Composers and Authors.

Germaine Tailleferre (1892–1983), the only woman in the group, understandably changed her name from the more colourful Taillefesse, which can mean 'arse-cutter' in French. She studied briefly with Ravel, and some critics claim she ended up as an Impressionist after all. Cocteau likened her compositions to pastels for the ears. Tailleferre was married briefly to an American writer and subsequently to a French lawyer, both of whom discouraged her from composing.

SEVEN

QUESTION 30

What are the 7 wonders of the ancient world?

The Great Pyramid of Cheops at Giza
The Hanging Gardens of Babylon
The Statue of Zeus at Olympia
The Temple of Artemis at Ephesus
The Mausoleum at Halicarnassus
The Colossus of Rhodes
The Pharos (Lighthouse) of Alexandria

IN HIS 'NATURAL HISTORY', Pliny the Elder tells of encountering the shattered fragments of the Colossus of Rhodes in the first century AD: 'Few men can clasp the thumb in their arms, and its fingers are larger than most statues. As for its broken limbs, their insides look like vast caves.'

In Pliny's time, the Colossus lay where it had fallen, toppled by an earthquake. Yet that didn't diminish the Roman's awe. The wonders tend to do strange things to people: about eighteen hundred years after Pliny made his observations, a decade-long obsessive quest to find traces of the Temple of Artemis at Ephesus drove the English archaeologist J. T. Wood to physical and emotional collapse. The pyramids, of course, have spawned overheated quests for gold, gods and cosmic enlightenment. And shards of the great lighthouse at Alexandria are even now being uncovered by deep-sea divers on the Mediterranean floor.

Each of the seven wonders of the ancient world was the product of singular architectural, engineering and artistic hubris. The sheer size of the wonders suggests that their makers had it in for Protagoras' anthropocentric notion that 'man is the measure of all things'.

In about 130 BC, the Greek poet Antipater of Sidon compiled a list of wonders very similar to our own. But as far back as the Greek historian Herodotus in the fifth century BC, legends abounded of magnificent sights that travellers had seen, sights (theamata) so arresting in their size and splendour that they were eventually called wonders (thaumata).

The Great Pyramid of Cheops at Giza. Until the nineteenth century, no one ever again built anything as tall as the tomb created by the Fourth-Dynasty Pharaoh Khufu, or Cheops, around 2560 BC. To Herodotus, the pyramids were almost as ancient as he is to us. The largest, the Great Pyramid, is by far the earliest of the seven wonders and also the only one still very much intact. For almost forty-four hundred years, the Great Pyramid, at 481 feet (now about 450), was the tallest edifice in the world – only twenty-four feet shorter than the United Nations Building in New York. What work of the twenty-first century will be standing in the year 6560?

Construction began with a series of stepped layers of stone. Then the spaces between the layers were filled in with gleaming white limestone from the hills east of what is now Cairo. The pyramid's sloping sides, intended to evoke the rays of the sun god Ra emanating from the apex to the ground, were set at an angle slightly less than 55°. The sides at the base are 756 feet long. Despite the ancient builders' lack of accurate surveying equipment, there's less than eight inches of variance between the shortest and longest sides. The base covers 13.1 acres, a space that can comfortably contain St Peter's in Rome, the cathedrals of Florence and Milan, Westminster Abbey and St Paul's of London.

The Great Pyramid required about 2.3 million granite blocks, each weighing an average of 2.5 tons. The blocks had to be moved on log rollers and sledges and then ramped into place, since neither the pulley nor the block and tackle would be invented for another twenty-five hundred years.

The historian Diodorus Siculus (fl. 60–30 BC) claimed 360,000 men worked on the pyramid, which took twenty years to complete.

Herodotus had estimated that a hundred thousand workers were needed and even recorded the vast sum it must have cost to feed them with radishes, onions and leeks. Modern scholars think the pyramids were built by a group of five hundred to a thousand craftsmen, assisted by five thousand to seven thousand workmen who came to labour on the monuments in shifts from all over Egypt. Contrary to earlier belief, these workers were not slaves. Their houses, recently unearthed, resemble the pyramids in miniature, complete with little false doors.

The entrance to the Great Pyramid was concealed on the north side, facing the pole star. Several corridors branched out inside the tomb. The largest, the Grand Gallery, angled upward into the heart of the pyramid. The gallery, 153 feet long and twenty-eight feet high, was a corbelled vault, unlike anything else in Old Kingdom architecture. It was up this ascending corridor that the funeral cortège moved, bearing the body of Cheops to its resting-place in the King's Chamber. Over their heads, giant blocks of granite perched on wooden beams.

The King's Chamber was designed in a 2:1 ratio – thirty-four feet, four inches long, by seventeen feet, two inches wide. It was nineteen feet, one inch high, and its flat roof comprised nine huge blocks that together weighed four hundred tons. After the funeral procession had descended, a team remained behind to dislodge the beams holding up the gallery's blocks of granite, thus plugging up access to the King's Chamber. The workmen then escaped through a narrow shaft hidden beneath a stone at the top of the Grand Gallery, which snaked down under the pyramid.

Despite these precautions, thieves plundered the pyramid within 250 years of its completion. They didn't find everything, however. In 1954, the solar boat of Cheops was discovered in an airtight pit beneath forty-one large blocks of limestone on the south side of the pyramid. Over a hundred feet long, it was made from 1,274 pieces of wood fitted together without a single metal nail. The vessel, which may have borne Cheops on the Nile to his entombment, enabled him to sail with the sun god beyond the grave.

The Hanging Gardens of Babylon. Relying on earlier sources, the

Roman historian Quintus Curtius Rufus (fl. mid-first century AD) claimed the trees of the Gardens were twelve feet in circumference and fifty feet tall. The tale of this forest of towering trees and tiered roof gardens rising high into the sky had already been told by the Greek poets, who embroidered it with the love of a king for his homesick lover.

The Hanging Gardens were said to be the work of Nebuchadrezzar II (reigned c.605–562 BC), King of Babylonia, whose mighty capital of Babylon was located on the Euphrates in what is now Iraq. This was the king who destroyed Jerusalem in 586 BC and led the Jews off into captivity. He apparently had a sentimental strain, though, for he was said to have built the gargantuan Gardens of trees, flowers and shrubs for his wife (or concubine), Amytis, who longed for the mountainous greenery of her homeland in Media (north-western Iran).

To Philo of Byzantium (late third century BC), the most fascinating feature of the Gardens built within the walls of the royal palace was their resting on stone columns so that people could stroll beneath the structure while workers ploughed and tended the fields overhead. He and a few other writers left circumstantial accounts of the Hanging Gardens (which seemed to 'hang in air'), touching on everything from the soil and root systems to the method of irrigation of the five landscaped brick terraces, each rising fifty feet above the other and connected by marble stairways. Modern scholars of hydraulics claim that a wooden piston pump run by a water-wheel would have had to raise the water of the Euphrates to a height of about three hundred feet to cisterns in the topmost terrace of the structure.

Despite the vividness of some ancient accounts, they are second-hand at best. No cuneiform inscription from Babylon even hints at the existence of such a garden, let alone offers an eyewitness description. Herodotus, who lived in the century after the Gardens were built, describes the city of Babylon without ever mentioning this wonder.

Of the seven, in fact, the Hanging Gardens alone are likely to be the stuff of legend. But the detailed descriptions still tantalise. 'The park extended four hundred feet on each side, and since the approach to the Garden sloped like a hillside and the several parts of the structure rose from one another tier on tier, the appearance of the whole resembled that of a theatre', wrote Diodorus Siculus in about 50 BC.

The Statue of Zeus at Olympia. 'Although the temple itself is very large, the sculptor is criticised for not having appreciated the correct proportions. He has shown Zeus seated, but with the head almost touching the ceiling, so that we have the impression that if Zeus moved to stand up he would unroof the temple.' The Greek geographer Strabo (c.63 BC–c. AD 24) put his finger on the strongest impression made on visitors by the statue of Zeus at the site of the sacred Olympian Games, which celebrated the lord of thunder: massive, irrepressible power.

The Doric temple of Zeus at Olympia, in western Greece, was completed around 460 BC by the architect Libon. It was not designed to house a congregation. Instead, on the middle day of the games (see Question 23), throngs would gather before a great altar outside the temple where one hundred oxen would be slaughtered and burned as a hecatomb offering to Zeus.

The people of Olympia turned to the Athenian sculptor Phidias to forge the image of the god. This designer of the sublime sculptures of the metopes, frieze and pediments of the Parthenon had been banished from Athens on a trumped-up charge of having stolen gold intended for the famous statue of Athene he had made for that temple. In Olympia, the chryselephantine (gold-and-ivory) statue of Zeus he completed in about 430 BC was built on a wood or stone core and rose to a height of forty feet, as tall as a four-storey building. Bare-chested, the god sat on a high cedarwood throne whose legs were decorated with images of Theban children seized by the Sphinx and with back-to-back winged figures of Victory (Nike). Seated figures of the Sphinx – a monster with a woman's head, a lion's body and an eagle's wings – supported the throne's armrests. Other images included those of Apollo, Artemis and Niobe and her slain children.

The Greek traveller Pausanias (fl. AD 150) wrote of the statue:

On his head is a sculpted wreath of olive sprays. In his right hand he holds a figure of Victory made from ivory and gold . . . In his left, he holds a sceptre inlaid with every kind of metal, with an eagle perched on it. His sandals and robe are made of gold, and his garments are carved with animals and lilies. The throne is decorated with gold, precious stones, ebony and ivory.

The Christian writer Clement of Alexandria (c.150–c.220) mentions that on the finger of Zeus were etched the words, 'Pantarkes is beautiful.' Pantarkes won the boys' wrestling contest at the eighty-sixth Olympiad (436 BC), and tradition has it that this was Phidias' tribute to his beloved. Another legend tells how after the image of the god was finished, Phidias asked Zeus for a sign of approval for his masterpiece. Immediately, a lightning bolt struck the black marble floor.

Zeus sat enthroned at Olympia for more than eight centuries. In AD 393 the Christian clergy persuaded Roman Emperor Theodosius I to close the temple and ban the pagan games. The statue was borne off to a palace in Constantinople where, in 462, a fire destroyed both palace and statue. The great temple itself at Olympia, bereft of its cult, succumbed to fire, flood, landslides and earthquakes.

The Temple of Artemis at Ephesus. There were actually two altars and one temple, and later two great marble temples, that rose and fell successively on the same site in Ephesus, a thriving Greek port in Ionia on the west coast of modern-day Turkey. The fourth edifice (called 'D' by archaeologists) was begun in the mid-sixth century BC, partly subsidised by fabulously wealthy King Croesus of Lydia. The architects were Chersiphron and his son Metagenes of Crete, and some of the greatest artists of antiquity, including Phidias and Polyclitus, worked on adorning the temple. This building was burned to the ground by Herostratus, a nobody whose successful claim to fame was his destruction of the temple so that posterity would remember his name. The fire occurred on 21 July 356 BC, supposedly the same night Alexander the Great was born. The legend arose that Artemis wasn't in Ephesus to protect her dwelling-place because she was assisting at the birth of the future mighty conqueror of Asia.

The late-classical temple (called 'E') was probably begun about 350

BC and incorporated many details of the style and design of its predecessor. Before approaching the temple, visitors stood far back in the outer courtyard to admire the decorated pediment high above. Sculpted Amazons framed the entranceway, which revealed a forest of gleaming marble columns.

Marble steps surrounded the building, the uppermost ending in a terrace 260 feet wide and 430 feet long. The temple itself was 180 by 350 feet. It's unclear whether the temple was completely roofed with tiled wood or if the inner sanctuary lay open to the sky. Inside, visitors walked amid 127 Ionic marble columns, sixty feet high and resting on sculpted rectangular bases. Each column was said to have been the gift of a different king.

In the centre of the colonnade, the *cella* of the temple most likely contained a cult statue of Artemis, who, at Ephesus, was actually an Asian mother goddess attended by eunuch priests, rather than the virgin goddess and huntress of Greece. The goddess was pictured with several rows of pendulous breasts – more than forty in all – amply deserving St Jerome's epithet for her, *Multimammia*.

'Great is Artemis of the Ephesians!' shouted the furious silversmiths of the city when St Paul's evangelising mission threatened their livelihood as makers of miniature silver shrines dedicated to their goddess (Acts 19:23–41). Yet the Temple of Artemis survived until AD 262, when it was ravaged by Ostrogoths. In 401, what remained of the once lovely structure, with its slender, elegantly fluted columns, was destroyed by order of St John Chrysostom.

The Mausoleum at Halicarnassus. This massive edifice of white marble, which gave its name to all subsequent large tombs, was the one wonder known to be built by a woman, Artemisia, the wife and sister of Mausolus, satrap of Caria (reigned 377–353 BC). Such love did she bear her brother–husband that she reportedly mixed his ashes with water and drank him down before raising the Mausoleum in Halicarnassus, now part of south-west Turkey.

The architect was thought to be Pythius of Priene, perhaps with Satyrus of Paros. The tomb's peculiar form may have resulted from an attempt to amalgamate the architectural features of three different civilisations — Lycian, Greek and Egyptian — in a trilayered rectangular structure. At its base, the Mausoleum measured about 127 by 100 feet. It was 140 feet high (about ten to thirteen storeys) and had three main parts: the base, a stepped podium sixty feet high; the middle layer, a colonnade of thirty-six Ionic columns, 37.5 feet tall; and, over this, a stepped, pyramidal roof. The roof's twenty-four steps rose 22.5 feet to a flat surface, on which, surmounting the entire tomb, stood a twenty-foot marble four-horse chariot — perhaps with statues of Mausolus and Artemisia in it. The burial chamber, with its sarcophagus of white alabaster decorated with gold, is believed to have been ensconced amid the columns on the podium.

The exterior of the Mausoleum was adorned with many friezes and free-standing statues, life-size or larger, of humans, lions, horses and other animals. The embellishment of each of the tomb's sides was said to have been assigned to one of four Greek sculptors: Scopas, Bryaxis, Timotheus and Leochares.

The tomb stood relatively intact until the thirteenth century, when portions of it collapsed in an earthquake. Ironically, it is these fragments, deeply buried, that constitute most of the remnants of the structure we have today. In the fifteenth century, what was left of the Mausoleum was used by the Knights of St John to erect and later fortify a massive castle. They quarried the tomb for stone and pulverised the sculptures for lime. A dozen slabs of a frieze vividly depicting the battle between the Greeks and Amazons were, with other elements such as statues of lions, built into the castle walls for decoration.

The frieze was extracted from the walls in 1846 and shipped to London's British Museum, where it is one of the glories of ancient Greek sculpture. In 1857, the British antiquarian Sir Charles T. Newton pinpointed the site of the Mausoleum and subsequently unearthed a hoard of architectural stones and statues (including those he claimed were of Mausolus and Artemisia). These priceless objects, too, followed the Amazon frieze to the British Museum.

The Colossus of Rhodes. In 305 BC, seventy thousand Macedonians led by Demetrius Poliorcetes ('Besieger of Cities') descended on the thriving island city of Rhodes. When an agreement was reached the next year, the attackers lifted the siege. Demetrius had been so impressed with the Rhodians' fortitude that he left behind his catapults, armoured towers and other siege engines.

The people of Rhodes sold the equipment and used the money to erect an enormous statue of their patron deity, the sun god Helios. They chose Chares of Lindus (a Rhodian city) for the task, and he and his bronze-casters worked for a dozen years (c. 292–280 BC). The bronze was fortified from within by giant blocks of stone and iron tie-bars, and the image was built upon itself: when the feet were completed, mounds of earth were piled around them so that the workers could move up to construct the ankles. As the statue rose, the completed parts lay buried.

The finished work stood 110 feet tall – easily the largest statue of antiquity. By comparison, the Statue of Liberty, 'The New Colossus', rises to a height of 152 feet. Little more is known for certain about either the appearance or location of the Colossus, other than that it never bestrode the entrance to any of the harbours of Rhodes.

The best guess is that the Colossus was a naked statue of the sun god, lifting a torch in one hand while the other held a spear at his side. His legs were placed close together to provide him with columnar stability.

The Colossus stood for little more than a half-century. A powerful earthquake hit Rhodes in about 224 BC, damaging the city and breaking the statue at its weakest point – the knees. The Rhodians received an offer from Ptolemy III of Egypt to cover all restoration costs for the top-pled monument. However, an oracle forbade them to rebuild the statue, which lay where it fell for nearly nine hundred years, much as Pliny the Elder experienced it.

In AD 653, the Arabs invaded Rhodes. They disassembled the remains of the broken Colossus, shipped them to Asia Minor, and sold them as scrap metal to a Jewish merchant from Emesa in Syria. All traces of the Colossus vanish behind the nine hundred camels that, legend has it, bore away the fragments.

The Lighthouse of Alexandria. The last of the seven wonders to be built was the first architecturally designed lighthouse in history. It took its name **Pharos** from the small island near the mouth of the Nile on which it was built – and gave its name to the French, Italian and Spanish words for lighthouse: *phare*, *faro* and *faro*.

Pharos lay before the harbour of Alexandria, the city founded in 332 BC by Alexander the Great immediately after his conquest of Egypt. The city grew rapidly and, since the Egyptian coastline offered few landmarks, the need soon arose to guide ships safely into harbour. Work on the lighthouse began under King Ptolemy I Soter, Alexander's boyhood friend who ruled Egypt from 305 to 282 BC. It was completed in about 280 BC under his son and successor, Ptolemy II Philadelphus (284–246 BC), and was designed (or perhaps paid for) by Sostratus of Cnidus.

Ancient coins show a three-tiered tower with rectangular windows on all sides. The lighthouse had three sections: the lowest was square, 183.4 feet high with a cylindrical core; the middle was octagonal with a height of 90.1 feet; and the third, twenty-four feet high, was cylindrical and encircled with a broad spiral ramp. A sixteen-foot statue stood at the top, perhaps of Alexander the Great or King Ptolemy I in the trappings of the sun god Helios.

The total height, including the foundation base, was about 384 feet, equivalent to a thirty-five-storey building. At night, a fire of resinous wood in the base of the Pharos was reflected by enormous mirrors, possibly of burnished bronze, at its top. Its beacon was said to be visible across the Mediterranean for thirty to forty miles. During the day, its mirrors reflected the sunlight, marking the port for sailors.

The Pharos was damaged in an earthquake in AD 956 and fell into ruin during other quakes in 1303 and 1323. An archaeological team of divers has recently uncovered more than twenty-five hundred architectural pieces beneath the waters around Pharos, including fifteen enormous granite blocks thought to be from the lighthouse, each weighing more than thirty tons. The discovery of many statues, sphinxes, obelisks and columns nearby could lead to a new understanding of the Pharos and the role it may have played as part of a civic or religious architectural complex.

The seven wonders of the world arrested onlookers like Pliny with their size and majesty and by the sublime ease with which they dismissed mundane notions of what human imagination and engineering could do. A wonder shocked by violating the continuity of scale between observer and observed.

How some of these artefacts were built remains a matter of intense debate. With others, we know how they were constructed and that they taxed the ingenuity of some of the most brilliant architects, engineers and sculptors the world has seen. Their ruin – except for the eternal pyramids – complicates our awe by confronting us with forces even more titanic than the wonders themselves.

What were the works of the 7 days of Creation?

1. Light
2. Heaven
3. Earth, seas and plant life
4. Sun, moon and stars
5. Sea life and birds
6. Land animals and mankind
7. Rest

THE SEVEN DAYS OF CREATION are described at the beginning of Genesis, the first book of the Bible. Although tradition attributes the authorship of Genesis to Moses, the leader and lawgiver of the Jews during their exodus from slavery in Egypt, it is actually a composite work.

The Genesis story of Creation is neither a historical account nor a scientific explanation of the origins of the world, a fact recognised even in the fifth century by St Augustine, who noted that some of the descriptions in Genesis diverged from the scientific knowledge of his day. None the less, many Jews and Christians still find profound truths about God, the material world and man in the biblical story of the seven days of Creation.

Genesis contains two Creation narratives. The first, which begins in Chapter 1 and describes the works of the seven days, is a much later text than the version of the so-called Yahwist (J) that begins in Chapter 2, verse 4b. The J text appears to contradict Chapter 1 in its claim that plant life, land animals and birds were created *after* Adam.

In Genesis 1, when God creates the heavens and the earth, the latter is at first 'a formless wasteland' in which 'darkness covered the abyss' of waters. This seems to refer to a kind of ur-matter, chaotically undifferentiated, to which God subsequently brings cosmic order. His first work, then, is to create **light** (the ordering principle par excellence), separate it from darkness, and call the light *day* and the darkness *night*: Thus, 'evening came, and morning followed – the first day'. A refrain now begins to punctuate the story, 'God saw that it was good,' referring to his various creations – until a cumulative statement, at the end of his labour, proclaims them in their totality to be 'very good'.

On the second day, order comes to **heaven**: 'Then God said, "Let there be a dome in the middle of the waters, to separate one body of water from the other." God called the dome *heaven*.' The ancient author was here expressing his belief that God set a dome or vault between the primordial waters now forming part of the sky (which supply rain to the earth) and the various waters remaining on earth itself.

Next, the **earth, seas and plant life**: 'Then God said, "Let the water under the sky be gathered into a single basin, so that the dry land may appear." God called the dry land *the earth*, and the basin of the water he called *the sea*. Then God said, "Let the earth bring forth vegetation: every kind of plant that bears seed and every kind of fruit tree on earth that bears fruit with its seed in it." ' On the third day, dry land is created and separated from the waters under the dome. With light, water and earth now available, plant life appears.

Only on the fourth day did God populate the sky with the **sun, moon and stars**: 'God made the two great lights, the greater one to govern the day, and the lesser one to govern the night; and he made the stars.' Note that the sun and moon are not named in the biblical text, since they were worshipped by neighbouring peoples as gods. Many sceptics have asked how light could have been created three days before the sun. John Milton tries to address the difficulty in *Paradise Lost* (7.245–9), where he claims that light

> . . . from her Native East
> To journey through the airy gloom began,
> Spher'd in a radiant Cloud, for yet the Sun
> Was not; shee in a cloudy Tabernacle
> Sojourn'd the while.

The creation of **sea life and birds** followed on the fifth day: 'Then God said, "Let the water teem with an abundance of living creatures, and on the earth let birds fly beneath the dome of the sky . . ." And God blessed them, saying, "Be fertile, multiply, and fill the water of the seas; and let the birds multiply on the earth." '

Finally came **land animals and mankind**: 'God made all kinds of wild animals, all kinds of cattle, and all kinds of creeping things of the earth . . . Then God said, 'Let us make man in our image, after our likeness. Let them have dominion over the fish of the sea, the birds of the air, and the cattle, and over all the wild animals and all the creatures that crawl on the ground." '

In this first account in Genesis, God created humans last – 'male and female he created them' – to imply they are the culmination of all his creatures. He endows them with a special dignity in making them overlords of the earth and all that lives on it and also directs them, as he did the animals, to be fruitful and multiply. But what does it mean to say that man was created in God's image and likeness? Does it refer to man's possession of a soul, reason and free will, all denied to brute beasts, or was the ancient author merely imagining God anthropomorphically in his own image?

Rest is the theme of the seventh day: 'So God blessed the seventh day and made it holy, because on it he rested from all the work he had done in creation.' God thus sets the example for the seven-day week of the Jews, whose Law requires six days of work followed by a holy Sabbath of rest, worship, prayer and religious study.

The entrance of evil, sin and death into God's 'very good' creation is explained in the story of the Fall of Man in the Yahwist account in Genesis 2–3. In this version, which predates Chapter 1 by many centuries, God creates a man, Adam, from the dust of the ground and places him in the Garden of Eden with instructions to cultivate it.

Eden is full of different kinds of succulent fruit trees, including the Tree of the Knowledge of Good and Evil, which Adam is forbidden to taste of or even touch. After the wild beasts and birds are created by God and named by Adam, God forms a woman, Eve, from the man's rib. She promptly succumbs to a beguiling serpent, who tricks her into eating

> . . . the Fruit
> Of that forbidden Tree, whose mortal taste
> Brought Death into the World, and all our woe,
> With loss of Eden . . .
>
> (*Paradise Lost*, 1.1−4)

Uxorious Adam eats some of it, too. The knowledge they gain results only in shame at their nakedness, causing them to sew themselves pathetic fig-leaf loincloths. God sentences the woman to pain in childbirth and lust for her husband, who now becomes her master. 'The master' must henceforth earn his bread with the sweat of his brow. He is informed that he will suffer death, and his sin of disobedience has shorn him of much of his former dignity: 'For dust you are, and unto dust shall you return.'

Christians who try to harmonise the seven days of Genesis too precisely with the aeons of evolutionary time sometimes cite 2 Peter 3:8: 'One day is with the Lord as a thousand years.' But all attempts to calibrate these metaphoric days with scientific time are foredoomed by St Paul's admonition that 'the letter killeth, but the spirit giveth life'.

What were the 7 hills of Rome?

Palatine	Esquiline
Capitoline	Caelian
Quirinal	Aventine
Viminal	

TO SETTLERS IN THE SECOND MILLENNIUM BC, some of these seven hills, 100 to 150 feet high and just east of the Tiber, offered easily defended sites overlooking a valley with access to the river trade. Much later, the hills of the Eternal City were enclosed by the Servian Wall (378 BC), mistakenly ascribed to Servius Tullius, Rome's sixth king (sixth century BC).

All palaces are named after the **Palatine**, hub of the seven hills, which probably took its name from Pales, a deity of uncertain sex who presided over shepherds and herds. It's traditionally the site of the oldest Roman settlement. The legend says that the twins Romulus and Remus resorted to augury to decide which of them should be king of a new city and give it his name. Remus, from the Aventine, first saw a sign from heaven – six vultures – but, immediately afterwards, Romulus saw twelve birds from his vantage point on the Palatine. In the ensuing discussion of the respective claims of priority or quantity, Remus was slain, and Romulus went on to found his city and name it Roma on 21 April 753 BC, according to unreliable sources.

Many centuries later, after Augustus' house on the Palatine was enlarged, it became the first palace (palatium) of the emperors to be located there. Other rich and famous residents of the Palatine included Crassus, Cicero and Mark Antony.

All capitols are named after the **Capitoline** (caput, 'head' or 'top'), the religious centre and citadel of ancient Rome. On one of its peaks rose the stupendous temple of Jupiter Optimus Maximus ('Jupiter Best and Greatest'), supposedly dedicated in the first year of the Roman republic

(509 BC), with side chapels for the goddesses Juno and Minerva. The temple was roughly two hundred feet on each side, and one hundred steps led up to its bronze gates. Roman magistrates offered sacrifice here upon entering office. Victorious generals who were awarded triumphs also sacrificed to Jupiter in this temple, which was destroyed by fire and rebuilt several times.

On another peak of the Capitoline was the *Arx* or stronghold of the city (the Roman 'Acropolis'). On yet a third stood the temple of Juno Moneta, which housed the mint of Rome. *Moneta*, which merely means 'admonisher', thus gave rise to our word *money*. On a more sombre note, traitors and murderers were flung from a cliff of the Capitoline, the Tarpeian Rock.

Petrarch was crowned Poet Laureate on the Capitoline in 1341. Here, in 1536, Michelangelo designed the superb square of the Campidoglio, flanked by three *palazzi*, one of which, the Capitoline Museum, is a treasury of ancient art. Here Edward Gibbon, in 1764, meditating on the ruins on the Capitoline and the vicissitudes of history, supposedly received the initial impetus for *The Decline and Fall of the Roman Empire*. On the Capitoline now stands the elaborately squat Monument to Victor Emmanuel II, the first King of Italy, completed in 1911. In pre-computer days, facetious Romans referred to the edifice as 'The Typewriter'.

The **Quirinal**, the northernmost hill of ancient Rome, was traditionally occupied by Sabines and named after Cures, the town from which the Sabines were supposed to have migrated to Rome. Or was the hill named after Quirinus, the Sabine god of war, who was eventually identified with the deified Romulus? Whatever the etymology, the Roman people were referred to in speeches and formal addresses as 'Quirites', apparently to commemorate their ancient assimilation with the Sabines, which occurred after the end of the strife occasioned by the abduction ('rape') of the Sabine women. In the late sixteenth century Pope Gregory XIII began building the Quirinal Palace on this hill as a papal summer home, which in 1870 became the residence of the King of Italy. The Italian President now lives there.

The **Viminal** was named after a copse of willow trees, *vimina*, that grew there. As far as the hills of Rome go, it wasn't very important.

The name **Esquiline** apparently stems from *excolere*, 'to cultivate'. It was the site of the villa and gardens of the archetypal literary patron Maecenas, who cultivated poets like Virgil, Horace and Propertius. Nero's monstrously huge and ornate *Domus Aurea* ('Golden House') was later built on the Esquiline and sprawled over adjoining areas – 125 acres' worth of palatial pleasure domes. 'Now I can live like a human being,' he commented.

The **Caelian** was named after Caelius Vibenna, an Etruscan who came to the assistance of a Roman king. His picturesque name in Etruscan was Kaile Fipne. The Caelian is now called the Lateran Hill.

The **Aventine**, home to a temple of Diana, was named after Aventinus, a Latin king buried there. This most southerly of the seven hills was given to the Roman plebeians to settle in 456 BC and remained a stronghold of the proletariat, though it's a fancy residential neighbourhood now.

What were the 7 liberal arts of the medieval curriculum?

Grammar
Rhetoric
Logic (these first three forming the trivium)
Arithmetic
Geometry
Music
Astronomy (these last four forming the quadrivium)

THE SEVEN LIBERAL ARTS were branches of learning considered appropriate for *liberi*, 'free men'. These arts — sometimes called the Seven Sciences — were the basis of education in the cathedral and monastic schools and, later, the universities of the Middle Ages. The Church long remained divided on whether the 'pagan learning' embodied in the seven arts should be embraced or rejected. Eventually, the consensus was for 'despoiling the Egyptians of their gold', that is, using the knowledge of the ancient Greeks and Romans for the Church's own purposes, much as the Jews in Exodus (12:35–6) departed from Egypt with the gold of their former heathen masters.

In the late twelfth and thirteenth centuries, someone who had studied the trivium of Latin grammar, rhetoric (Latin literature) and Aristotelian logic at a university received a baccalaureate or Bachelor of Arts degree. Those who then ploughed through the quadrivium received their master's degree (*Magister Artium*, 'Master of Arts'), allowing them to teach. (A *magister* was a schoolteacher.) Hardy souls who continued their studies could choose to specialise in theology at a university such as that of Paris, civil or canon law at Bologna, or medicine at Salerno. Graduates would receive a doctorate in their field of study. Some of these men would choose to teach at a university (*doctor* meant professor), whereas others pursued careers as prelates, ecclesiastical or civil lawyers, or physicians.

How did this grouping of the arts originate? In Book 7 of the *Republic*, Plato (c.429–347 BC) includes in the education of his ruling elite the studies that came to be called the seven liberal arts. Several centuries later, the Roman encyclopaedist Varro (116–27 BC) dealt with them systematically (plus architecture and medicine) in his *Disciplines*. St Augustine (354–430), a professor of rhetoric before his conversion, wrote works on grammar, rhetoric, logic and music – parts of an encyclopaedic work on the liberal arts modelled on Varro's book.

Yet another writer influenced by Varro, the fifth-century Neoplatonist Martianus Capella, composed *The Marriage of Mercury and Philology*, a long, allegorical farrago of Latin prose and verse in which Mercury, god of eloquence, marries the learned maiden Philologia ('the science of words'). Each of the seven handmaidens of Philologia corresponds to one of the liberal arts and delivers an interminable harangue on her own particular charms. Later writers who composed influential works on the seven arts were Cassiodorus (c.490–c.583) and Isidore of Seville (c.570–636).

What was so special about these seven arts? Let's start with the **trivium**. In the Middle Ages, it served as the 'threefold way' for mastering the verbal skills and reasoning tools needed to delve into study of the Bible, theology and the Latin classics – or to preach an effective sermon. It thoroughly grounded students in

Reading, writing and speaking Latin

Using figures of speech and narrative strategies to make their writing and speaking aesthetically pleasing ('the sugar-coated pill')

Thinking logically, so that they could state an argument clearly, develop it, sustain it with proofs or examples, and refute counter-arguments.

Certainly the trivium didn't have much relevance to 'the real world' and so became an easy target of ridicule for the likes of Rabelais in a later age. But without the verbal and reasoning skills so obsessively, even lunatically, cultivated by medieval scholars, the achievements of the scientific revolution beginning in the mid-seventeenth century might have been postponed or stillborn.

In the Middle Ages, students usually learned the rudiments of Latin **grammar** from the fourth-century text of Donatus. Advanced students moved on to the bulkier grammar of Priscian (fl. *c.* AD 500), which incorporated a copious anthology of Roman authors. This book became synonymous with Latin grammar, so that 'to crack Priscian's pate' meant to make an egregious mistake in Latin. Dante puts Donatus in his *Paradiso* and Priscian in his *Inferno*, reflecting an ambivalence about grammarians that many of us still share.

Rhetoric didn't always have pejorative connotations. What Cicero called 'The Queen of the Arts' was an invaluable tool for presenting ideas effectively and elegantly in public speaking, verse and prose. The goals of rhetoric were to teach, delight and, above all, persuade an audience to adopt or shun a course of action. Its three main divisions were (1) arrangement or organisation, (2) amplification or abbreviation of classical passages on a particular subject to suit one's own purposes, and (3) style and its ornaments, such as figures of speech.

In the ancient world, Aristotle's *Rhetoric* was a classic exposition, along with the *Institutes of Oratory* (*c.* AD 95) of the Roman rhetorician Quintilian, who also wrote on the six other liberal arts. Medieval students of rhetoric were particularly fond of Cicero's *On Invention*, the *Rhetorica ad Herennium* (misattributed to Cicero) and Horace's *Art of Poetry*. Rhetoric, 'the most precious gift of the gods' (Quintilian), remained a required course at Jesuit colleges well into the twentieth century.

The names of the many rhetorical figures still offer incomparable means of displaying one's erudition and classical education:

> Aposiopesis, a sudden breaking-off of speech: 'Of all the dirty – I'll rip your lungs out, Jack!'
> Catachresis, a mixed metaphor: 'The very heart of the digestive system is, of course, the stomach.'

Litotes, understatement expressed by negation of what is
meant: 'Not bad at all, that Sistine Chapel.'

Paronomasia, a sesquipedalian word for a pun.

Synecdoche, a part for the whole or the whole for a part:
'Jennifer memorised all sixty-one lists – what a brain she is!'

Among the debating tricks developed by rhetoricians over the ages is
this neat example from the Greek Sophist Gorgias (c.483–c.376 BC):
'You should kill your opponents' earnestness with jesting and their jesting with earnestness.' Note that this infuriating trait didn't shorten his
enormous life span at all.

While rhetoric persuades via the emotions, **logic** persuades by reason. Thousands of medieval thinkers learned how to split hairs from
Latin translations of Aristotle's impenetrable works on logic – bleakest
of all, the *Posterior Analytics* – collectively known as the *Organon* ('tool' or
'instrument' of investigation). The author of *The Consolation of Philosophy*,
Boethius (c.480–524), 'the last of the Romans and the first of the Scholastics', translated into Latin Aristotle's works on logic and composed his
own works in the field. These, with other Latin translations of Aristotle's
logical treatises and of countless Arabic commentaries on them, became
grist for the ever-grinding mills of the Scholastic philosophers.

The self-appointed task of these 'Schoolmen' was to reconcile the
revealed truths of Christianity with Aristotelian logic and science, often
by using acrobatically creative reasoning to prove that yes was no. (In
fact, one of Peter Abelard's most important works bears the title *Sic et Non*
– 'Yes and No'.) This tendency wasn't restricted to Christianity: avid
medieval Aristotelians included the Jewish scholar Moses Maimonides
and, among many Islamic thinkers, Avicenna and Averroës.

The aim was a noble one: if the main tenets of a religious creed could
be shown to accord with 'science' (then represented by the philosophy
of Aristotle), religion was not merely a belief or opinion, but a demon-
strable system of truths. Thus, only a dunce could doubt its claims, since
they were as self-evident as the theorems of geometry – to those who
knew how to 'do the proofs'. By the thirteenth century, the intellectual

obsession with Aristotelian logic almost drove the study of Latin humanistic literature from the universities.

The **quadrivium** was the 'fourfold way' to knowledge – largely mathematical knowledge, since music and astronomy were considered applied maths. Boethius wrote textbooks on the arts of the quadrivium, a word he apparently coined. His basic text on **arithmetic** became a manual for medieval schools. Although it was more Pythagorean/Platonic (dealing with the philosophy of numbers) than computational, it did include practical knowledge relating to the calendar. Since clumsy Roman numerals were still used for computing, the Venerable Bede (673–735) wrote a handy work on how to do sums on one's fingers. Only in 1202 did Leonardo Fibonacci introduce Arabic numerals (ultimately of Indian origin) into Europe.

Over the doors of Plato's Academy was the inscription 'Let no one ignorant of geometry enter.' Plato didn't consider **geometry** one of the practical arts – which he scorned – but an abstract study that allowed students to understand relations among ideal forms. The immutable entities of geometry permitted a glimpse into the perfect world of essences and eternal Ideas – the Good, True, Beautiful and Just. But by far the most influential writer in the field of geometry was Euclid (fl. c. 300 BC). The complete text of his *Elements* first became accessible to the Scholastics when it was translated into Latin in the early twelfth century.

Boethius (or a later writer) composed an elementary treatise on **music** that long remained a standard text at Oxford and Cambridge. The study of music included practical instruction in the Church's plainsong and other liturgical applications, as well as theoretical work on the mathematical basis of music, ultimately harking back to Pythagoreanism. In the eleventh century, the Italian monk Guido d'Arezzo worked out a protomodern system of musical notation. We also owe to Guido the names of *re, mi, fa, sol* and *la*, which, along with the precursor of *do* (*ut*), were taken from the first syllables of six half-lines of a Latin hymn to St John the Baptist.

The indefatigable Boethius also compiled a Latin work based on Greek **astronomy**, mainly on Ptolemy's *Almagest* (second century AD).

The *Almagest*, completely translated into Latin only in the twelfth century, was used to track the course of the heavenly bodies and determine the positions of more than a thousand stars. In the middle of the next century, John of Holywood wrote a commentary on the *Almagest* that became the basic text of elementary astronomy for almost four hundred years. Ptolemy's system of the universe, with the earth enthroned at the centre of the cosmos, became the official version sanctioned by the Church.

And so the great synthesis that Thomas Aquinas had attempted in his *Summa Theologica* — the reconciliation of Greek science with Christian theology — was specifically extended to astronomy, too. Here, the integration of pagan science with Christian metaphysics involved harmonisation of Aristotle's theory of the heavens, Ptolemy's hard astronomic data, and the traditional teachings of the Church. Ptolemy also wrote on astrology, which many ancient and medieval scholars considered to be applied astronomy.

Our word *trivial*, first attested in 1589, originally meant 'commonplace, the kind of thing likely to be encountered on the street' — more precisely, at a *trivium* or crossroad. But by that time, most humanist thinkers regarded the old educational system of the seven arts, with its emphasis on Aristotelian logic, as essentially trivial.

Where do the English names of the 7 days of the week come from?

Sunday (Old English, Sunnandaeg): Sun's day
Monday (Monandaeg): Moon's day
Tuesday (Tiwesdaeg): Tiw's day
Wednesday (Wodnesdaeg): Woden's day
Thursday (Thuresdaeg): Thor's day
Friday (Frigedaeg): Frigg's day
Saturday (Saeternesdaeg): Saturn's day

OUR SEVEN-DAY WEEK harks back to the Sumerians and Babylonians, who even designated one as a day of leisure. Although astronomy dictates that we have a 365-day year, there's no scientific reason for a seven-day week. None the less, the Babylonians named the days of their week after the sun, moon and five planets they knew.

Early in the fourth century AD, the Romans adopted this system of naming the days after these same heavenly bodies, which had already been named after gods. In addition to **Sun's day** and **Moon's day**, the Romans had Mars' day, Mercury's day, Jove's (Jupiter's) day, Venus' day, and **Saturn's day**. The Latin names of the five weekdays are still ensconced in the French, Italian and Spanish words for those days.

While English has kept the days named in honour of the sun, moon and Saturn (Roman god of agriculture and father of Jupiter), the names of the remaining four are based on the Anglo-Saxon names for various Norse gods. Tuesday – **Tiwesdaeg** – memorialises Tiw (or Tiu), the Saxon version of the Norse god of war, Tyr. The son of Odin (Woden), Tyr was also a protector of justice and peace treaties.

On one occasion his fellow gods rather unkindly took advantage of Tyr's reputation as a guardian of good faith when they used the magic thread *gleipnir* (spun from the footfalls of cats, beards of women, spit of birds, breath of fish and roots of stones) to bind the fierce wolf-monster Fenrir (sometimes called Fenris-wolf), sired by Loki. All in jest, the gods explained to Fenrir. Despite the thread's insubstantial appearance, cagey Fenrir would play the game only if Tyr placed his forearm in the wolf's mouth. When Fenrir realised he'd been tricked and was firmly bound, he bit off Tyr's right hand. Fenrir remained captive until the apocalyptic battle – Ragnarok – between the gods (called the Aesir) and, on the other side, the giants and forces of Hel, Queen of the Underworld, led by mischievously malicious Loki. The war god Tyr corresponds to the Roman god Mars, and thus Mars' day (*dies Martis*) became our Tuesday.

The chief Norse god Odin was the ultimate source of **Wodnesdaeg**. Known as the All-Father, the cultured, refined but promise-breaking Odin has only one eye, having traded the other for a drink at the Well of Wisdom in an effort to postpone the day of doom, Ragnarok. Each evening, two ravens perch on his shoulders and whisper hoarsely in his ears. The birds, named Hugin and Munin ('thought' and 'memory'), fly all over the earth during the day, observing humans, and then report back to him on what they've observed. By hanging on a tree for nine agonising days and nights, wounded by a spear, Odin earned the knowledge of runes, and by stealing the skaldic mead of the Giants he became the patron of poets. Odin also feasts all brave dead warriors brought to him at Valhalla by the Valkyries, 'choosers of the slain'. Because Odin/Woden was a match for the Romans' shrewdest god, Mercury, their *dies Mercurii* became our Wodnesdaeg.

The strongest of the Aesir was the thunder god, Thor, from whom **Thuresdaeg** takes its name. The son of Odin, Thor is often depicted as the antithesis of his father – coarse, uncouth and endowed with huge appetites. His massive belt is the source of his power, and he is invincible because of his iron gloves. Thor's hammer, Mjöllnir, which he throws to create thunderbolts, returns to him every time he hurls it, much like a boomerang. Jove's day (*dies Jovis*) became Thuresdaeg because the Saxons considered Thor analogous to the Roman thunderer god Jupiter.

Frigg (or Frigga), who gave her name to **Frigedaeg**, was Odin's wife, Queen of the Aesir, goddess of fertility and, by most accounts, an excellent mother, forever mourning Loki's treacherous murder of her son Balder. She is described as wise and silent, sitting for hours on end spinning gold thread.

Frigg is a somewhat nebulous figure whose identity may have fused with that of Freya, the Norse Venus. Freya was far less virtuous than Frigg and considerably more colourful – driving a wagon pulled by lynxes and refusing to settle down with any of her numerous gentlemen friends. Is Friday – *dies Veneris* – named after model-wife Frigg or promiscuous Freya? Scholars disagree, although most believe the two goddesses gradually coalesced in the minds of the Teutonic peoples who worshipped both of them.

What are the 7 sacraments?

Baptism   Holy Orders
Penance   Matrimony
Holy Eucharist   Extreme Unction
Confirmation

THE WORD SACRAMENTUM originally referred to a military oath of allegiance taken by Roman soldiers at the start of a new campaign. In Roman Catholic tradition, however, which is the main point of view adopted in this essay, a sacrament is a sacred mystery, or, in the words of the catechism, an 'outward sign instituted by Christ by which invisible grace and inward sanctification are communicated to our souls'.

Catholics believe that the priest who administers a sacrament acts only as an instrument of Christ. The Church's commitment to this belief is exemplified by its rejection of Donatism, a fourth-century heresy according to which a sacrament is void if administered by a 'bad' priest.

Baptism (or christening) is the first and most necessary sacrament. In John (3:5), Christ says, 'In all truth I tell you, no one can enter the kingdom of God without being born through water and the spirit.' Indeed, he himself insisted that his cousin, John the Baptist, baptise him in the River Jordan. Baptism cleanses from the soul all taint of original sin – the legacy of Adam and Eve's disobedience of God. When those who are baptised have water poured over their head, or are fully immersed, they are said to be reborn into the life of Christ so as to share in his Resurrection. This rite of purification is also a rite of initiation into the Church for newborns as well as for older converts, whose personal sins are also forgiven. In early Christianity, baptism was probably reserved for adult converts. After the third century, however, a newborn Christian was assigned spiritual parents – godparents – who accepted baptism in the child's name. Baptism, confirmation and Holy Orders can be received only once because their imprint on the soul is said to be indelible.

Christians derive the authority to baptise from the words of Christ before his ascension: 'Go, therefore, make disciples of all nations; baptise them in the name of the Father and of the Son and of the Holy Spirit' (Matthew 28:19). This sacrament can be administered by a layperson in an emergency.

The rite of **penance** or confession, now often called reconciliation, is the sacrament by which Christ, through his priestly representative, forgives the sins of the contrite. In early Christian times, persons deemed to be sinners were assigned notoriously humiliating reparations, including fasting and public denouncement. These were replaced in later centuries by auricular confession, the private admission of sins to a priest (hence the confessional booths in Catholic churches).

Mortal sins, like murder, blasphemy, adultery and theft, are so serious that, unless forgiven in the sacrament of penance, the sinner has no chance of attaining Heaven. Venial sins are less heinous – fibbing, backbiting, quarrelling, a raunchy thought here and there – and do not bar Heaven, but the Church urges that they, too, be confessed. The process begins with an examination of conscience, in which the penitent reviews recent life events in light of the Ten Commandments (see Question 53) and the teachings of the Church, developing contrition for any sins committed. The penitent then approaches the confessional (or, more likely today, a reconciliation room) and confesses the sins to a priest, who may discuss ways to avoid these transgressions and then offers absolution with the words, 'I absolve you from your sins in the Name of the Father, and of the Son, and of the Holy Spirit.' A similar rite is practised in the Eastern Orthodox Churches, but the formula of absolution is more humbly phrased: 'May God, through me, a sinner, forgive thee.'

Most other Christian churches offer public prayers for the forgiveness of sins, but not private confession as in the Catholic Church, claiming that only God has the power to forgive sins. Catholics counter that the priest is merely Christ's representative and cite the words of Christ to his apostles: 'If you forgive anyone's sins, they are forgiven; if you retain anyone's sins, they are retained' (John 20:23). And the epistle of James (5:16) says, 'So confess your sins to one another, and pray for one another to be cured.'

Christians believe that the following Gospel passage describes Christ's institution of the **Holy Eucharist**, also known as Holy Communion or the Lord's Supper: 'This is my body given for you; do this in remembrance of me' and 'This cup is the new covenant in my blood poured out for you' (Luke 22:19–20). Christ seems to be asking his followers to commemorate and re-enact the Last Supper by sharing bread and wine. Most Christians believe that reception of the Eucharist (Greek, *eucharistia*, 'a giving of thanks') unites them more fully with Christ and each other. A rite of praise and thanksgiving, the Eucharist is, with baptism, one of only two sacraments recognised by nearly all Christians as established by Christ.

That's where the agreement ends. Catholics believe that in each celebration of the Eucharist, Christ, joined by the congregation, again offers himself to God the Father, as he did in the sacrifice of the Cross. According to the doctrine of impanation, the Church teaches that, with the priest's words 'This is my body . . . this is my blood', the bread and wine on the altar literally become the body and blood of Christ. In this miracle of transubstantiation, all that remain of the bread and wine are their physical appearances. For centuries, only the clergy received Communion under 'both species' of bread and wine; the laity received only the bread. This was somewhat amended by the Second Vatican Council. Communion in both species is not the norm at many Sunday Masses (probably because of logistical concerns) but may be reserved for special occasions such as weddings and First Communions. According to Church law, Catholics must receive the Eucharist at least once a year, during the Easter season.

The dogma of the Real Presence is also maintained by the Eastern Orthodox Churches, and the Anglican and Lutheran traditions have similar beliefs. Martin Luther (1483–1546) preached the doctrine of consubstantiation – that Christ is truly present 'in, with and under the bread and wine', which coexist with but are not transformed into his body. John Calvin (1509–64) taught that the Eucharist is a spiritually charged metaphor symbolising unity with God but that it does not represent the actual physical body of Christ. This is the view of most Protestants today.

Confirmation involves the laying-on of a bishop's hands and anointment with chrism, a mixture of consecrated olive oil and fragrant balsam. The Holy Spirit, the third person of the Holy Trinity, is said to descend, strengthening the soul and conferring additional grace beyond that received at baptism. The sacrament is usually administered in early adolescence, marking the beginning of adult Christian life, when one is 'sealed with the Holy Spirit' and becomes obliged to witness and spread the faith. As a reminder of the possibility of persecution for the faith, the bishop may also administer a slight tap on the cheek.

The Twelve Apostles (see Question 59) were the first to receive what is now called confirmation. Just before his ascension, Christ told them, 'You will receive the power of the Holy Spirit which will come on you, and then you will be my witnesses' (Acts 1:8). About ten days later (or about fifty days after Christ's Resurrection – on Pentecost, from the Greek for 'fiftieth day'), the Apostles were meeting when the sound of a mighty wind filled the room, 'and there appeared to them tongues as of fire; these separated and came to rest on the head of each of them. They were all filled with the Holy Spirit and began to speak different languages' (Acts 2:3–4). In Acts 8, the Apostles Peter and John pray that the Holy Spirit may descend on some converts in Samaria who had only been baptised. Since Catholics consider bishops to be the successors of the Apostles, only bishops can administer confirmation.

Holy Orders confers the powers of the Catholic priesthood: to change bread and wine into the body and blood of Christ, administer baptism, grant absolution, witness marriages and anoint the sick. A new priest is thought to receive a permanent charism (grace from the Holy Spirit). Although this charism can never be revoked, a priest can be suspended and forbidden from administering the sacraments if, for example, he breaks his vow of celibacy and marries. Like confirmation, Holy Orders can be conferred only by a bishop. During the rite, the candidate lies prone before the altar while the bishop imposes his hands and anoints him. The Church teaches that Christ made the Apostles priests when he gave them the power to change bread and wine into his body and blood at the Last Supper and to forgive sins after he rose from the dead.

Priests don't perform the sacrament of **matrimony**. In the exchange of mutual promises, the wife administers God's grace to her husband, and the husband does the same for her, while the priest acts only as the Church's witness. The Catholic Church considers marriage indissoluble, citing Christ's words in Matthew 19: 'What God has joined together, man must not separate' and 'If a man divorces his wife for any cause other than unchastity, and marries another, he commits adultery.' Although the Church does not recognise divorce, a marriage can be declared null and void if certain conditions are met. Today, psychological problems that keep a person from making a valid marriage contract are probably cited most often in declarations of annulment, at least in the United States. Conservative Catholics believe that annulment has become too easy, while those whose marriage has been annulled at the request of their partner may feel demeaned by the Church's declaration that their marriage never existed.

The Church takes James 5:14–15 as the basis for **Extreme Unction**, now called the Anointing of the Sick:

Any one of you who is ill should send for the elders of the church, and they must anoint the sick person with oil in the name of the Lord and pray over him. The prayer of faith will save the sick person and the Lord will raise him up again; and if he has committed any sins, he will be forgiven.

Anyone in danger of death because of an accident, illness or old age is eligible for this sacrament, which can be received as often as necessary. The purposes of the anointing are to console the dying person, instil the patience to bear suffering, and prepare the soul to meet its Maker.

Who were the 7 against Thebes?

Polynices	Parthenopaeus
Adrastus	Hippomedon
Capaneus	Amphiaraus
Tydeus	

THE TWIN SONS of the incestuous King Oedipus and Queen Jocasta of Thebes, **Polynices** and Eteocles, agreed to share the crown in alternate years after their father's banishment. But when Eteocles refused to resign the kingship at the appointed time and expelled his brother, Polynices raised an army with the help of his father-in-law, King **Adrastus** of Argos. Adrastus also enlisted five other captains who agreed to help place the exiled Polynices on the Theban throne. These chiefs became known in Greek myth as the Seven against Thebes. When they arrived at the city, each of the leaders stationed himself and his troops at one of its seven gates.

It was a smashing defeat for Greece's Magnificent Seven. **Capaneus** boasted that he would scale the walls of Thebes in spite of Zeus, who promptly killed the blaspheming braggadocio with a lightning bolt. (His fierce hubris later earned him a place in Dante's *Inferno*.) King Adrastus' other son-in-law **Tydeus** (the father of Homer's Diomedes) was fatally wounded, but before dying he had the grim satisfaction of eating the brains of his killer Melanippus, who had been beheaded in the meantime. The goddess Athene was bringing a salve to cure Tydeus but was so disgusted by his savagely vengeful meal that she let him die.

Parthenopaeus was the son of the Greek hero Meleager and the virgin huntress Atalanta, who had a fling after meeting at the famous Calydonian Boar Hunt, in which many mythic dignitaries came to Meleager's aid when a fierce boar was ravaging his kingdom of Calydon. Parthenopaeus, whose name means, according to Robert Graves, 'son of a pierced maidenhead', was a handsome blond much loved by women and men alike, but he died at Thebes when a flung boulder smashed his proud head. And **Hippomedon**, despite his huge stature, also found a gory death beneath the walls of the besieged city.

To avert further bloodshed, the feuding brothers Polynices and Eteocles agreed to resolve the war by single combat – and proceeded to kill each other in a furious battle. King Adrastus' brother-in-law, the prophet and ex-Argonaut **Amphiaraus**, foreseeing his own death at Thebes, had tried to evade conscription, but his wife Eriphyle was bribed by Polynices with a magical necklace to persuade her doomed husband to join the expedition. As he fled in a chariot from his Theban foes, Amphiaraus was swallowed up in a chasm that Zeus mercifully opened up in his path. King Adrastus, the only one of the Seven to survive, was spirited away on his flying white horse Arion.

One of the seven extant plays of the Greek tragedian Aeschylus (525–456 BC), *Seven against Thebes*, is a curiously static, undramatic treatment of the legend, first performed in 467 BC. With its accompanying (now lost) tragedies of *Laius* and *Oedipus*, it won first prize that year at the Greater Dionysia, the Athenian spring festival at which plays were presented. Like his masterpiece, the three plays of the *Oresteia*, which deal with the curse on the House of Atreus through the three generations of Atreus, Agamemnon and Orestes (see Question 10), Aeschylus' Theban trilogy explored the curse on the House of Thebes in the three generations of Laius (murdered by his son), Oedipus (an unwitting incestuous patricide), and Eteocles and Polynices (mutual murderers in fulfilment of Oedipus' curse on them for exiling him after his disgrace and self-blinding).

Seven against Thebes consists mainly of descriptions of the heraldic devices on the shields of the seven champions, of their impious boasts against Thebes, and of Eteocles' assignment of a Theban champion (including himself) to confront each of them. The play may have been in part a plea to strengthen the Acropolis of Athens against attack.

The tragedy closes with the dirge of a chorus of Theban women and of Antigone and Ismene over the corpses of their brothers Eteocles and

Polynices. At the very end of the play, the Theban state decrees that Eteocles will be granted solemn burial with all honours, whereas the body of Polynices will be cast out unburied to glut the dogs and birds. This is too much for Antigone, who asserts that she will disobey the decree and bury her brother, traitor or not. Her defiance later provides the impetus for Sophocles' complex exploration of the relationship between the laws of the state and the rights of the individual conscience in *Antigone* (c.442 BC).

In his epic poem, the *Thebaid*, the Latin poet Statius (c. AD 45–96) describes how, when Eteocles and Polynices are burned on the same funeral pyre, the flame enveloping their corpses rises double-crested at its peak – a final index of their undying mutual hatred.

There's a sequel, too. The sons of the Seven, called the Epigoni (the 'after-born' or 'successors'), had better luck against Thebes when they sacked it ten years later in a sort of copycat war. Our word *epigone* means a follower or inferior imitator, but usually of a thinker or creative artist rather than a warrior.

Who were the 7 Sages of Greece?

Solon of Athens
Pittacus of Mytilene
Bias of Priene
Cleobulus of Lindus

Periander of Corinth
Chilon of Sparta
Thales of Miletus

LORE, HISTORY AND LEGEND agree there were Seven Sages of Greece but differ on the exact roster. Plato's list in the *Protagoras* has been followed here, except that his Myson of Chen – about whom little is known – has been bumped by Periander, a colourful tyrant with a spectacularly awful personal life who was often considered one of the Seven.

Wait a second, you say. Who are these people? Where are Socrates, Plato, Aristotle and a host of others? They're not here because this group consists of seven men who all lived about 600 BC, more than 150 years before Socrates flourished. Second, at the time their 'wisdom' was celebrated, this word had more to do with mastery of the busy world of law and commerce than with contemplative profundity. The Sages were all eminent public personages in their time. Four of them – Pittacus, Cleobulus, Periander and Chilon – were tyrants (legitimate rulers with far-reaching powers) or magistrates. Solon was an innovative lawgiver, Bias seems to have been a pleader of just causes, and Thales was a renowned scientist, philosopher and mathematician.

The Seven were also refreshingly free of hubris. The story goes that some young men found a golden tripod in a catch of fish. They consulted Apollo's oracle, who said it should be given to 'whoever is wisest'. They gave it to Thales, who declined the honour. Each of the other Sages followed suit. When it finally came to Thales again, he declared that Apollo was wisest and sent the prize to the god's sanctuary at Delphi.

Another quality the Seven shared was a quick-witted penchant for shrewd one-liners that got repeated all over the Mediterranean. Plato observed that the style of the ancient Sages tended to be brief but pungent, in the laconic mode of the Spartans. As we listen to their quips and pithy wisdom, bear in mind that the Sages weren't chat-show hosts or media sports pundits. All, even the theoretical scientist Thales, were men of action. Some, like Solon, lived with a brilliance and vibrancy undimmed 2,600 years after their time. Indeed, Solon didn't just endow his people with a new legal order, he also had the wit to survive the political turbulence his laws provoked.

'No great statesman has ever risen higher above the mere lust for power than Solon,' wrote historian Werner Jaeger. It wasn't always easy, however, for **Solon of Athens** (c.630–c.560 BC) to steer clear of the fray: 'I put myself on guard at every side, and turned among them like a wolf inside a pack of dogs.' That's Solon in one of his few surviving poems, describing how he managed to avoid being murdered by either of the warring Athenian factions. He had failed to satisfy both the wealthy and the poor, who were threatening to destroy each other and Athens itself.

The Athenians had turned to Solon when the city was being torn apart by a political, economic and social crisis. The rich owned most of the land, and the poor owed them money. When the poor had no more land to sell for paying their debts, and could produce no more food to bring to market, they sold themselves into slavery. Athens was on the brink of becoming a city of nothing but masters and slaves.

Solon owed his prestige to the often fickle goodwill of the people, who respected him for spurring the city to reconquer from the Megarians the nearby island of Salamis, Solon's birthplace. According to the ancient biographer Diogenes Laertius, the people sought to make Solon tyrant of Athens, but he refused, saying that tyranny was 'a very fair spot, but it had no way down from it'.

He also realised that, 'acting where issues are great, it is hard to please all'. His ultimate success was at least partly due to his mastery of double-talk. Plutarch credits him with inventing the political euphemism. For example, he called cancelling the debts of the poor *seisachtheia* – a 'relief' or 'disencumbrance'. Solon again relied on verbal legerdemain in attempting to appease the warring Athenian classes by telling them there could never be strife when things were 'even'. The wealthy thought he meant 'in fair proportion', but the poor took him to mean 'absolutely equal'. Into a single word Solon packed two mutually incompatible political solutions: the promise of perpetuating hierarchical order and the commitment to eliminate class distinctions.

In the end, Solon freed people from monetary debt but did not redistribute land, as his poor supporters expected of him. His compromise set him smack in the middle of the pack of dogs, but eventually both factions went along with him.

Solon's laws defy facile categorisation. For example, he ordained that

A magistrate found intoxicated should be put to death
Prostitution be legalised and taxed
Anyone catching an adulterer in the act could kill him on the spot
It was a crime to speak evil of the dead
Dowries for women other than heiresses were banned because marriage was for love, not gain
Women who went out were allowed no more than three articles of dress and no more than an obol's worth of food and drink.

Solon also introduced the use of wills to control inheritance. Before, everything had reverted to the family, but Solon prized friendship above family, and affection above the arbitrary dictates of kinship. By making every man's estate truly his own, he broadened the individual's scope of choice, expanding the notion of individuality itself.

Solon gave Athens more than just a law code to replace that of Draco, whose draconian enactments prescribed the death penalty for most offences. He gave the city a vision of the body politic as a whole that was dependent on the integrated functioning of all its members. All citizens had to be involved, if in nothing else, as jurors. The best city, he said, was one 'where those not injured try and punish the unjust as much as those that are'. For this reason, neutrals in a time of sedition were disenfranchised. Citizens no longer had the option to sit on the fence when the survival of their country was at stake.

Asked what made an orderly state, Solon replied, 'When the people obey the rulers, and the rulers obey the laws.' But Solon was always anchored in the all-too-human world of *realpolitik*. Unlike Minos, Hammurabi and Numa, Solon made no claim that his laws were delivered to him by a god. He remained plain-spoken to the end. Asked if he had given the Athenians the best laws he could give, Solon said, 'The best they could receive.'

When Solon finished hammering out his laws, he sailed from Athens, having demanded of the city a commitment to abide by them for ten years. He then travelled the world. A famous, and no doubt apocryphal, anecdote tells of his coming to the resplendent court of King Croesus of Lydia. As the Greek historian Herodotus tells the story, Croesus asked, 'Who is the happiest man you have ever seen?'

Solon named an obscure Athenian who had had an honourable death. Croesus then enquired, 'Who is the second happiest?' Solon named Cleobis and Biton, two brothers who died in their sleep in the prime of their youth just after drawing the cart of the goddess Hera. Croesus then angrily demanded, 'What about me?' Noting that victory is not awarded to a wrestler still in the ring, Solon replied, 'We call happy only a person to whom God has given happiness right up to the end.'

His words proved prophetic years later, when Croesus had been crushed in battle by Cyrus the Great. As the Persian conqueror was preparing to burn him alive on a pyre, Croesus, in his anguish, called out Solon's name three times. Cyrus stopped the proceedings and, on hearing the story from Croesus and reflecting on how it could someday apply to himself, spared the broken King's life.

Solon's innate scepticism about the ephemeral perks of life allowed him to see through the vain pretence of politics. After he refused to become tyrant of Athens, the city came under the spell of Pisistratus, who feigned being wounded to drum up support for his tyranny. Solon called his bluff, saying, 'This is a bad copy of Homer's Ulysses; you do to trick your countrymen, what he did to deceive his enemies.' When the people put Pisistratus in charge, Solon wrote poems castigating them for their folly. For his part, Pisistratus courted Solon assiduously and retained many of his laws. This may or may not have had anything to do with the story that, long before, Solon had been Pisistratus' lover.

Though he refused the reins of power, Solon exerted an influence that outlived that of his contemporaries. The city whose laws he shaped has shaped western culture more than any other. In a phrase whose terse audacity might have pleased Solon himself, Werner Jaeger calls him 'the first Athenian'. But Solon himself should have the last word, this time on successful ageing: 'As I grow old, I keep learning so many new things.'

Like Solon, **Pittacus of Mytilene** (c.650–570 BC) was a moderate democratic reformer. His bailiwick was Mytilene, the chief city of the island of Lesbos and home of the early Greek lyric poets Sappho and Alcaeus (see Question 50). Pittacus was famed for his courage and morality. His most memorable law doubled the penalty for all offences committed while under the influence. His sayings include the sad but true observation, 'Hard it is to be noble,' and an early version of Horace's *carpe diem* advice: 'Seize time by the forelock.'

Plutarch relates how when Pittacus was entertaining some friends one evening, his wife burst in, furious about something. As he watched her overturn the dining-table, Pittacus said, 'No one's life is perfect. Anyone with only my troubles is very well off.' Spoken like a true sage.

Little is remembered of **Bias of Priene** in Caria (fl. 570–550 BC). His main claim to fame seems to be how he answered a riddle. Asked which part of the sacrificial animal is best and which is worst, he cut out the tongue and sent it back as his answer to both questions. Someone else asked him which creature is the most formidable. 'The tyrant is the most formidable wild creature', he replied, 'and the flatterer is the domesticated creature most to be feared.' A saying often attributed to him is 'Most men are bad'; he combined this with the advice to live as if our life span will be both long and short. Another piece of sagacity reminds us that 'the most unfortunate of men is he who has not learned how to bear misfortune'. Bias also shrewdly observed that 'power proves the man', and he seems to have coined an early form of the proverb 'Too many cooks spoil the broth.'

Another fairly obscure Sage was **Cleobulus of Lindus** on the island of Rhodes (fl. 580 BC). Besides being tyrant of Lindus, strong and handsome Cleobulus was a lyric poet and the man who foreshadowed Aristotle's golden mean and Horace's *aurea mediocritas* with his dictum 'Moderation is best.' He was also famed for his riddles, such as, 'One father, twelve children, each of them with thirty children, partly black and partly white; and though immortal, they all die.' The answer? 'The year.'

Periander of Corinth ruled his bustling city from about 625 to 585 BC in one of the longest dictatorships in the history of Greece. He was the Greek Citizen Kane – a titan of commerce who came to a tragic end.

Periander had no use for idleness in his subjects, focusing on a vigorous expansion of Corinth's economic base. His motto was 'Forethought in all things'. He built triremes, sailed the seas, established state coinage, and lowered taxes to promote industry. For a time, Periander's Corinth was the foremost city in Greece. But he wasn't just a Corinthian Bill Gates. He also undertook great public works, protected small business by limiting the number of slaves any one man could employ, and made the wealthy contribute to a gigantic golden statue. Yet this busiest of the Greeks also spoke for every true Mediterranean when he said, 'What a beautiful thing leisure is!'

Periander's legend has a darker side. Herodotus tells of how he sent a messenger to Thrasybulus, master of Miletus, for advice on how to rule. Instead of offering precepts, Thrasybulus took Periander's messenger for a walk in a field, during which he lopped off the tallest ears of wheat and flung them away. When the messenger reported this to Periander, he at once took the meaning and went on a bloody, systematic purge of all the most powerful and prominent citizens of Corinth.

Periander is also said to have thrown his wife, Melissa, down a flight of stairs, killing her. After her death, he was unable to find something and sent envoys to the oracle of the dead to discover where he had mislaid it. The shade of Melissa rose up from Hades, refusing to answer the question and complaining she was forced to wander in the underworld naked and cold because her husband 'had put his loaves in a cold oven'. When he heard this, Periander knew his envoys were telling the truth because only Melissa knew that he had made love to her corpse.

Then, says Herodotus, Periander summoned the Corinthian women to what they believed was a festival and ordered them stripped of their clothing and jewels. As he burned their sumptuous silks in her honour, Periander prayed to his dead wife. Propitiated, she told him where to find what he was looking for.

Tragedy attended the relations of Periander with his son Lycophron. At a young age, when the boy learned his father had killed his mother, he refused to have any dealings with him. Periander drove him into exile, but when he was very old he sought to make peace with him and make him tyrant of Corinth. Lycophron steadfastly refused, saying he would never set foot in Corinth as long as Periander lived there. Finally, Periander offered to exchange places, making Lycophron tyrant of Corinth, while Periander himself would go into exile in Corcyra. But when the people of Corcyra learned of the plan, they put Lycophron to death, just to keep the dangerous old lion out of their country.

Herodotus called **Chilon of Sparta** (fl. c.556 BC) the wisest of the Seven Sages, but little is remembered of him today. A Spartan magistrate (an ephor) and a philosopher, Chilon is credited with radically altering Spartan foreign policy, leading to the creation of the Peloponnesian League.

Chilon is known for several bits of wisdom, including 'Look to the end' and 'Speak no evil of the dead' – which accords with one of Solon's laws and anticipates the Roman admonition *de mortuis nil nisi bonum*. He also provides a Greek version of 'Judge not, lest ye be judged,' which goes, 'Do not malign your neighbour if you do not want to hear distressing words in return.'

Aristotle ascribed one of the two most famous Greek precepts to Chilon: *meden agan* – 'nothing in excess' – a basic tenet of Aristotelian ethics. Diogenes Laertius, however, thought Solon first said it. The other fundamental tenet, 'Know thyself,' *gnothi sauton*, was variously attributed to Solon or Thales and inscribed on the temple of Apollo at Delphi.

It should be clear by now that Wisdom in the sixth century BC was not an ascetic clambering out of Plato's Cave to attain a vision of the timeless world of transcendental Forms. The wisdom of the time was a far more rough-and-tumble thing, often born in the heat of political action.

The seeming exception was **Thales of Miletus** (c.624–c.546 BC). Possibly of Semitic descent, Thales lived in Ionia, the west coast of what is now Turkey. He was the first of a triad of Milesian wise men (the others being Anaximander and Anaximenes) who attempted to explain the origin and composition of the universe in natural terms – the world's earliest known physicists. Plutarch made the point that Thales was different from the other Sages: 'It is probable that, at that time, Thales alone had raised philosophy above mere practice into speculation; and the rest of the wise men were so-called from prudence in political concerns.'

A famous anecdote about Thales offers a glimpse into how early Greeks tended to view this abstract speculation of his. When the venerable sage was taken out of doors by an old woman to observe the stars, he promptly fell into a ditch. To his cry for help, the woman responded, 'How can you expect to know all about the heavens, Thales, when you can't even see what's right in front of your feet?'

Aristotle called Thales the founder of physical science, but the Ionian thinker's approach was more poetic and gnomic than systematic. Although none of his writings survive, what we know of his thought reveals a philosopher seeking the broadest truths. He was perhaps the first western man to reduce the multiplicity of observed phenomena to a single principle.

For Thales, that principle was water, which he claimed was the origin of all things (see Question 14). In the nineteenth century, Nietzsche was still struggling with how this seemingly preposterous fancy gave rise to Greek philosophy. He concluded that 'Everything is water' was actually a major step in thought for three reasons: 'It enunciates something about the origin of things; it does so without figure and fable; and in it is contained, if only in chrysalis form, the idea that everything is one.'

Among the Sages, Thales makes the perfect book-end to Solon. While the great Athenian enmeshed himself in the densest political thickets, producing laws of extraordinary specificity to foster individual freedom, Thales remained detached, seeking the broadest possible generalisation to penetrate beneath appearances and suggest their underlying unity.

An anecdote illustrates some of the differences between Solon and Thales. Solon is urging Thales to marry, mustering all the usual arguments. One day, Thales pretends he's just learned that the Athenian's son has died. Solon collapses in grief, giving Thales his opening: marriage binds us to the world, and thus to sorrow. Thales became a touchstone on the question of 'to marry or not to marry'. Montaigne, a married man, claimed Thales said it best: 'When he was young and his mother urged him to marry, he answered that it was not yet time; and when advanced in years, that it was too late.' Francis Bacon shortened that to 'A young man, not yet; an old man, not at all.'

Thales was far more than a nerdy ivory-tower intellectual. In his own day, he was celebrated as a multifaceted genius who astonished the Greeks with real-world achievements. As an engineer, he is said to have diverted the River Halys from its course so that an army could ford it. As a mathematician, he developed abstract geometry from his study of Egyptian land measurements. By measuring the length of a pyramid's shadow at a time of day when the length of a man's shadow was equal to his height, Thales was able to determine the height of the structure. As an astronomer, he predicted the year (though not the month or day) of the total solar eclipse of 28 May 585 BC.

His versatility extended to the business world. Aristotle tells the story of how sceptics were tweaking Thales, alleging philosophy was useless because it had left him a poor man − saying, in effect, 'If you're so smart, why aren't you rich?' But from his knowledge of the stars, Thales knew a bumper crop of olives was coming. He raised a little capital and put deposits on all the olive presses in Miletus and Chios. Anyone who needed them to make oil had to pay him a rental fee. By thus cornering the market, he made a killing, demonstrating that philosophers can become wealthy if they want, but that they have better things to do with their time.

Nowhere is Thales more inscrutable than when it comes to divinity. The statement that 'All things are full of gods' was attributed to him. He was also reputed to maintain there was no difference between life and death. 'Why, then, don't you kill yourself?' someone asked. 'Because there's no difference,' he replied.

However else he differed from the other Sages, Thales shared their gift for the memorable one-liner. Asked what was difficult, Thales responded, 'To know oneself.' What was easy? 'To give advice.' Why had he no children? 'Because I loved children.' Thales is even said to have written a song that elevates the Sages' terse style into a rule of life:

> Many words do not declare an understanding heart.
> Seek one sole wisdom,
> Choose one sole good.
> Thus will you check the tongues of chatterers
> Prating without end.

QUESTION 38

What are the 7 deadly sins?

Pride   Avarice
Envy   Gluttony
Wrath   Lust
Sloth

POPE ST GREGORY THE GREAT (reigned 590–604) distinguished these seven as capital or deadly sins. Much later, St Thomas Aquinas (1225–74) called special attention to two of them in his *Summa Theologica*: **avarice**, or covetousness, and **pride**, or vainglory.

In elaborating on what St Paul had said in 1 Timothy (6:10) – that the love of money is the root of all evil – Aquinas asserts that 'by riches a man acquires the means of committing any sin whatever, and of sating his desire for any sin whatever, since money helps a man obtain all manner of temporal goods'. It all begins with pride, though: 'Now man's end in acquiring all temporal goods is that, through their means, he may have some distinctive perfection and excellence . . . Pride, which is the desire to excel, is said to be the beginning of every sin.'

For Aquinas, much of the meretricious danger of the seven deadly sins derives from their proximity to good, and he observes that many sins are committed in the pursuit of some laudable end. To strive for 'excellence of honour and praise' is a fine goal, he seems to say, until sought inordinately by vainglory and expressed by boasting – when it becomes the deadly sin of pride. Similarly, avarice is an inordinate desire for satiety, and though the desire for meat and drink is natural, crossing the line to **gluttony** is sinful. Sexual intercourse preserves the species, but obsession with 'the venereal pleasures' is **lust**. Both gluttony and lust aim at an overabundance of pleasure.

According to Aquinas, **sloth** is a spiritual laziness, the failure 'to acquire spiritual goods because of the attendant labour'. He cites an earlier theologian to the effect that sloth is an oppressive sorrow, a 'sluggishness of the mind which neglects to begin good'. It is evil because it 'oppresses man so as to draw him away entirely from good deeds'.

Of **envy** Gregory the Great says that the 'self-inflicted pain wounds the pining spirit, which is racked by the prosperity of another'. It was the serpent's envy of Adam and Eve in the Garden of Eden that brought sin and death into the world. Envy is the companion of sloth, claims Aquinas: 'Sloth is grief for a Divine spiritual good, so envy is grief for our neighbour's good.'

Compound envy with angry, self-righteous recrimination, and **wrath** is the result. What makes wrath so sinful, according to Aquinas, is the guise of good masking wicked intent: 'The angry man desires another's evil under the aspect of just revenge.'

Perhaps the most interesting aspect of Aquinas' understanding of the seven deadly sins is his observation that they are all derived from love. In his system, the soul experiences no passion that does not have its origin in some form of love, either praiseworthy or reprehensible.

Dante (1265–1321) relied heavily on this aspect of Aquinas' thought in his *Purgatorio*. He conceives of Purgatory as a huge terraced mountain rising from the sea at the antipodes of Jerusalem. Souls being punished for the sinfulness they displayed during life must work their way up the seven terraces, each of which corresponds to one of the deadly sins.

Dante's guide Virgil echoes Aquinas – quite a trick for an ancient Roman born centuries earlier – when he explains that 'love must be the seed in you of every virtue and of every action deserving punishment'. Thus, each deadly sin in the *Purgatorio* is an example of love gone wrong. Misdirected egocentric love is exemplified by the most reprehensible of the deadly sins – pride, envy and wrath. Sloth is defective love, a half-hearted effort to pursue good, plying 'too slack an oar'. Avarice, gluttony and lust – the results of excessive love – are, in this scheme, the least blameworthy of the deadly sins. As Dante's sinners make their reparations, they climb to the top of the mountain, where the Garden of Eden is located, and from there ascend to Paradise.

Dante the literary character tells us a bit about Dante the poet in the

Purgatorio. On three terraces, Dante joins the penitents in expiating his own sins, notably those of pride, wrath and lust. On the last terrace, populated by the lustful, Virgil insists that Dante literally walk through fire for the sake of his beloved Beatrice.

A number of other medieval literary works deal with the seven deadly sins. *The Vision of Piers Plowman*, ascribed to William Langland, is a long allegorical English poem of the late fourteenth century containing a dream vision of the sins personified as contemporary types – Gluttony who, on his way to church, is tempted into a beer-house; Sloth as a priest who knows Robin Hood poems better than his prayers. And in the last and longest of Geoffrey Chaucer's *Canterbury Tales*, the virtuous Parson delivers a deadly prose sermon on penitence and the deadly sins, a tedious finale to a consummate masterpiece.

What are the 7 virtues?

Faith	Prudence
Hope	Fortitude
Charity (Love)	Temperance
Justice	

TO COMBAT THE SEVEN DEADLY SINS (see Question 38), we must have recourse to the seven virtues. These are the three theological virtues of faith, hope and charity (or love), grafted on to the four cardinal virtues of Plato – justice, prudence, fortitude and temperance. The word *cardinal* comes from the Latin *cardo*, or hinge, and it is applied to Plato's four virtues because all moral development hinges on the possession of these qualities. The Church Fathers, steeped in the classics, couldn't resist appropriating these venerable virtues of the Greeks, but subordinated them to three new virtues of their creed.

Justice, the most important virtue for Plato (c.429–347 BC), is the epic goal he sets his teacher Socrates questing for in the *Republic*. Plato believed that justice in a society results from everyone's working at the specific job for which he or she is most qualified and from the harmonious interplay among the other three cardinal virtues – each of which is crucial for one or more of the three classes of citizens in the ideal state. Thus, the prudence of the rulers, the fortitude of the warriors or soldiers, and the temperance (moderation of appetites) of the merchant and artisan class, as well as of the other two classes, maximise the chances that a society will be truly and fully just.

As described in Book 4 of the *Republic*, **prudence** (good counsel or wisdom) 'resides in those Rulers whom we . . . call Guardians in the full sense'. Plato differentiates the knowledge possessed by the ruling class from the knowledge of carpenters, farmers and smiths. The particular knowledge of rulers – wisdom – is the defining characteristic of a specially trained and naturally qualified elite: 'If a state is constituted on natural principles, the wisdom it possesses as a whole will be due to the knowledge residing in the smallest part, the one which takes the lead and governs the rest.'

Plato compares the courage, or **fortitude**, instilled in the warriors to the immersion of white wool in permanent purple dye: 'Their convictions about what ought to be feared and on all other subjects might be indelibly fixed, never to be washed out.' During their indoctrination, says Plato, warriors should be taught that things that coarsen or debase are rightly feared and should be assiduously avoided. Suffering and death, on the other hand, confronted bravely, can ennoble the soul and help save the state and thus are not proper objects of fear.

Temperance is defined by Plato as the mastery of our better selves over the faculties inclined to indulge our pleasures and appetites. Intemperance, he says, is found 'chiefly in children and women and slaves and in the base rabble of those who are free men only in name'.

While Plato's cardinal virtues doubtlessly existed as pure Ideas or Forms in some abstract world beyond the senses, their earthly counterparts were intended to guide human conduct in the here and now. In contrast, the Christian theological virtues redirect human aspirations to the metaphysical realm.

The best-known celebration of the three theological virtues, **faith**, **hope** and **charity**, is found in St Paul (1 Corinthians 13). The message is unambiguous: 'If I speak in human and angelic tongues, but do not have love, I am a resounding gong or a clashing cymbal . . . If I have all faith so as to move mountains, but do not have love, I am nothing. If I give away everything I own . . . but do not have love, I gain nothing . . . So faith, hope and love remain, these three; but the greatest of these is love.'

St Ambrose (339–97), Doctor of the Church and Bishop of Milan, was probably the first to incorporate the Platonic cardinal virtues into Christian thought. St Augustine of Hippo (354–430), who was converted and baptised by Ambrose, continued the work of adapting the cardinal virtues to a Christian context in *The City of God*. Temperance – *sophrosyne* in Greek – is said to 'bridle our fleshly lusts', and he cites

St Paul's war between the flesh and the spirit. Prudence, says Augustine, helps us recognise good and evil and make the correct choice between them. Justice refers to the proper hierarchical subordination of the soul to God, of the body to the soul, and of the body and soul together to God.

Augustine's explanation of fortitude, broadened from its original military focus, is the ultimate reality therapy and an odd kind of comfort. Doesn't fortitude's very function, he asks, 'to bear patiently with misfortune', constitute 'overwhelming evidence that human life is beset with unhappiness, however wise a man may be?' He sums up by relegating the cardinal virtues to their new subsidiary roles in the Christian schema: 'No wisdom is true wisdom unless all that it decides with prudence, does with fortitude, disciplines with temperance and distributes with justice is directed to that goal in which God is to be all in all in secure everlastingness and flawless peace.' Indeed, the book of Proverbs, which is partly a paean to wisdom, proclaims that 'the beginning of wisdom is the fear of the Lord'.

St Thomas Aquinas (1225–74), in his *Summa Theologica*, distinguishes the theological virtues – faith, hope and charity – from the intellectual, or moral, virtues of Plato and of Aristotle's *Ethics*. The moral virtues pertain to our human nature, says Aquinas, and are useful for attaining human happiness by perfecting our intellect and will. They are accessible to pagans, too. In contrast, God alone infuses the theological virtues in us to perfect our souls – our supernatural selves – and to help us achieve supernatural happiness by directing us back to our source, himself.

In the *Paradiso*, Dante (1265–1321) must pass his 'oral exams' on faith, hope and charity before he can attain the Beatific Vision of God. His questioners are St Peter on faith, St James on hope and St John the Apostle on love. Why did Dante pick these examiners? The trio of Peter, James and John were chosen by Jesus to be present at the Transfiguration and the Agony in the Garden and appear to be the leaders of the Twelve (see Question 59). Peter surely knew the pitfalls of lost faith. The first of the Apostles to recognise Christ's divinity – 'Thou art the Christ, the Son of the living God' – he then experienced a notorious lapse (and lack of fortitude) on the night of Jesus' arrest. James was the first Apostle to be martyred, the ultimate exemplification of Christian hope in an afterlife of eternal rewards. And St John was 'the disciple whom Jesus loved'. He is shown resting his head on Christ's shoulder in many depictions of the Last Supper and is also the Apostle to whom Jesus entrusted his mother just before his death on the cross. Dante passes all three of his exams with flying colours.

In about 1306, Giotto (1266–1337) painted frescoes of the seven virtues and seven vices. These masterworks adorn the Arena (or Scrovegni) Chapel in the Church of the Annunziata at Padua. Giotto's patron, Enrico Scrovegni, was a Paduan moneylender whose usurious father had earned a humiliating role in Dante's *Inferno*, perhaps prompting Enrico to reach into his pockets and lavishly demonstrate his faith, hope, charity and, most of all, prudence.

What are the 7 ages of man according to Shakespeare?

The infant
The whining schoolboy
The lover
The soldier
The justice
The lean and slippered Pantaloon
Second childishness and mere oblivion

THE SPEAKER IS JAQUES, melancholic social critic of Shakespeare's romantic comedy *As You Like It* (1599–1600), set mainly in the Forest of Arden. Responding to the banished Duke's comment that

> This wide and universal theatre
> Presents more woeful pageants than the scene
> Wherein we play in,

Jaques, a lord sharing the Duke's exile, sums up the pathetic lives of men in the play's best speech (2.7.139–66):

> All the world's a stage,
> And all the men and women merely players.
> They have their exits and their entrances,
> And one man in his time plays many parts,
> His acts being seven ages. At first **the infant**,
> Mewling and puking in the nurse's arms.
> Then **the whining schoolboy**, with his satchel
> And shining morning face, creeping like snail
> Unwillingly to school. And then **the lover**,
> Sighing like furnace, with a woeful ballad
> Made to his mistress' eyebrow. Then **a soldier**,

Full of strange oaths and bearded like the pard,
Jealous in honour, sudden and quick in quarrel,
Seeking the bubble reputation
Even in the cannon's mouth. And then **the justice**,
In fair round belly with good capon lined,
With eyes severe and beard of formal cut,
Full of wise saws and modern instances,
And so he plays his part. The sixth age shifts
Into **the lean and slippered Pantaloon**
With spectacles on nose and pouch on side,
His youthful hose, well saved, a world too wide
For his shrunk shank, and his big manly voice,
Turning again toward childish treble, pipes
And whistles in his sound. Last scene of all,
That ends this strange eventful history,
Is **second childishness and mere oblivion**,
Sans teeth, sans eyes, sans taste, sans everything.

This Shakespearean pessimism is counterbalanced elsewhere by the demoniacal power of his titanic heroes, the banter of his gentle clowns and wise fools, and, most of all, the floodlight beauty of his romantic heroines, the loving, long-suffering women who suffuse his stage with an incomparable humanity: 'How far that little candle throws his beams!' observes Portia in The Merchant of Venice. 'So shines a good deed in a naughty world.'

As You Like It is a pastoral romance based on a novel by Thomas Lodge (Rosalynde, 1590). In the play, the usurping Duke Frederick has banished his elder brother, the rightful Duke, who has fled to the Forest of Arden with some faithful followers. The exiled Duke's daughter Rosalind has been allowed to remain at court because she is the best friend of her cousin Celia, Duke Frederick's daughter.

Meanwhile, Orlando, the younger son of a man who had been an ardent supporter of the banished Duke, is being so mistreated by his elder brother Oliver that he decides to flee to the Forest of Arden, but not before he and Rosalind fall in love. When Duke Frederick discovers Rosalind's interest in the son of his dead enemy, he banishes her, too. Celia and Touchstone, the court clown, flee with her – to the Forest of Arden. Soon Frederick and Oliver also set out for the forest to finish off their enemies. After the requisite number of disguises, confusions of identity, and wooing scenes, the play's major reversals occur. Orlando saves the sleeping Oliver from a lioness, and the two brothers are reconciled. Duke Frederick, conveniently converted by an old hermit living in the forest, embraces the religious life and restores his brother to the dukedom. The world-weary Jaques announces his intention to join the reformed Frederick.

Four couples pair off at the end. Orlando wins his beloved Rosalind, having carved her name on innumerable trees and fastened countless lousy love poems on them. The new, improved Oliver marries Celia. The clown Touchstone ties the knot with the underwashed country wench Audrey. The shepherd Silvius finds nuptial bliss with the shepherdess Phebe.

Shakespeare introduces his creation of Jaques into his borrowed plot to deflate the excesses of romantic love and the pastoral pretensions of the banished Duke's entourage in the forest. The pastoral convention, harking back to Theocritus and Virgil, maintained that the simple ways of country folk were saner than those of their citified counterparts. (Recall the fable of the city mouse and the country mouse.) Jaques serves to remind the back-to-nature enthusiasts surrounding him, who believe that 'sweet are the uses of adversity' and who find

> ... books in the running brooks,
> Sermons in stones, and good in everything

that the human condition – no matter where – is hopelessly flawed. His role is to mock the romanticisation of rustic life and 'the green world', which Shakespeare none the less presents as a corrective to the cruel, cynical, power-mad existence of urban courts.

True, Jaques is a rather absurd egoist, strutting around the forest in his affected melancholy and refusing to 'adapt'. Rosalind ridicules him – and so does Shakespeare. Even his name may owe something to *jakes*, a coarse Elizabethan word for a privy. Yet, although the plot doesn't require him at all, Jaques remains an intriguing misanthrope who comments wryly on the goings-on around him, especially in his prolonged meditation on the banality of life and the silly parts it makes men play.

In comparing the world to a stage, Jaques makes use of a Renaissance commonplace with Hebrew, Greek and Roman antecedents. Shakespeare's more immediate inspiration, however, may have been the motto of the new Globe Theatre: *Totus mundus agit histrionem* ('All the world plays the actor'). The roles are played out in the seven ages the ancient Romans identified as infancy, childhood, adolescence, youth, manhood, old age and decrepitude.

And so, in early life, men are helpless, whimpering, puking burdens to their caregivers and whiny, reluctant schoolboys. Then they graduate to sighing over women and writing steamy love poems. Next they're swaggering, irascible soldiers, eager for fame though it may involve becoming cannon fodder. If they survive that stage, they settle down to paunchy, trim-bearded burgherhood, boring everyone with their proverbs and clichés. But soon they shrivel up into foolish old coots, wearing clothes that went out of style decades ago and speaking in the shrill tones of little boys again. Finally, they undergo total privation: a toothless second childhood and general system failure.

Shortly before his speech, Jaques overhears Touchstone say,

> And so, from hour to hour, we ripe and ripe,
> And then, from hour to hour, we rot and rot,
> And thereby hangs a tale.

Jaques hangs his tale of the seven ages on this theme and makes us wonder about the futility of it all.

What were the 7 metals of alchemy and their associated gods and planets?

Gold: Apollo, the sun
Silver: Diana, the moon
Quicksilver: Mercury
Copper: Venus

Iron: Mars
Tin: Jupiter
Lead: Saturn

> The bodyes sevene eek, lo! hem heere anoon:
> Sol gold is, and Luna silver we threpe,
> Mars iren, Mercurie quyksilver we clepe,
> Saturnus leed, and Juppiter is tyn,
> And Venus coper, by my fader kyn!

GEOFFREY CHAUCER, 'The Canon's Yeoman's Tale'

THE IDENTIFICATION OF the seven 'planets' of medieval astronomy with the seven metals of alchemy has its roots in ancient pseudo-science and Roman mythology. The theoretical basis of alchemy was fairly consistent among the ancient civilisations that practised it, including China, India and Greece. It was believed that basic elements such as earth, water, air and fire could be combined in various ways to create all material things (see Question 14). The goal of alchemy was the trans-mutation of base elements such as lead into precious ones like silver and gold. Alchemical beliefs usually merged with astrological ones, allowing medieval protoscientists to posit correspondences among the elements, metals, planets and human temperaments.

The connection between **gold** – long regarded as the most precious of metals because of its beauty, durability, malleability and purity – and Apollo, god of light, is relatively straightforward. Often called Phoebus ('brilliant' or 'shining'), Apollo was perhaps the most revered of the Graeco-Roman gods, as gold was the most cherished metal.

Apollo, playing his golden lyre, was also identified with the sun's disc and with Helios, the god who drove the chariot of the sun across the sky each day.

Lustrous **silver** was readily associated with the moon's sheen and the Roman moon goddess, Diana, Apollo's twin sister (see Question 57). This was a tidy sibling arrangement, given their respective linkings with the sun and moon. Diana was also goddess of the hunt, driving her hounds to the chase from a silver chariot. The moon's inevitable associations with night, witchcraft and magic led to the belief that those who fell under the influence of the moon – luna in Latin – ended up as moonstruck lunatics.

The ancients believed the highly toxic metallic element **quicksilver**, or mercury, warded off evil spirits and had potent medicinal properties. It took its name from the mischievous, quick-witted god Mercury, Heaven's speedy messenger who flew to his tasks with the aid of winged shoes. The Romans also named the planet closest to the sun, the fastest object they observed in the sky, after swift Mercury (see Question 51). Our word mercurial, meaning rapidly changeable or fickle, reflects the alchemical and astrological associations that accrued around the god, the planet and the element, with its alternating liquid and solid states.

The alchemists associated **copper** with Venus, Roman goddess of love, because her sacred land was the island of Cyprus, Rome's source for this metal. The Romans called copper aes Cyprium ('metal of Cyprus') and then just cuprum, ancestor of our word. Venus was sometimes called 'the Cyprian' because of her important shrine and cult at Paphos, on Cyprus. In its guise of the evening star (Hesperus or Vesper), the planet Venus is the brightest heavenly body, except for the sun and moon, and summons humans to love. Presumably, Venus herself was the first, but not the last, to have a venereal disposition.

Iron was associated with Mars, god of war and protector of Rome, because of its use in weapons. The planet Mars was probably linked with the war god because of its reddish colour. Wherever Mars walked on the battlefield, blood was said to ooze from the ground. People born under the influence of Mars are, of course, martial.

173

The association between **tin** and the god of gods, Jupiter, or Jove, remains obscure. Tin is a soft metal, most often used in alloys. Bronze, well known to the ancients, is an alloy of copper, Venus' metal, and tin. Perhaps the link between Jupiter and tin alludes to the god's predilection for changing himself into other beings – swans, eagles, bulls and even mortal men – so as to escape his wife Hera's notice while he was busy seducing goddesses, nymphs, women and handsome boys. It's easy to see why those lucky enough to be born under the sign of Jove are jovial.

The heavy metal **lead** was associated with Saturn, the slowest of the planets to wend its way across the heavens. Alchemists considered lead the oldest of metals and thus linked it with primeval Saturn, the dethroned old father of the chief god Jupiter. Those born under the influence of the planet Saturn are saturnine – gloomy and taciturn, true 'heavies' – though Longfellow was obviously thinking only of gloomy and not of taciturn when he addressed Dante, author of the vast *Divine Comedy*, as 'O poet saturnine'. Even today, the term *saturnism* might be used by a pedantic, classically minded physician as a synonym for lead poisoning.

What were the 7 French dynasties?

Merovingian	Bourbon
Carolingian	Bonapartist
Capetian	Orléanist
Valois	

I N THE BEGINNING (58–51 BC), Julius Caesar conquered Gaul, which included the territory of modern-day France. The Romans ruled and Romanised Celtic Gaul for about five hundred years before it was overrun by Germanic barbarians – the Visigoths, Burgundians and Franks. The Salian branch of the Franks was ruled by the Merovingians, who took their name from Merovech or Merowig, king of the Salian Franks (448–56; dates of rulers are of reigns).

The **Merovingian dynasty** (481–751) was inaugurated by the greatest of their kings, Clovis I (Ludwig, Louis; 481–511), the founder of the Frankish (French) monarchy. Clovis enlarged Merovech's domain enormously to contain all of northern and south-western Gaul. This redoubtable barbarian seized Reims, had himself crowned there in 481, became a Christian with three thousand of his soldiers in 496, killed a slew of rival kings and relatives, and made Paris his capital. But his successors in the late seventh and eighth centuries became 'do-nothing kings' who were supplanted in everything but title by their Carolingian mayors of the palace (chief ministers), such as Pepin of Héristal and his son Charles Martel.

In 751, the last Merovingian king, Childeric III, was deposed by the son of Charles Martel, Pepin the Short (751–68). The **Carolingian dynasty** (751–987) was thus formally established after many progenitors had served as de facto rulers. Pepin's son, the incomparable Charlemagne (768–814), became King of the Franks in 768 and was crowned Emperor of the reconstituted Western Roman Empire on Christmas Day of 800 by Pope Leo III in St Peter's in Rome. Charlemagne's empire included

France, Germany, northern Italy, part of northern Spain and the Low Countries, and his main capital was at Aix-la-Chapelle (Aachen). Besides conquering, this Charles the Great, who tried hard but never learned to write, founded schools, attracted Europe's leading scholars and poets to his court, supported the arts, and presided over what has been called the Carolingian Renaissance. He was succeeded in 814 by Louis I the Pious, who ruled a united empire until 840. In 843, Louis's three sons divided the empire by the Treaty of Verdun. By 870, the Carolingian family had established separate French and German ruling lines.

The last Carolingian ruler of France, Louis V, died in 987. Hugh Capet (987–96) was offered the throne and became first king of the **Capetian dynasty** (987–1328). Although Dante claims Capet was the son of a Parisian butcher (*Purgatorio* 20.52), he was actually a descendant of the counts of Paris – and, in fact, ruled only a small kingdom around the city. The rest of France was in the possession of hundreds of feudal lords, big and small. Succeeding Capetian kings absorbed surrounding principalities and increased the power of the monarchy. Some noteworthy kings of this dynasty were Philip II, Louis IX and Philip IV.

Philip II, called Philip Augustus (1180–1223), seized Normandy from England's pathetic King John in 1204; received the submission of Maine, Anjou and Touraine; flattened southern France in the 'Albigensian Crusade'; and still found time to organise the University of Paris. Louis IX (1226–70), canonised as St Louis in 1297, took over much of southern France for the Crown (1229), was captured in Egypt by the Saracens in 1250 while on the Seventh Crusade, and died of the plague in Tunis while on another crusade in 1270.

The ruthless Philip IV (1285–1314), called 'the Fair', as in handsome, not as in fair play, took Gascony and Bordeaux from the English. In 1302, in a bid for popular support, he summoned the first Estates-General (legislative assembly), comprising members of the nobility, clergy and bourgeoisie. Philip was termed 'the new Pilate' by Dante (*Purgatorio* 20.91) for his imprisonment and disgraceful treatment of Pope Boniface VIII. In 1305, Philip made the papacy a tool of the French monarchy, and in 1309 he instituted the so-called Babylonian Captivity of the Popes in Avignon, which lasted until 1376. The crowning achievement of his reign was his destruction of the Knights Templar, instigated by his desire to seize their immense riches and capped by his witnessing the burning at the stake of their grand master Jacques de Molay in 1313.

In 1328, Philip of Valois, grandson of an earlier Capetian king, became King of France as Philip VI, inaugurating the **Valois dynasty** (1328–1589). The first half of this dynasty's reign was plagued by the Hundred Years' War against the English (1337–1453). During the latter part of the war, in 1429, Joan of Arc helped France's irresolute Dauphin defeat his English enemies at Orléans and finally get crowned at Reims as Charles VII (1422–61). The unification of France was achieved after the English were expelled from French territory (except Calais, which they held until 1558); Louis XI (1461–83) defeated Charles the Bold, Duke of Burgundy, and snatched his domains; and Charles VIII (1483–98) married Anne, Duchess of Brittany, thereby uniting her lands to the French crown.

The great Valois King Francis I (1515–47) conquered Milan in 1515 and then spent the rest of his reign waging wars against Charles I, the Habsburg King of Spain (also known after 1519 as Holy Roman Emperor Charles V). Francis found time to preside over the introduction of the Italian Renaissance into France with his patronage of artists like Leonardo da Vinci, Benvenuto Cellini and Andrea del Sarto, and his building of Chambord and Fontainebleau. He also patronised homegrown wits like François Rabelais. Francis's son, Henry II (1547–59), the husband of Catherine de' Medici and lover of Diane de Poitiers, was killed in a jousting tournament. Henry's son, Francis II (1559–60), was briefly married to Mary, Queen of Scots, and died at the age of sixteen. Catherine persuaded her next son who succeeded as king, Charles IX (1560–74), to order the massacre of the French Protestant Huguenots on St Bartholomew's Day, 24 August 1572. Catherine's third royal son, Henry III (1574–89), was stabbed to death by a Dominican monk in 1589 for having named a Protestant successor.

With the extinction of the Valois line in that year, the **Bourbon dynasty** (1589–1792, 1814–30) began with Henry of Navarre, a descendant of the French kings of the fourteenth century. This Henry IV (1589–1610), leader of the Huguenots, converted to Catholicism in 1593 to consolidate his precarious hold on the throne – 'Paris is well worth a Mass', he supposedly said. Henry went on to antagonise his Catholic subjects by the Edict of Nantes (1598), guaranteeing religious freedom to the Protestants and ending the Wars of Religion, which had raged since 1562. After Henry's assassination in 1610 by the religious fanatic François Ravaillac, his second wife, Marie, another Medici, became Regent of France for seven years.

The absolutism of the Bourbon kings asserted itself during the reign of Henry IV's son, Louis XIII (1610–43), who had the benefit of Cardinal Richelieu's Machiavellian statesmanship in suppressing revolts of the nobility and breaking the power of the Huguenots. Absolutist Richelieu also founded the absolutist French Academy in 1635.

Sicilian-born Cardinal Mazarin, who became chief minister after the death of Richelieu, guided the destinies of the young Louis XIV until 1661. Louis XIV, *Le Roi-Soleil* ('The Sun King') and *Le Grand Monarque*, reigned seventy-two years (1643–1715), longer than any monarch in European history. This King identified the state with himself (*'L'État, c'est moi'*), revoked the Edict of Nantes in 1685 (thus exiling three hundred thousand of his most productive citizens, the French Protestants), fought four expansionist wars that prostrated his country's finances, built Versailles and made it the most magnificent (and extravagant) court of Europe, lavishly patronised all the arts in an age that produced the likes of Corneille, Racine and Molière, and fornicated to his royal heart's content. He ruled so long he was succeeded by his great-grandson, Louis XV.

During Louis XV's reign of fifty-nine years (1715–74), this debauched king dallied with Madame de Pompadour, Madame du Barry and a host of others; lost Louisiana to the Spanish, and Canada and possessions in India to the English; and further depleted the finances. Things got even worse during the reign of his grandson, the hapless Louis XVI.

A maladroit king who loved to tinker with locks, Louis XVI (1774–92) married Austrian archduchess and airhead *extraordinaire*, Marie Antoinette. He actively supported the colonists against the English in the

American Revolution, but this only buried France deeper in its financial hole. On 4 May 1789, desperate for new taxes, Louis convoked the Estates-General for its first meeting since 1614 – and by 14 July the royal prison of the Bastille was being stormed.

France and the morals of the royal court were bankrupt. The legitimacy of the *ancien régime* had been shaken by the anti-absolutist and anticlerical teachings of thinkers like Montesquieu, Voltaire, Diderot, d'Alembert, Rousseau, Baron d'Holbach, Condorcet and scores of others. The wealthy but disfranchised bourgeoisie smouldered with resentment. The American Revolution had pointed the way. The result of this situation was the knock-your-head-off cocktail known as the French Revolution of 1789 – a necessary evil that was a mishmash of idealism, sadism, hysteria, fanaticism, militarism, nationalism, propaganda, egalitarianism, science-worship, anarchy, purges, Robespierrism and political theatre that set the pattern for even more ghastly re-enactments the world over, well into our times. Louis XVI and Marie Antoinette, guillotined in 1793, joined thousands who lost their heads for the sake of liberty, equality and fraternity.

A French Republic was established in 1792, a Directory in 1795, and a Consulate in 1799. General Napoleon Bonaparte, famed for his Italian campaign of 1796–7, thought the time ripe for his seizure of absolute power as First Consul by his *coup d'état* of the 18th Brumaire of the Year VIII (as the French revolutionary calendar styled 9 November 1799). The attempt to found a **Bonapartist dynasty** (1804–14, 1852–70) began in earnest in May 1804 with Napoleon's crowning himself Emperor of the French. After spreading French law, civilisation and terror through most of Europe, and winning crushing victories like Austerlitz against the Austrians and Russians (1805) and Jena against the Prussians (1806), Napoleon's military machine got stuck in Spain and ruined in Russia. He abdicated on 6 April 1814. From his exile on the island of Elba, he returned to Paris on 20 March 1815 for his 'Hundred Days' before his final defeat at Waterloo in Belgium on 18 June at the hands of the Duke of Wellington. This time 'Boney', as the English called him, was exiled to the island of Saint Helena in the south Atlantic, where he died in 1821.

Napoleon had wanted the King of Rome, his infant son by his second wife, Marie Louise of Austria, to succeed him as Napoleon II, but this plan was thwarted by the Allies. Instead, they restored the Bourbon monarchy by trotting out Louis XVIII (1814–24), brother of the executed Louis XVI. (The son of Louis XVI and Marie Antoinette, 'Louis XVII', never ruled and died at the age of ten.) Louis XVIII was fairly reactionary, but his brother, who succeeded him as Charles X (1824–30), wanted to roll back the clock to well before 1789 and was overthrown in the July Revolution of 1830.

The throne was now offered to the Duke of Orléans, a descendant of Louis XIII, who ruled as King Louis-Philippe, the 'Citizen King' and the only **Orléanist monarch** (1830–48). Louis-Philippe, whose accession the wily politician Talleyrand supported 'for want of a better and fear of a worse', was popular at the beginning of his reign. None the less, economic instability, the growing power of the bourgeoisie, and Louis-Philippe's indifference to the people's clamour for universal manhood suffrage led to his overthrow in the February Revolution of 1848.

The Second Republic, established in 1848 with Napoleon's nephew, Louis Napoleon Bonaparte, as president, gave way to Louis's *coup d'état* on 2 December 1851, and his establishment of the Second Empire, with himself as Emperor Napoleon III (1852). In comparing this Bonapartist coup with that of Napoleon I, Karl Marx commented that when history repeats itself, it does so as farce. Napoleon III sent military expeditions into Europe, Asia and Africa, and vainly tried to obtain French control of Mexico via his puppet-emperor Maximilian. France's defeat in the Franco-Prussian War (1870–1) resulted in the loss of Alsace and Lorraine and in Napoleon III's being taken prisoner by the King of Prussia at Sedan. The Emperor was deposed in September 1870, and the Third Republic was established.

After the liberation of France from the Germans in World War II, the Fourth Republic was proclaimed (1946). This lasted until France's embroilment in a ghastly war with its Algerian colony led to the establishment of the Fifth Republic (1958–), with Charles de Gaulle as deviser of its constitution and first president.

What are the 7 voyages of Sinbad the Sailor?

1. To the Indian Ocean, where he and other crew members 'go ashore' on a whale they suppose to be an island
2. To a desert island, where he sees a roc's egg, and then to the Valley of the Diamonds
3. To the land of a huge cannibal, who devours Sinbad's companions
4. To an island, where he marries a rich woman and is lowered into the Cavern of the Dead with her body after she dies
5. To a desert island, where he kills the Old Man of the Sea
6. To a rocky coast, where he sees the banks of a river glittering with precious stones
7. To an island in the China Sea, where he finds men who sprout wings and fly for one day each year

THE STORY OF SINBAD THE SAILOR is found in *The Arabian Nights* (*The Thousand and One Nights*), a large collection of stories originating mostly in Arabia, India or Persia, and written in Arabic in the fourteenth to sixteenth centuries. The tales were introduced into Europe by the free translation (twelve volumes, 1704–17) of Antoine Galland, which was soon cast into other European languages. The best-known English translation is the unexpurgated version (fifteen volumes, 1885–6) by Sir Richard Burton. The specific tales making up the collection have been highly fluid throughout the centuries, however, and the closest approximation to a standard Arabic text was compiled only towards the end of the eighteenth century in Egypt, probably in Cairo.

The frame story, of Persian origin, tells how King Shahriyar becomes disgusted with female infidelity when he catches his Queen in the act. After putting his wife to death, he decides to marry a different virgin each night and kill her the next morning to make sure she can't cheat on him. After three years of this, when virgins are becoming extremely rare, the vizier, who is charged with procuring them, lets his daughter Shahrazad (Scheherazade) convince him that she knows how to get the better of the King. When the King marries her, Shahrazad keeps his interest piqued – and postpones her death – by telling him a long series of tales, making sure to leave him hanging by never providing the ending for any story on the same night she begins narrating it.

One of her series of tales concerns Sinbad (or Sindbad), a fictional merchant of Baghdad who went on seven marvellous sea voyages during the reign of Harun al-Rashid (Caliph of Baghdad, 786–809). His adventures are probably based on tall tales brought back by Muslim seamen who traded with India, China and the islands of the Far East in the eighth to tenth centuries. Another major influence seems to have been watered-down versions of Homer's *Odyssey* that had become part of Muslim legend. The adventures of Sinbad the Sailor, probably at first an independent work, are narrated on seven successive days by the protagonist himself to teach a poor man, Sinbad the Porter, that great wealth and fame like his are won 'only after long toil, fearful ordeals and dire peril'.

First voyage. Sinbad, son of the chief merchant of Baghdad, dissipates his patrimony with riotous living like a true prodigal. Selling what remains, he buys some merchandise and decides to try his luck trading abroad. After taking a river-boat down the Tigris to Basra (as he does on all his voyages), he sets sail on the open sea in a merchant ship that puts in at numerous shores. Disembarking on a little island as lovely as the Garden of Eden, Sinbad and his companions light a fire for cooking and start exploring – when the captain screams to them from the ship that the island they're on is really a whale. The fire must have annoyed the leviathan, because it now submerges violently, leaving Sinbad clinging to a wooden tub while watching the ship and its crew speed away. He floats to a densely wooded island where huge mares are tethered to trees so that 'sea horses' will come and mate with them and sire priceless colts and fillies. This is the native industry of the land of King Mahrajan, who soon promotes Sinbad to Comptroller of Shipping. In this capacity,

Sinbad meets a sea captain who still has aboard his ship some merchandise belonging to a drowned merchant named Sinbad. After the recognition scene, a happy ending ensues when Sinbad sells his salvaged goods at a nice margin and sails home with his old mates.

Second voyage. Sinbad soon begins to experience wanderlust, so he buys some wares to trade with and sets out to sea again. After landing on an uninhabited island, Sinbad discovers on awakening from a nap that his ship has sailed off without him. While reconnoitring, he comes across a huge white dome, fifty paces in circumference, and sees an enormous bird flying above it. He realises the bird is a roc, which is known to feed its young on full-grown elephants, and the 'dome' is the roc's egg. Hoping to escape from the deserted island, Sinbad attaches himself to the roc by tying one end of his unwound turban to one of the bird's talons and the other around his waist. The roc flies off and soon deposits Sinbad in a valley strewn with diamonds but surrounded by insurmountably steep cliffs. When Sinbad notices a skinned sheep carcass come tumbling down the mountainside, he remembers a story about the Valley of the Diamonds and how men would fling sheep carcasses into it so that the diamonds at the bottom would stick to their soft flesh. When rocs and huge vultures swooped down on the meat to bring it to their nests, the men waiting above would make a great commotion to frighten off the birds and make them drop the diamond-studded sheep. After unwinding his trusty turban, Sinbad uses it to tie himself to the sheep carcass – but not before cramming his pockets with a fortune in diamonds. Sure enough, a vulture takes the bait, gets Sinbad out of the valley, and is shooed away by the diamond merchants, who eventually take the newly wealthy Sinbad home.

Third voyage. Sinbad gets bored at home again. This time, his ship is attacked by dwarf apes with gleaming yellow eyes who set him and his companions ashore on an island and make off with the ship. The stranded men enter a vast building, where soon they see a giant come in, who proceeds to kill the three fattest men on successive nights and roast them on a spit for his supper. This story sounds a lot like the encounter of Odysseus and his men with the cannibalistic Cyclops, except that this giant has two eyes. A curious detail is that the men are not trapped inside but actually leave the monster's 'palace' for a while to build a raft for their escape. Returning to exact their vengeance, they wait until the monster falls asleep (he's not drunk on wine in this version) and then put out his eyes with the red-hot spits he's been using to barbecue their companions. As they push off on the raft, the monster and a fellow monstress hurl rocks at them, scoring direct hits on all but two of them and Sinbad, who manage to arrive at another island. There Sinbad's remaining companions are swallowed whole by a largish serpent. Next day he is rescued by the ship whose crew had inadvertently abandoned him on Roc Island on his second voyage. Since his merchandise is still on board, he trades with it, grows rich, and returns to Baghdad.

Fourth voyage. This man never learns. After setting out to sea again, Sinbad's ship is destroyed by a storm. He and some others manage to reach an island where naked savages bring them to their king. When they're offered food, Sinbad's buddies eat ravenously, but he abstains, revolted by the food's appearance. Good thing. The other men can't stop eating: soon they're transmogrified into hoggish beasts devoid of reason that are taken out to pasture and then fed on by the King (who roasts his captives) and his followers (who prefer their meat *carpaccio*). Escaping from this nasty locale – which bears a resemblance to the island in the *Odyssey* where Circe changes Odysseus' men into swine – Sinbad meets some decent folk who take him to a neighbouring island. There he teaches the King and all the other dignitaries the use of saddles for their horses, thus becoming the richest man of them all. The King is so fond of Sinbad that he wishes him to marry a beautiful young noblewoman, though Sinbad is homesick and sorely misses his first wife. (This is somewhat reminiscent of Odysseus' desperate longing for Ithaca and his wife Penelope after spending seven years as Calypso's kept man.) But when his new wife dies, Sinbad must adhere to a strict custom of the country – equal-rights suttee. After his wife's body is thrown into a deep burial pit, Sinbad is lowered into it by a rope and provisioned with only seven loaves of bread and a pitcher of water. But, like Odysseus, Sinbad is resourceful, a man 'of many twists and turns', so when a widow is lowered down with her food and water, he bashes in her skull with the leg-bone of a skeleton and appropriates them. He does the same to other widowed unfortunates and survives for many weeks. One day he sees a wild beast in the cavern that has been attracted by the stench of carrion and tunnelled through the rocky wall of the pit. Easing his way through the tunnel – after cramming his pockets with food and the jewels and pearls that have been buried with the corpses – Sinbad makes his way to a seashore, from which he is soon rescued by a ship, etc.

Fifth voyage. Was Sinbad sick and tired of all these scrapes with death? Why, he was just warming up. This time, he ends up on a deserted island, where he sees the tell-tale white dome that indicates a roc's egg. Much to his horror, his companions amuse themselves by smashing the shell with rocks, dragging out the roc chick, and cooking it up. When they set out to sea, vengeful parent birds follow the ship with boulders in their talons and bomb it to pieces. Sinbad alone escapes by floating to an island on a piece of wreckage. (This episode is similar to the gods' destruction of Odysseus' ship by a lightning storm after his men have eaten the sacred oxen of the Sun.) On the island is a decrepit old man sitting by a brook who asks Sinbad to ferry him across by bearing him on his shoulders. Once in the saddle, this Old Man of the Sea (the epithet of Proteus in the *Odyssey*) refuses to dismount and torments Sinbad by clasping him about the neck and chest with his surprisingly strong legs. After many weeks of schlepping the Old Man around and doing his bidding, Sinbad manages to make some wine in a gourd and get him drunk (like Odysseus with the Cyclops). When the monster plops to the ground, Sinbad smashes his skull to pieces with a stone, becoming the first victim of the Old Man of the Sea to escape with his life. After being rescued by a ship, Sinbad comes to the City of the Apes. There he earns his passage-money home in the following way. Like the residents, he fills up a sack with pebbles and slings it over his shoulder. Proceeding to a coconut grove far from the city, where the towering trees are impossible to climb, the men pelt the monkeys in the tree-tops with their pebbles. In retaliation, the monkeys bombard them with coconuts, which the crafty men gather and bring to market. On his way home to Baghdad, Sinbad trades the coconuts for spices and then pays some divers to fetch him up a fortune in pearls.

Sixth voyage. *Déjà vu* all over again. Sinbad's ship breaks up on a rocky coast in a fierce gale, but he manages to clamber ashore. There he finds a river that flows into a mountain gorge. Unlike other rivers, this one's banks are covered with rubies, emeralds and pearls. Sinbad decides to follow the river's course into the gorge, hoping its outlet is frequented by ships. The rocky shore is also supplied with rare Chinese aloes and ambergris, so he builds a raft and piles it high with these commodities – and many sacks of jewels, too. On re-emerging from the gorge, he is kindly received by some Indians and Abyssinians. They take him to their King, who makes him a trusted courtier and decides to send a magnificent gift to Harun al-Rashid. Sinbad accordingly sails back home to Baghdad and obtains an audience with the famed Caliph. Harun orders that Sinbad's adventure be inscribed on parchment in letters of gold for the edification of posterity.

Seventh voyage. Though past the prime of life, Sinbad still hasn't seen enough of the world and its ways. He sails to the China Sea, where a tempest rages near the Realm of Kings, burial place of Solomon. A whale much bigger than Moby-Dick swallows their ship, but Sinbad dives off just in time and escapes to an island. He builds a raft and sails it down a river towards the interior, where he is saved from flying off a precipice by a group of men who trap his raft in their net. A venerable old man takes him to the city and regales him with food, drink, a bath and servants. Imagine Sinbad's surprise when, at an auction, his raft garners him eleven hundred pieces of gold – it was made of rare sandalwood, it turns out – and the buyer is the old man himself. Sinbad's generous friend wants him to marry his beautiful young daughter – his sole heir – and become in time chief merchant of the city. Sinbad joyfully accedes to the old man's wish, and he and his bride live together happily. He soon discovers, however, that the men of this land grow wings once a year and fly around for a whole day. Sinbad begs a friend to take him along, so on the appointed day he grabs hold of the man's waist and soars upward with him. They fly so high that Sinbad hears the angels singing hymns to Allah. He can't resist shouting out his praises, too. At that, his friend plummets from the sky and leaves Sinbad on a mountain-top, calling down curses on him as he flies away. After Sinbad meets what seem to be two angels – one of whom gives him his golden staff and points him on his way – he bumps into his winged friend who, no longer angry, explains that the mention of Allah's name always has this depressing effect on his countrymen's flying abilities. Sinbad's wife later explains that their fellow citizens – all except her deceased father – are brothers of Satan. (Now she tells him!) After selling their houses and goods, they flee to Baghdad, where Sinbad, who has been away twenty-seven years on this voyage, vows to stay put. Sinbad the Porter, who has been treated to all these inspiring tales, becomes a bosom friend of wise old Sinbad the Sailor.

After 1,001 nights of storytelling, including the tales of Aladdin and the Enchanted Lamp (did you know Aladdin was Chinese?) and Ali Baba and the Forty Thieves, Shahrazad reveals to the King the three sons she has borne him in the meantime and begs for her life for their sake. But the King has already fallen in love because he has found her to be 'chaste and tender, wise and eloquent'. The irresistible magic that Shahrazad weaves with her words is an apt emblem of the narrator's art.

EIGHT

What are the components of the Noble Eightfold Path of Buddhism?

Right views   Right livelihood
Right intentions Right effort
Right speech   Right mindfulness
Right conduct   Right concentration

THE LAST OF the Four Noble Truths of Buddhism* promises a way of escape from the endless cycle of birth, suffering, death and re-birth. This is the Noble Eightfold Path, the quintessential Buddhist guide for living. Those who follow this path assiduously achieve nir-vana, the cessation of all selfish desire and thus of suffering. The ultimate goal is maha-parinirvana, 'great total extinction', which for Buddhists is hitting the jackpot and for most westerners is more terrifying than death itself.

How can humans empty themselves of desire? Darwinians and Nietzscheans would claim this is a contradiction in terms. Buddhists contend that desire results from misunderstanding the nature of the universe and of what is called the self or soul (atman) in Hinduism, the parent religion of Buddhism. Everything that seems to be is actually in a state of becoming; nothing is stable or simple in its essence, everything is impermanent and composite, subject to decay. Even the self is a delu-

* The other three are: first, life is full of suffering; second, the cause of suffering is craving which leads to the cycle of rebirth; and third, craving and suffering can be annihilated.

sion: we are shifting, momentary conjunctions of various substances, perceptions, memories, emotions. This self that does not have a unitary existence, which is actually a 'no-self' (*anatman*), then makes the mistake of desiring other things that are no less evanescent and 'unreal'. The worst form of desire is sexual, since it results in bringing more suffering creatures into the cycle of reincarnation.

Along with the Four Noble Truths, Buddha revealed the Noble Eightfold Path to his five original disciples in his first sermon after attaining Enlightenment under the bo tree. The Eightfold Path divests the individual of selfish desire by its influence in three areas of human life: morality, mental discipline and wisdom. Morality or ethics (*sila*) includes right speech, conduct and livelihood. **Right speech** is that which avoids lies, gossip, backbiting and verbal abuse. **Right conduct** involves following the 'Five Moral Rules', which forbid killing any living thing (the law of *ahimsa*), stealing, making false statements, drinking intoxicating beverages and indulging in unchaste behaviour. **Right livelihood** means refusing to earn a living by improper means, such as hoodwinking people with astrology or fortune-telling. It also enjoins the virtues of compassion (a great moral imperative in Buddhism), friendliness to all, joy in the joy of others, forgiveness of enemies, and serenity.

Mental discipline or training (*samadhi*) comprises **right effort**, **right mindfulness** and **right concentration**. These require the practice of yoga, a system of mystic meditation adopted from Hinduism. By concentrating the mind on a single stable point or subject, yoga induces varying stages of trance or self-hypnosis that free the mind from the distractions of the external world and habituate it to exist without desiring the world's specious pleasures.

Wisdom (*prajna*) or intuitive insight results from right views and intentions. **Right views** imply an understanding of the Four Noble Truths, the impermanence of all things, and the doctrine of karma. **Right intentions** are crucial because the law of karma is based on the intention or motive governing deeds and not necessarily on the deeds themselves. Depending on the goodness or evil of intentions in their current life, people can be reborn as gods, humans, animals, hungry ghosts or hell-dwellers. Of course, the ultimate goal is the total shedding of any attachment to desire and life, so that karma ceases to be generated and the Wheel of Rebirth (*samsara*) is permanently broken. This state of nirvana can occur on earth, though the individual who has attained it still lives on (like the Buddha after his Enlightenment), or it can mark the final extinction of the illusory self (as at the Buddha's death).

But if the self or soul is an illusion, what gets reborn in *samsara*? This is a weak spot in Buddhist metaphysics. Just as the ancient Greek philosopher Heraclitus said that one could never step into the same river twice because its waters are always flowing, so Buddhists claim that although the reborn soul partakes in a continuity of sorts, it is not the selfsame identical soul as before. Think of it as the flame of a candle that has been lit from that of another candle. In fact, only those who have attained Enlightenment can even remember any of their thousands of previous existences.

Strict adherence to the Noble Eightfold Path implies a rigorous discipline incompatible with the demands of everyday family life. Members of the *sangha*, the Buddhist monastic order, have always had a much better shot at it.

What are the 8 Beatitudes?

Blessed are the poor in spirit: for theirs is the kingdom of heaven.

Blessed are they that mourn: for they shall be comforted.

Blessed are the meek: for they shall inherit the earth.

Blessed are they which do hunger and thirst after righteousness: for they shall be filled.

Blessed are the merciful: for they shall obtain mercy.

Blessed are the pure in heart: for they shall see God.

Blessed are the peacemakers: for they shall be called the children of God.

Blessed are they which are persecuted for righteousness' sake: for theirs is the kingdom of heaven.

JESUS ADDRESSES THE CROWDS with these words in the Sermon on the Mount in the Gospel of Matthew (5:3–10). Some have called the Beatitudes the charter of Christianity, which sets forth the essential characteristics of those who will attain salvation. Since Matthew, who wrote one of the two Gospel versions of the Beatitudes, is addressing Jewish Christians, he attempts to draw a parallel between Christ and Moses (see Question 21). He thus sets the scene on a mountain to remind his readers of God's giving the Ten Commandments (see Question 53) to Moses on Mount Sinai (according to the account in Exodus) or Mount Horeb (according to the account in Deuteronomy).

Although readers were to understand that Christ was presenting them with a new set of precepts, Christ himself insists that he came to fulfil and broaden, not abolish, the Mosaic law. In any event, the literary device of the beatitude is fairly common in the Old Testament: the first Psalm begins, 'Blessed is the man that walketh not in the counsel of the ungodly.'

Luke's version of the Beatitudes (6:20–3) includes only four blessings:

Blessed are you who are poor, for the kingdom of God is yours.
Blessed are you who are now hungry, for you will be satisfied.
Blessed are you who are now weeping, for you will laugh.
Blessed are you when people hate you, and when they exclude you and insult you, and denounce your name as evil on account of the Son of Man.

These are followed by four corresponding woes:

But woe to you who are rich, for you have received your consolation.
But woe to you who are filled now, for you will be hungry.
Woe to you who laugh now, for you will grieve and weep.
Woe to you when all speak well of you, for their ancestors treated the false prophets this way.

This version, part of what is known as the Sermon on the Plain, is addressed to the disciples only, not the multitudes. Some biblical scholars consider Luke's Sermon on the Plain the ordination sermon for the Twelve Apostles (see Question 59), since Christ had just selected them from the larger group of disciples.

Note that in Matthew's text the emphasis is on the self-effacement, victimisation and benevolence of those who are blessed. Half of the Beatitudes promise purely spiritual rewards, while the rest set their more tangible consolations in an indeterminate future. Luke's version, nuanced somewhat differently, addresses itself to the poor and hungry (rather than 'the poor in spirit' and those who 'hunger . . . after righteousness'), while inveighing against the well-fed, self-satisfied burghers of the day.

Matthew's Beatitudes are part of the larger framework of Christ's reevaluation of acts of piety as practised by the Pharisees – almsgiving, prayer and fasting. In the Sermon on the Mount, Christ exhorts his disciples to perform these acts unobtrusively so that only God is aware of them. He contrasts this with the behaviour of 'the hypocrites', whose pious deeds are meant to elicit public admiration – the only benefit, Christ says, that they will receive, since 'they have their reward already'.

But the Beatitudes have failed to provide solace to many of 'the wretched of the earth', and the values they embody have even been subjected to derision. The German philosopher Friedrich Nietzsche (1844–1900) – who in *The Antichrist* cast himself in the title role and claimed that the only character in the entire New Testament worthy of respect was Pontius Pilate – believed that Christian virtues such as meekness, mercifulness and peacemaking constituted a 'slave morality', the antithesis and subversion of the noble, heroic, proud and warlike aristocratic code of ancient Rome. In his view, the Christian ethic was nothing more than a clever, resentful ploy to make the strong feel guilty about their ruthless superiority. As a consequence, natural leaders strove to become more like the helpless weak, who had everything to gain from the newly found altruism of their masters.

NINE

QUESTION 46

Who were the 9 great gods of ancient Egypt (The Great Ennead)?

Atum	Osiris
Shu	Isis
Tefnut	Seth
Geb	Nephthys
Nut	

A N ENNEAD is a Greek-derived word for a collection of nine things – in this case, gods. The ancient Egyptians used nine to indicate a great number (like the Hebrew forty), since it is the product of three (the number of plurality) multiplied by itself. They thus tended to group their gods in enneads to indicate 'the totality' of their deities (more than two thousand!). The Great Ennead, the grouping of nine that arose in Heliopolis during the First Dynasty (c. 3000 BC), was the principal one and by no means confined to that locality alone.

In the cosmogony of Annu, the Egyptian city that the Greeks called Heliopolis ('City of the Sun'), **Atum** was the primeval earth hill, the creator of the world who rose from the waters of the god Nun ('the primordial ocean'). After lonely Atum masturbated and swallowed his own seed – an act sometimes attributed to the god Khepera – he gave rise to the god of air, **Shu**, and his twin, **Tefnut**, the goddess of moisture. These coupled and brought forth **Geb** or Seb (male, 'earth') and **Nut** (female, 'sky').

The goddess Nut was depicted in art as a naked woman arched across the heavens over her husband, the earth. Her fingertips and toes rested on Geb at the four cardinal points, and her torso was bordered with stars. Nut swallowed the sun each night and gave birth to it again in the morning. Because she was identified with the cosmic cow of the sky, she was sometimes represented as bovine. The coupling of earth and sky resulted in the birth of Osiris and Seth (males) and Isis and Nephthys (females), who paired off as married couples.

Osiris, or Ausar ('many-eyed'), the best loved of the gods and Lord of the Dead in the underworld, was identified at first with the deceased King but later with all dead Egyptians, who were referred to as 'Osiris So-and-So', much as we would say 'the late Mr Jones'. Osiris was a god of vegetation and agriculture who caused the fertilising Nile to overflow each year. Although he died each winter, he was resurrected as the new crop in the following year. As such, he was one of the august company of Mediterranean 'corn gods', including Tammuz, Adonis, Attis, Dionysus, Zagreus and the goddess Persephone. Osiris was depicted as a green mummified man wearing a crown and wielding the sceptre and scourge of kingship. In a related aspect of Osiris (his procreative forces), his embodiment was the sacred Goat of Mendes in the Nile delta, a beast that was allowed to indulge in ritual copulation with the most exceptionally beautiful women of the region.

In the underworld, an enthroned Osiris presided over the ceremony of the Weighing of the Heart of every dead Egyptian. Anubis, the jackal-headed god, balanced in a huge set of scales the heart (deeds) of the deceased against an ostrich feather of Maat, goddess of justice and truth. Then Thoth, the god of the moon, wisdom and writing, usually portrayed as an ibis-headed man or a baboon, meticulously recorded the verdict. If the heart of the dead person counterbalanced Maat's feather, all was well for that soul for all eternity.

When the insane Persian King Cambyses conquered Egypt (525 BC), he scornfully killed the holy black bull at Memphis that represented the god Apis, a major manifestation of Osiris. None the less, the cult of Isis and Osiris lived on for many centuries, not only in later Alexandrian Egypt but also in Greece and the Roman Empire until Christianity ousted it.

Isis, or Auset ('throne'), wife and sister of Osiris and mother of Horus, is often portrayed as a woman with the hieroglyph for throne on her head. In later Egyptian art, she merges with Hathor, or Het-heru, the goddess of love, beauty, music and the dance, whose name means 'house of Horus'. Both the wet-nurse and the wife of Horus, Hathor was identified by the Greeks with Aphrodite.

The Greek writer Plutarch offers a somewhat garbled version of the most important Egyptian myth in his essay 'On Isis and Osiris'. Here is his story as modified by other Greek and Egyptian sources.

Osiris was a wise king of Egypt who, while travelling abroad, left the state in the hands of his sister-wife Isis. His younger brother Seth fell in love with Isis and decided to make himself king. After Osiris' return, Seth and seventy-two other conspirators invited him to a banquet at which a magnificent chest was offered to whichever guest fitted in it most closely. The conspirators were all too short for it, but the chest turned out to be just right for Osiris. Suddenly the conspirators clapped the lid on the chest, nailed it down, and soldered it with lead. After they flung it into the Nile, it drifted out into the Mediterranean, landing at Byblos on the Phoenician coast (north of modern Beirut). The chest came to rest against a tamarisk tree, which gradually incorporated it into itself.

The King of Byblos had the splendid tree cut down and used for a pillar in his palace, but Isis persuaded him to surrender it to her. Once back in Egypt, she managed to get herself pregnant by the dead Osiris; the child she bore was named Horus.

Evil Seth soon discovered Osiris' corpse, which he dismembered into fourteen pieces and scattered all over Egypt. Isis recovered all of them except the penis, which had been eaten by the fish of the Nile. She made an image of that and, with the help of Nephthys, Horus and Thoth, instructed Anubis in how to reassemble and mummify Osiris' body. Osiris revived and became the ruler of the dead in the underworld. He was thus the first mummy, and each subsequent mummified Egyptian hoped to share in his resurrection and eternal life. The Mysteries of Osiris were the greatest of all Egyptian festivals, including an eight-act drama on his life, death, mummification and resurrection.

Meanwhile Horus had grown up, and he fought a battle with his uncle Seth that lasted many days, during which Horus lost an eye and Seth his testicles. When the earth god Geb was asked to arbitrate, he decided that Horus should succeed his father Osiris as king of both Upper (southern) and Lower (northern) Egypt, a union which took place historically in about 3200 BC under King Menes.

Horus was originally a falcon sun god and chief god of Lower Egypt who became identified with the Egyptian King at the very beginning of the First Dynasty. In later myth, he merged with another Horus, the son of Isis and Osiris who avenged the latter's murder. He thus became identified with the living Egyptian King, whereas the dead King became Osiris and ruled the underworld.

Horus, usually portrayed as a falcon or falcon-headed man and representing the rising sun, was identified with Apollo by the Greeks. He was also often pictured in Egyptian art as a child being suckled by Isis or held in her lap, uncannily prefiguring medieval Christian representations of the Madonna and Child. This domesticated version of Horus presented quite a contrast with jackal-headed Anubis, ibis-headed Thoth, ram-headed Khnum, crocodile-headed Sobek, the cat-headed goddess Bast and, in the words of the Roman poet Juvenal, all the other 'monsters adored by demented Egypt'.

Seth or Set was the god of storms, darkness, war, confusion and the sterile desert beyond the Nile valley. He was originally a god of Upper Egypt, and his struggle with Horus may have been based on an actual invasion of Upper by Lower Egypt in about 4245 BC. Seth was sometimes represented as a man with a big-eared head resembling that of a donkey.

Nephthys, or Nebt-het ('lady of the house', that is, the house of Osiris), was the sister of Isis, Osiris and Seth, and wife of the last, although she always supported Isis and Osiris against murderous Seth and helped restore Osiris to life. Plutarch claims she gave birth to Anubis by Osiris, though Egyptian texts state Anubis was the son of Ra, the god of the sun at noontime.

Who were the 9 Muses, and what were their associated arts?

Calliope: epic poetry
Urania: astronomy
Clio: history
Terpsichore: dance
Melpomene: tragedy

Thalia: comedy and pastoral
  poetry
Euterpe: lyric poetry and
  flute music
Erato: love poetry
Polyhymnia: sacred songs

O for a Muse of fire, that would ascend
The brightest heaven of invention . . .

SHAKESPEARE, *Henry V, Prologue*, 1–2

IT'S ENTIRELY FITTING THAT THE MUSES, the lovable, (usually) nurturing patronesses of the arts and goddesses of creative inspiration and intellectual activity, should be the daughters of Zeus by the Titaness Mnemosyne, the goddess of memory. From their mother, the Nine learned about all that had transpired in the world since the beginning of time, including stories of the Titans and the ascendancy of the Twelve Olympians (see Question 57). The ancient lesson seems to be that an amply stocked memory is crucial for breathing life into the arts, whether one is creating or appreciating them.

The Muses were born in Pieria, sometimes thought to be on the slopes of Mount Olympus in Thessaly, home of the Greek gods. From Pieria, they migrated to the spring Aganippe and the fountain Hippocrene on Mount Helicon in Boeotia. The spring of Castalia on Mount Parnassus, site of Apollo's oracle at Delphi, was another of their haunts. Whoever drank from a sacred spring or fountain of the Muses was immediately suffused with artistic inspiration. Hippocrene ('horse fountain') was created by a hoof-stamp of the winged horse Pegasus – another potent symbol of inspiration – when he alighted on Helicon.

The Muses were not only inspirers but consummate performers, often entertaining the gods during their feasts on Olympus. Homer imagines Apollo, god of music and poetry, and sometimes called Musagetes ('leader of the Muses'), accompanying them on the lyre as they sing with ineffable voices.

It was on Mount Helicon that the Boeotian poet Hesiod (fl. c.700 BC) claimed the Muses manifested themselves to him. Hesiod, author of the didactic agricultural poem The Works and Days, was the first to reveal the names of the Muses in his long poem on the origin of the gods, the Theogony, which the Nine Sisters supposedly bade him compose.

Calliope ('beautiful voiced') was chief of the Nine – Ovid calls her maxima – and Muse of epic poetry. In this latter capacity, she was invoked by Virgil in the Aeneid and by Dante in the Purgatorio. In late ancient sculpture, she was often depicted with a scroll, stylus and tablet.

When Zeus asked Calliope to arbitrate in a dispute between Persephone and Aphrodite over Adonis, the wise Muse decreed that the gorgeous young man should spend four months with Persephone, four months with Aphrodite, and the remainder of the year on his own, presumably recovering. Neither goddess gave much heed to Calliope's directive.

The most famous offspring of all the Muses was Orpheus, in most accounts the son of Calliope and Oeagrus, King of Thrace. So ravishing was the music he made on the lyre presented to him by Apollo that it enchanted not only wild beasts but even trees and rocks.

His joy was complete when he took as his bride the lovely tree nymph Eurydice, but she died of a serpent bite on their wedding day. Confident of the persuasive power of his music, Orpheus descended to Tartarus, hoping to mollify Hades, god of the underworld. At the sound of his plaintive song, the three-headed guard-dog Cerberus let him pass, and the savage Furies wept blood. At the behest of his Queen, Persephone, Hades allowed Eurydice to depart on one condition: that Orpheus wouldn't look back at her until they had both returned to the upper world. As they approached the land of the living, Orpheus turned to make sure Eurydice was following behind – and she was gone in an instant, with time only to say 'Farewell'.

After returning brokenheartedly to Thrace, Orpheus gave offence to a band of frenzied Maenads, female followers of Dionysus (Bacchus), the god of intoxication and revelry, either for speaking out against their orgiastic rites or for shunning the company of women. The fierce Maenads tore Orpheus limb from limb and flung his head into the River Hebrus. After drifting out to sea, still singing, it came to rest on the island of Lesbos, which later gave birth to Greece's first great lyric poets (see Question 50). John Milton evokes the dismemberment of Orpheus in *Paradise Lost* (7.32−8), where he speaks of

> . . . the barbarous dissonance
> Of Bacchus and his Revellers, the Race
> Of that wild Rout that tore the Thracian Bard
> In Rhodope, where Woods and Rocks had Ears
> To rapture, till the savage clamour drown'd
> Both Harp and Voice; nor could the Muse defend
> Her son.

The Muses gathered Orpheus' limbs and buried them at the foot of Mount Olympus, a favourite haunt of melodious nightingales. His lyre was placed in the heavens as a constellation. The Maenads were turned into oak trees.

Urania ('heavenly') was sometimes depicted pointing to a globe. As the Muse of astronomy, she was able to predict the future by scanning the stars. Milton invokes her at the beginning of *Paradise Lost* as the 'Heav'nly Muse', but in a Christianised guise that makes her the inspirer of Moses and other Hebrew prophets. In his invocation to Book 7 of the poem, at the midpoint of his poetic task, he calls on Urania again.

Clio ('she that extols'), the Muse of history, is often pictured unfolding a scroll or holding a water clock. According to some accounts, Clio was the mother of Linus, the archetypal musician who invented rhythm and melody, sang the story of the Creation and taught Orpheus and Thamyris their musical wizardry. Apollo himself was so jealous of Linus that he killed him. (This Linus must be distinguished from another musical Linus who was slain by Heracles – see Question 58.)

Terpsichore ('she that rejoices in the dance') was often depicted dancing and holding a lyre. From her, we got our word *terpsichorean* ('pertaining to dancing'). In some stories she is the mother of the Sirens, the half-bird, half-woman creatures who used their incomparably lovely voices to lure unwary mariners to their death. Odysseus, however, managed both to listen to their song and to evade their trap by having himself tied to the mast of his ship while his men stopped up their ears with wax.

Melpomene ('she that sings'), the Muse of tragedy, is pictured holding a tragic mask and sometimes poising a dagger at her breast. She wears a vine wreath because of its association with Dionysus, god of wine, in whose honour festivals featuring tragic dramas were held. Melpomene's footgear is the cothurnus (or buskin), the thick-soled laced boot worn by tragic actors to endow them with a suitable stature. Although the tragic Muse seems to have been too depressed and introspective to take a lover, some think that she, rather than Terpsichore, was the mother of the Sirens.

Thalia ('festive' or 'flourishing') is usually pictured in the environs of a comic mask in artistic renditions of her. She may wear the low shoe or slipper of comic actors (called the sock) and hold a small rustic drum or shepherd's crook, indicating her dual role as Muse of both comedy and pastoral poetry. Some say she was the mother by Apollo of the Corybantes, attendants of the Phrygian nature goddess Cybele, 'the Great Mother'. The Corybantes accompanied Cybele over her mountain haunts with lit torches and wild, intoxicated dancing to the crashing sound of flutes, horns, drums and cymbals. Later, the name was applied to Cybele's priests, who castrated themselves in the orgiastic frenzies of their rituals.

Euterpe ('she that gladdens'), the Muse of lyric poetry, is often depicted with a double flute, which she is said to have invented. Unmarried like the rest of the Muses, Euterpe became yet another single mother in the family when she gave birth to Rhesus. On the very night he arrived to aid the beleaguered city of Troy in the Trojan War, the sleeping Rhesus was slain by the Greek warriors Odysseus and Diomedes, who sneaked up on his camp (Iliad, Book 10). His snow-white, wind-swift horses were then driven off before they could taste the grass of Troy or drink its waters; an oracle had foretold that if they managed to do this, Troy could not be taken. But Odysseus and his partner in crime made a total monkey out of Rhesus.

Erato ('passionate'), Muse of erotic poetry, is pictured with a lyre. You would figure the inspirer of so many amorous ditties would have some scandalous story of her own, but none has surfaced so far.

Polyhymnia ('rich in hymns') is often depicted wearing a garland of roses and looking terribly serious. This Muse of sacred songs is, according to various accounts, the mother of Triptolemus, who invented farming; of Orpheus; or even of Eros himself, though that honour is almost always assigned to Aphrodite.

Usually benevolent and kindly, the Muses sometimes displayed the vengeful haughtiness at the heart of most creative artists who know their true worth. Ovid tells how Pierus, King of Macedonia, named his nine daughters (collectively known as the Pierides) after the Muses. When they later presumptuously challenged the real Muses to a singing contest, they of course lost. Calliope and her sisters turned the King's daughters into chattering magpies, a myth recalled by Dante at the beginning of his *Purgatorio* as an object lesson on the importance of humility. A similar fate befell the Sirens, who also unsuccessfully challenged the Muses and had their wing feathers plucked by the victors, who used them to make crowns for themselves. Some versions of the story have the Sirens plummet into the sea and drown as a result of this encounter.

Another unfortunate soul was the mythic poet Thamyris, who dared claim he was more skilled than the Muses at composing verse. He, too, lost the contest – and his vision, voice and poetic craft as punishment. Milton, speaking of his own blindness in *Paradise Lost*, invites comparison with two famed Greek poets: 'Blind Thamyris and blind Maeonides' – the last word being an epithet of Homer.

The followers of Pythagoras, as well as Plato and Aristotle, officially organised their schools as associations for the cult of the Muses (*thiasoi*), and our word *museum* comes from the Greek *Mouseion* – 'home of the Muses'. Today, if these mythological deities still linger in our consciousness, it is because they evoke music, poetry, knowledge, wisdom, beauty, grace, inspiration. And which of us, at some point in our life, hasn't longed, not just for any garden-variety Muse, but a Muse of fire?

What are the 9 orders of angels (from lowest to highest)?

Angels	Dominations
Archangels	Thrones
Principalities	Cherubim
Powers	Seraphim
Virtues	

ANGELS DATE BACK at least to the time of Zoroaster (or Zarathustra), prophet of Zoroastrianism, which dominated the religious life of the Persian Empire from about the sixth century BC to the seventh century AD. This tradition was messianic and included themes of resurrection, reward and punishment, and cosmic conflict between a benevolent god of light, Ahura Mazda (later called Ormazd), and his antithetical evil counterpart, Ahriman. The Talmud points to Babylon as the source of angels (or at least of their names), but by 539 BC Babylonia was already part of the Persian Empire.

In fact, angels with proper names don't enter Jewish tradition until after the return of the Jews from their Babylonian captivity in 538 BC. The Hebrew word for angels is *malakhim*, or messengers (Greek, *angeloi*), and that is a primary role of theirs in the Old Testament. In the book of Daniel (8:17), Gabriel explicates visions and prophecies for Daniel, who faints in his presence. Michael is identified as 'the Great Prince, defender of your people' in the same book (12:1). And Raphael, who appears in the apocryphal book of Tobit (Chapter 5), is engaged by Tobit to be a guide and protector for his son Tobias as he journeys to Media. Raphael also acts as a matchmaker on this trip and restores old Tobit's sight. Angels in Jewish tradition were anthropomorphised, pictured as eating and drinking with Abraham, wrestling with Jacob, and even becoming objects of lust in Sodom.

In addition to these close encounters, the Old Testament records several awesome apparitions. The **cherubim**, who wield a flashing sword to keep the banished Adam and Eve away from the Tree of Life, make up a living chariot for Yahweh called the Merkabah in Ezekiel 10. In this astonishing vision, God and his sapphire throne are pictured high above four winged cherubim, each covered all over with eyes and having four faces: those of a cherub (an ox in Ezekiel 1), man, lion and eagle. Each cherub is beside a whirring topaz wheel – which is 'like a wheel inside a wheel', also covered with eyes and alive with the spirit of the angels. Hot coals lie scattered among the cherubim, and the sound made by their wings rivals the 'voice of God Almighty when he speaks'.

In Isaiah (6:2), the **seraphim** have six wings: two to cover their faces, two to cover their feet and two for flying. Seraphim are 'the burning ones' in Hebrew, and Isaiah is purified when one of them takes a live coal with tongs and touches it to the prophet's lips.

We read about messenger angels and archangels in the New Testament, too. Gabriel announces to Mary that she is to bear the son of God. An unnamed angel in white robes greets women mourning at Jesus' empty tomb, reassuring them that Christ has risen from the dead. St Paul mentions principalities, powers, virtues, thrones, dominations and archangels in Ephesians (1:21), Colossians (1:16) and 1 Thessalonians (4:16). In the book of Revelation, which contains a vision of Michael battling Satan, we encounter fantastic creatures like those described in the Old Testament.

Paul evidently acquired his knowledge of the various orders of angels when he was rapt into heaven – 'whether in the flesh, I know not' – and allowed to view the full angelic panoply. St Ambrose (339–97) was apparently the first to enunciate a nine-order schema, which was greatly elaborated by Dionysius the Areopagite, ostensibly an Athenian convert of Paul's who had imbibed detailed knowledge about the angels directly from him. His work, On the Celestial Hierarchy, was translated from Greek into Latin by Johannes Scotus Erigena (c.810–c.77), an Irish theologian and philosopher who was one of a handful of western Europeans of the time who were fluent in Greek. Only in the mid-fifteenth century, with the development of Greek philology, did scholars examining the original text of Dionysius realise that its verbal forms were typical of Syria in about AD 500. The author, who could not have been a contemporary of Paul's, was probably a Syrian monk born centuries later – hence his current name, Pseudo-Dionysius.

None the less, Erigena's translation made Pseudo-Dionysius' book a widely accessible authority on angels, whom it divided into three choirs, each with three orders. The Councillors of God comprised the seraphim, cherubim and thrones. The Governors were the dominations, virtues and powers. Principalities, archangels and angels were the Messengers of God.

Unaware of relying on an impostor, St Thomas Aquinas (1225–74) cited Pseudo-Dionysius hundreds of times in his Summa Theologica. Aquinas maintained that angels, created for God's glory, were pure spirits capable of masquerading as corporeal beings when expedient, usually to break the ice with humans. Each individual angel, he said, really represented a distinct species, and their number surpassed all reckoning. According to Aquinas, angels know neither the future nor the thoughts of humans, but they do have full knowledge of themselves, which allows them to understand and accept their limitations. As a result, lower-order angels accept their place without envying high-ranking colleagues. Aquinas also assigned a division of labour to the angelic orders: love to the seraphim, sight (or knowledge) to the cherubim, support to the **thrones**, leadership to the **dominations**, execution of commands to the **virtues**, judgement to the **powers**, guidance of nations to the **principalities**, guidance of leaders to **archangels**, and guidance of other humans to **angels** ('guardian angels').

These nine orders were also thought to be the Intelligences or Movers of the nine heavens or spheres, which contained, in ascending order, the orbits of the moon, Mercury, Venus, the sun, Mars, Jupiter, Saturn, the fixed stars and the crystalline sphere (or primum mobile, 'the first moving thing'). Unmoving Earth was at the centre of this cosmos. The immediate dwelling of God, the unmoved Mover, was beyond the material universe of time and space in the Empyrean, the tenth heaven of pure spiritual fire and light, where the redeemed share in the Beatific Vision.

The orders of angels were delegated to the various heavens, from the lofty seraphim in charge of the *primum mobile* to the humble angels governing the sphere of the moon. By striving to attain to God and by fervently loving and contemplating him, the angelic orders caused their spheres to revolve in perfect circular orbits – infinitely fast in the *primum mobile* and more slowly in each descending sphere (the diurnal orbiting of the sun bringing night and day). In a celestial trickle-down effect, each sphere imparted God's love, as motion, to the sphere below it, along with his grace and effulgence. At the centre was the ultimate recipient of these divine, angelic and astrological influences, the Earth and its inhabitants. This wheels-within-wheels effect, with each sphere revolving at a different speed and producing a different note, created the exquisitely harmonious music of the spheres, which crude human ears haven't been able to hear since the expulsion of Adam and Eve from Eden.

What else do we know about these creatures? Fully one-third of the angels were said to have followed Lucifer (Satan), the most glorious seraph and victim of his own overweening pride, into hell (Revelation 12:4, 7–9). Some churchmen argued that Satan's rebellion against God and his fall occurred immediately after the first instant of his creation, when he pronounced (or thought) his '*non serviam*' ('I will not serve', Jeremiah 2:20). Dominations were considered the first angels to be created, although no consensus exists on when. We know the names of seven archangels: Michael, Gabriel, Raphael, Uriel, Chamuel, Jophiel and Zadkiel. And only angels and archangels speak to humans. In Islamic tradition, the four archangels are Gabriel (Jibril), the transmitter of divine revelations; Michael (Mikal), the warrior; Azrael (Izra'il), the angel of death; and Israfel (Israfil), who will sound the trumpet in Jerusalem on Resurrection Day.

On the *Celestial Hierarchy* and Aquinas' countless pronunciamentos on angels had quite an impact on subsequent literature. Dante (1265–1321) adopted the nine-order, three-choir view of the angels and heavenly spheres in his *Paradiso*. There Beatrice shows Dante the souls of the saved residing in the sphere that best corresponds to their character in life: for example, wise theologians and religious writers (including Dionysius and Aquinas), who shed intellectual light on God's mysteries, in the heaven of the sun; martial champions of God in that of Mars. Beatrice mentions Dionysius as the thinker who elucidated the angelic hierarchy and describes how Pope Gregory the Great had a laugh at his own expense when he got to Heaven and saw first-hand the errors he had made in attempting to classify the angels in his writings. We are also told that each of the three angelic choirs contemplates a separate person of the Trinity.

Since medieval times, writers have felt increasingly free to tamper with the orthodox view of angels. John Milton, for example, surely made Aquinas turn over in his grave by claiming in *Paradise Lost* (1667) that angels were sexually active (even if only with other angels, and rather ethereally).

Who were the 9 Worthies?

Hector of Troy	Judas Maccabaeus
Alexander the Great	King Arthur
Julius Caesar	Charlemagne
Joshua	Godfrey of Bouillon
King David	

> For it is notoirly known through the universal world that there
> been nine worthy and the best that ever were, that is to wit, three
> Paynims [pagans], three Jews and three Christian men.
>
> WILLIAM CAXTON,
Preface to Sir Thomas Malory's
Le Morte d'Arthur (1485)

THE NINE WORTHIES is a medieval list of the world's greatest warriors, composed with an eye towards the three historical groups that had contributed most to medieval culture. The ever-symmetrical medieval mind is revealed in the allocation of exactly three Worthies to each of the three groups: pagan warriors of antiquity, Old Testament warriors and warriors of the Christian era.

Hector of Troy, a son of King Priam, is the greatest Trojan warrior in Homer's *Iliad*. Aided by conniving Aphrodite, Hector's brother Paris had eloped with Helen, most beautiful of women, who was daughter of Zeus and Leda and wife of Menelaus, King of Sparta. The Trojans refused to return Helen, and for ten years they fought off an allied Greek army for possession of her. Unlike his brother Paris, who preferred to make love, not war, Hector battled the Greeks valiantly, even though deeply torn by his devotion to his wife Andromache and infant son Astyanax. After being deserted by Apollo and betrayed by Athene, he was slain on the battlefield by Achilles, who was by far the greatest warrior at Troy. Bereft of its champion, Troy fell soon thereafter.

Hector is often seen as the noblest, most chivalrous warrior in the *Iliad*, fighting in what he recognised to be an unjust cause only for the sake of his honour and that of Troy. None the less, his blustery, swaggering challenges to his foes gave us the verb *to hector*. But why wasn't Achilles picked as the first Worthy?

Several reasons. The brooding, wrathful, vengeful Achilles was the antithesis of the medieval knightly ideal. More important was the association between the Trojan people and the founding of Rome – as immortalised in Virgil's *Aeneid*, the Latin epic that relates how Trojan Aeneas, cousin of Hector and survivor of the destruction of Troy, arrives in Italy and founds a dynasty that leads to Romulus and Remus, the mythical founders of Rome. And Rome, in the fullness of time, became the seat of Christianity. In addition, many communities of western Europe claimed a Trojan origin. For example, Brut (or Brutus), the fabled founder of the British race, was said to be a great-grandson of Aeneas and an ancestor of King Arthur. Layamon's *Brut*, an English late-twelfth-century long poem based on a work by the French poet Wace, recounted this myth.

Alexander the Great, born in 356 BC and tutored by Aristotle, was the son of King Philip II of Macedon. This kingdom controlled Greece by the time Philip was assassinated in 336 BC as he prepared to attack the Persian Empire. Alexander, who claimed descent from Achilles through his mother Olympias, a queen of Epirus, carried out his father's plan, invading Asia Minor in 334 BC, where, according to legend, he cut the Gordian knot. The knot had been fastened between the yoke of a wagon and its pole by the peasant Gordius, later King of Phrygia and father of Midas. It was said that the man who could undo the knot would rule Asia. Alexander sliced through it with a quick blow of his sword. He then trounced King Darius III and his Persians at the battle of Issus and took, in succession, Syria, Tyre (in modern Lebanon), and Egypt, where he founded Alexandria in 332 BC.

After decisively defeating the Persians at the battle of Arbela in 331 BC and Darius' subsequent death, Alexander declared himself successor to the Persian throne and spent the next seven years conquering and consolidating his claims eastward as far as north-west India – where his men refused to march any further – and then returning westward again. He married Darius' daughter and presided over a celebration honouring nine thousand of his men who had already married women of the former Persian Empire, 'the marriage of East and West'. Alexander died of typhoid fever or malaria at the age of thirty-two in Babylon on 10 June 323 BC, in the palace of Nebuchadrezzar II. His empire soon fragmented into separate states ruled as hereditary monarchies founded by his generals.

As the greatest conqueror and general of the ancient world, Alexander was a shoo-in for the Worthies competition. The Middle Ages teemed with freely embellished narratives about him, such as the *Roman d'Alexandre*, a long French poem of the twelfth century. Alexander was also famed as a magnanimous conqueror who was especially kind to captured Persian noblewomen.

Roman general and statesman **Julius Caesar** (100–44 BC) rounds out the pagan portion of the list of Worthies. A brilliant politician and orator, Caesar was elected consul and, with Pompey and Crassus, formed the cabal known as the First Triumvirate. As proconsul of Gaul, he conquered an area from the Rhine to the Pyrenees. The Senate, fearing his power and veteran troops, recalled him to Rome. Knowing this would involve laying aside his army command and subjecting himself to retaliatory criminal prosecutions, Caesar made the fateful decision to cross the Rubicon – at that time the border of Italy – and embroil Rome in civil war. He defeated Pompey and other opponents in a series of swift campaigns in Greece, Africa, Asia Minor and Spain, and had himself proclaimed dictator. Detested by republican and senatorial aristocrats, Caesar was assassinated by a group of them led by Brutus and Cassius on 15 March 44 BC.

Here was another natural to make the Worthies team. As a general and conqueror, Caesar ranks second – perhaps – only to Alexander, and he claimed descent, through the Julian clan, from Iulus, the son of Trojan Aeneas. In the Middle Ages, Caesar was also considered the first Roman Emperor (though that distinction actually belongs to his successor,

Augustus), and the Emperors were thought to have bequeathed their temporal power over the empire to the Popes.

Joshua, first of the Old Testament Worthies, was the successor of Moses who brought the Israelites into the Holy Land. Marching behind the Ark of the Covenant, Joshua led his people across the Jordan River under miraculous circumstances, the very waters pausing in their course to allow the crossing. According to the book named after him in the Bible, Joshua conquered Jericho — where the walls came tumbling down at the blowing of rams' horns and the shouting of the Israelites — and overran Canaan, distributing the land among the twelve tribes of Israel. Historians and biblical scholars agree that the process was accomplished more gradually. None the less, the Israelites had a solid foothold in Palestine by the thirteenth century BC. Joshua, the warrior who conquered the Holy Land, was the ideal type of medieval hero in that he succeeded in an undertaking that successive waves of Crusaders tried to accomplish over the course of several hundred years.

King David, the second Israelite King, reigned from about 1000 BC until his death in 962 BC. A musician and probably the author of some of the Psalms, David united Israel with its capital at Jerusalem. In Jewish tradition, he is the King *par excellence*, and the authors of the New Testament claim Jesus was his descendant. Although David started out as a shepherd, he became an aide to King Saul, married the King's daughter, and forged a classic friendship with Saul's son Jonathan.

When David slew the giant Philistine Goliath with only some stones and a slingshot, old King Saul became furiously jealous — 'Saul has slain his thousands', the Israelite women sang, 'and David his ten thousands' — forcing the young man to flee to the desert of Judah. There, leading a band of outcasts, David protected the locals from marauders and gained a reputation as a patriot. Although he was anointed by the prophet Samuel in Bethlehem while the manic-depressive Saul was still alive, David was not proclaimed king until after the deaths of Saul and Jonathan, both slain fighting the Philistines.

David conquered Jerusalem and made it the capital of his newly united kingdom. His family, however, was wormwood to his heart. His son Absalom killed David's eldest son, Amnon, after the latter had raped his half-sister Tamar. When Absalom was killed by one of David's generals after the young man had rebelled against him, the grief-stricken king mourned him in the words of bereft fathers since time immemorial: 'My son Absalom! My son! My son Absalom! Would I had died in your place! Absalom, my son, my son!' The adulterous relationship between David and Bathsheba led to the murder of her husband, Uriah, but also to the birth of their son Solomon, who succeeded David as king.

David is perhaps the most intriguing character in the Old Testament. In the Goliath story, he is the vulnerable but courageous young man who conquers despite overwhelming odds. Countless Renaissance statues attest to the symbol he gave humanity, that of the brave champion, armed only with a righteous cause, defeating tyranny and oppression. To the medieval world he had been the perfect poet, musician and king; conqueror of Jerusalem; and ancestor of the Saviour.

Judas Maccabaeus, the mighty Jewish patriot, fought decisively against the Hellenistic Syrians, led by Seleucid King Antiochus IV Epiphanes, who tried to impose the pagan Greek religion and other related practices on the Jews. Maccabaeus, whose name probably means 'Hammer', defeated Seleucid armies four times and, in December of 164 BC, presided over the purification and rededication of the Temple of Jerusalem, an event commemorated by the eight-day Festival of Lights, or Hanukkah. The movement led by Maccabaeus and his brothers Jonathan and Simon eventually resulted in a short period of political and religious independence for the Jews. The resonance that Judas Maccabaeus had for the Middle Ages involved his being a brave, virtuous warrior who routed the foreign overlords of the Holy Land and rededicated its holy sites, much as the Crusading nations had attempted to do.

King Arthur was probably a historical figure, although much Arthurian lore and the stories of his Round Table are largely Welsh and medieval concoctions (see Question 60). His exploits attained legendary status partly because the times in which he lived were decisive for British history. The occupying Roman legions had pulled out by about AD 410, and the cultural and linguistic character of Britain was to undergo a profound change during the several hundred years that followed.

Arthur, who was most probably Welsh, gained a reputation as a magnificent warrior while fighting against the invading Saxons during the late fifth and early sixth centuries AD. Fairly reputable historical evidence credits him with a major victory at Mount Badon in 490 (or 518) and another triumph in 511 (or 539) at the battle of Camlann, where he reportedly died. He was probably an extremely adept general serving under British kings, and his fame lived on as a powerful symbol of British resistance to invaders. There arose a vast literary tradition dealing with him, his knights, and the quest for the Holy Grail. In his character of Worthy, Arthur appears in an anonymous fourteenth-century English poem, *The Alliterative Morte Arthure*, where he dreams of Fortune's wheel and sees the six pagan and Jewish Worthies on it, already fallen from their high estate, and the three Christian Worthies, with himself at the very top, heading for predominance.

Besides Arthur's exploits and the renowned chivalry of at least some of his followers, his links to Christianity secured him a notch on the list of Worthies. Thus, the traditional number of his Round Table inner circle of knights, twelve, is the same as that of Christ's Apostles (see Question 59). There's even an empty chair left at the table, the Siege Perilous, which calls to mind the treachery of Judas Iscariot. In addition, the Grail was usually understood as the cup that Christ used at the Last Supper and in which Joseph of Arimathea caught some of his blood at the Crucifixion. The lance often associated with the Grail was the one that had pierced Christ's side while he was on the cross. Joseph of Arimathea is mentioned in the Gospels as having requested Christ's body from Pontius Pilate and buried it in 'his new tomb that he had hewn in the rock' (Matthew 27:57–60). This is none other than the Holy Sepulchre, ultimate goal of Crusaders, which establishes a circuitous but undeniable link between Arthur and medieval Christian 'Holy Wars'.

Charlemagne (reigned 768–814), sometimes called *Rex pater Europae*, 'the King Father of Europe', was the son of Pepin the Short, who had been anointed King of the Franks by the Pope (see Question 42).

Charlemagne was unique in his time in that he considered himself to have official Christian endorsement of his role as warrior king of the Franks. In addition, he endeavoured to make his court a centre of Christian learning, and he generously subsidised the arts. A very tall, strong, cheerful man, he spoke Latin and read Greek, although he apparently never learned to write.

The empire Charlemagne carved out for himself was the largest in the West since the fall of Rome. He defeated the Germanic Lombards in Italy. He forcibly converted the Saxons to Christianity, thereby neutralising them as opponents. His defeats of the Slavs and other peoples allowed him to open an important Danubian trade route to Constantinople. He conquered the Danes and Bavarians and marched into northern Spain, eventually uniting all Christian lands in western Europe except southern Italy, part of Spain and Britain. Charlemagne was crowned Emperor Charles I of the Holy Roman Empire on Christmas Day of 800 by a grateful Pope Leo III, who had been reinstated in Rome by Charlemagne's forces. Charlemagne's vast empire survived as a unity for only a few decades after his death before splitting into essentially French and German components.

Like Alexander the Great and King Arthur, Charlemagne was at the core of an immense cycle of medieval legends, romances and *chansons de geste*, most famously *La Chanson de Roland*. In most of the tales he is portrayed as the ideal Christian King who battles against pagans and, especially, Moors – co-religionists of the Saracens who held the Holy Land.

This brings us to the Worthy most directly associated with the Crusading ideal, **Godfrey of Bouillon** (1060–1100), Duke of Lower Lorraine and leader of the First Crusade. A descendant of Charlemagne, Godfrey became the first Latin ruler of Palestine when his armies captured Jerusalem from the Saracens in 1099. When offered the title King of Jerusalem, he refused it in favour of *Advocatus Sancti Sepulchri*, 'Protector of the Holy Sepulchre'. After taking Jerusalem, Godfrey engineered truces with the Muslim cities of Ascalon, Caesarea and Acre, and repelled an Egyptian attack. He set a precedent by making himself a vassal of the Patriarch of Jerusalem, thereby making life difficult for subsequent civil and religious leaders who sought control in Jerusalem. Godfrey appears as the saintly hero and perfect Christian knight of Italian poet Torquato Tasso's late-Renaissance epic, *Gerusalemme Liberata* (*Jerusalem Delivered*, 1581).

An extended reference to the Worthies appears in Shakespeare's *Love's Labour's Lost*. In this early comedy, King Ferdinand of Navarre and three of his young nobles agree to eschew the company of women for three years to devote themselves to study. Ferdinand has forgotten, however, that he has a previous engagement with the Princess of France and her ladies-in-waiting, who prove most intriguing to the King and his friends. In the midst of the farcical goings-on, the pedantic schoolmaster Holofernes (famed for his teacherly exclamation, 'O thou monster Ignorance, how deformed dost thou look!') musters a troupe of blockheads to present a pageant of the Nine Worthies in honour of the Princess and her ladies. The list of Worthies differs from the traditional one in that it includes Hercules and Pompey the Great. The pageant lays an egg immediately when the first yokel introduces his character as 'Pompey the Big'. It's all downhill from there – for the pageant, but also for the medieval conception of the Worthies themselves as bigger-than-life embodiments of martial valour.

Who were the 9 lyric poets of ancient Greece?

Sappho	Bacchylides
Alcaeus	Alcman
Anacreon	Stesichorus
Simonides	Ibycus
Pindar	

THE GOLDEN AGE OF the ancient Greek lyric – a poem sung to the accompaniment of a lyre – stretched about 150 years from the mid-seventh century to the end of the sixth century BC. Long afterwards, the scholars and critics of Alexandrian Egypt canonised a list of nine who had excelled in that genre. Like many others, these poets turned away from the stately dactylic hexameters of epic and didactic verse (Homer and Hesiod), perfecting instead the lyric forms, moods and voices that were to dominate European poetry up to the fall of Rome and beyond.

Sappho (c.620–c.550 BC), the original 'lesbian', was born on the wealthy and sophisticated island of Lesbos off the coast of Asia Minor and lived most of her life in its capital, Mytilene. She wrote exquisitely passionate poems to and about the members of a musical and poetic society for highborn girls. (Some say it was a cult – a *thiasos* – of Aphrodite and the Muses, others liken it to a finishing school, and still others speculate it was just a coterie.) No one knows whether Sappho's mad crushes resulted in physical intimacy, but it certainly seems like it from her surviving poetry.

Sappho does mention a daughter, Cleis, but the traditional name of her husband, Kerkylas of Andros ('prick from the Isle of Man'), has the earmarks of Athenian wit about it. There's no truth in Ovid's story in his *Heroides* (ultimately derived from the Greek playwright Menander) that Sappho committed suicide by leaping from the Leucadian rock, off the coast of Epirus, after being abandoned by a much younger lover, the handsome boatman Phaon. Her literary remains, in the Aeolic dialect of Lesbos, consist almost entirely of fragments.

Standing at the origin of western love poetry, Sappho is one of its most poignant exemplars – a woman mourning past loves and the devastation they have wrought in her soul and body. Many of her poems invoke Aphrodite and speak of the girls – Atthis, Anactoria, Gongula – whom she loved with a passion that makes her tremble at the mere memory of it: 'I was in love with you once, Atthis, long ago.' The poet whom Plato dubbed 'the Tenth Muse' (see Question 47) was the first to call love 'bitter-sweet'.

Sappho's poem beginning 'Phainetai moi kenos isos theoisin' ('He seems to me an equal of the gods') inspired one of the loveliest lyrics of the Roman poet Catullus (c.84–c.54 BC), who translated it into Latin in his poem 51 ('Ille mi par esse deo videtur'). Sappho enviously describes a beloved girl sitting across from a man, probably her bridegroom. He must be a god, Sappho thinks, if he can enjoy the girl's presence without going to pieces, whereas the poet experiences an upheaval in all her senses if only she catches a glimpse of her. Here is John Addington Symonds's translation, which, despite the archaisms, deftly suggests the movement of the original stanzaic structure and metre, the sapphic strophe:

> Peer of gods he seemeth to me, the blissful
> Man who sits and gazes at thee before him,
> Close beside thee sits, and in silence hears thee
> Silverly speaking,
>
> Laughing love's low laughter. Oh this, this only
> Stirs the troubled heart in my breast to tremble!
> For should I but see thee a little moment,
> Straight is my voice hushed;
>
> Yea, my tongue is broken, and through and through me
> 'Neath the flesh, impalpable fire runs tingling;
> Nothing see mine eyes, and a noise of roaring
> Waves in my ear sounds;

Sweat runs down in rivers, a tremor seizes
All my limbs, and paler than grass in autumn,
Caught by pains of menacing death, I falter,
Lost in the love-trance.

Sappho's repudiation of the epic ideal of life is evident in her poem beginning 'Some say the fairest thing upon the dark earth is a troop of horsemen or a host of foot-soldiers, and others again a fleet of ships, but for me it is my beloved.' In her invocation to the goddess of love beginning 'Splendour-throned, deathless Aphrodite, child of Zeus, weaver of wiles' ('*Poikilothron' athanat' Aphrodita, pai Dios doloploke'*), Sappho begs the goddess to appear, as in the past, and reassure her that the latest object of her affection will soon stop fleeing her and reciprocate her love. Sappho's magic touch is evident even in this simile comparing a bride to an apple, which is all that remains of another of her poems:

Like the sweet apple which reddens upon the topmost bough,
A-top on the topmost twig, — which the pluckers forgot somehow,
— Forgot it not, nay, but got it not, for none could get it till now.

translated by
DANTE GABRIEL ROSSETTI

Her poems are perfused with the scent of flowers, especially the hyacinth and the rose. She calls women and goddesses 'rosy-ankled' and 'rosy-armed', and she transfers Homer's epithet, 'rosy-fingered', from the dawn to the much more romantic moon. Although this brief lament is perhaps not by Sappho, it evokes her style and tone:

The moon has set, and the Pleiades.
It is midnight. Hour
drags on after hour.
And I lie alone.

'Raise high the roof beam, carpenters' is the beginning of a Victorian-era translation of an epithalamium (wedding song) by Sappho. (J. D. Salinger used the phrase as the title of an ironic story about a cancelled wedding ceremony.) The rafters have to be hoisted higher because 'Like Ares comes the bridegroom, taller far than a tall man'.

Sappho is the earliest western poet to claim that her verse will confer immortality on her: 'When I die, I shall not be forgotten.' As long as people love (and read), she won't be.

Invariably associated with Sappho is **Alcaeus**, a contemporary of hers who also lived in Mytilene and wrote love lyrics, among many other types of poems. From early youth, Alcaeus was a leading member of the aristocratic faction and fought with words and weapons against the popular party. Whether in or out of exile, he inveighed against Pittacus, one of the Seven Sages who was made tyrant of Mytilene (see Question 37). He wrote barbed political songs and describes in one of his fragments his delight in the gleaming weapons and war gear in an armoury. Alcaeus was the first poet to use the 'ship of state' metaphor in reference to the political turbulence of his time. His great Roman admirer Horace (65–8 BC) elaborated on it in his first book of *Odes*, poem 14.

The lighter side of Alcaeus found expression in the theme that Horace later epitomised in the words '*carpe diem*' ('seize the moment') (*Odes* 1.11). Alcaeus exhorts us to take a carefree attitude towards life – though *he* didn't – since we are all poised on the brink of an inexorable abyss. Horace was also greatly influenced by Alcaeus' drinking songs (*scolia*), such as the one beginning 'Drink, Melanippus, and be drunk with me'. In one poem, Alcaeus urges his readers to throw a log on the fire and drink wine as a defence against the rain and ice of winter. In another, he reminds men to drink wine in the summer as a defence against the parching heat and the excessive sexual demands of women, who grow particularly amorous at that season. In yet another, he reminds us we don't have to wait for nightfall to begin drinking. The classical scholar Werner Jaeger wrote that Alcaeus' *scolia* call for 'a Dionysiac intoxication to drown the cares of the world'.

Anacreon (c.570–c.490 BC) was from Teos, an Ionian city in Asia Minor. He fled to Thrace with his fellow Greeks when the Persians conquered Teos, spent time at the court of Polycrates of Samos (where Ibycus was also a resident), and ended his days in Athens as a friend of Simonides. In his Ionic dialect, Anacreon celebrated wine, women, song and young boys. One of his poems describes how he sets his sights on a pretty girl, only to discover she's from Lesbos and thus prefers 'to make eyes at the ladies' instead. In another, he speaks of a scornful Thracian 'filly' who needs a skilled horseman like him to mount her. The pathos of old age closing in on a sensualist is the theme of yet another poem. The pleasures of love are now just a memory, and mournful Anacreon can look forward only to the terrors of death, which are always present to him, and the dark pit of no return. The *Anacreontics*, sixty Greek poems in the style of Anacreon written many hundreds of years after his death, were influential in the English lyric of the seventeenth century, especially in the work of the Cavalier poets, Robert Herrick, Sir John Suckling and Richard Lovelace.

Simonides (c.556–468 BC), from the Ionian island of Ceos off the coast of Attica, was one of the first Greek poets to earn his living by writing verse. He was also one of the most versatile, composing victory odes, hymns, drinking songs, elegies, dirges, epitaphs, epigrams – even a couple of tragedies. He went to Athens in 490 BC, where he excelled in dithyrambs (poems in honour of Dionysus), became a patriotic Pan-Hellenic spokesman during the Persian Wars, and enjoyed the friendship of the pre-eminent general and statesman Themistocles. In 476 BC, at the age of eighty, he went to the court of Hiero I of Syracuse in Sicily, where his nephew and fellow Top Niner, Bacchylides, joined him. Simonides was renowned for the pathos and mellifluousness of his verse. In his poem 38, Catullus speaks of a poetic composition 'sadder than the tears of Simonides'.

Simonides was also a brilliant, learned man who pulled no punches. In one of his poems, he calls Cleobulus of Lindus, one of the Seven Sages, a fool because he had claimed in an epitaph that the commemorative statue raised above a tomb would last as long as the sun, moon and sea (see Question 37). On a different occasion, he corrects another Sage, Pittacus of Mytilene, who had written that 'hard it is to be noble'. Simonides' view is more pessimistic. In certain circumstances, it's not only hard, it's impossible:

> Yes, every man is worthy if his luck is good,
> and bad if it goes badly.

Simonides will thus not throw his life away striving for perfection, since it is

> beyond their power who win
> the bread of life from spacious earth.

The fragment ends with a reminder that not even the gods can fight against Necessity (*ananke*). In another poem, he tells us that Virtue (*arete*) is rare. It abides with the gods but with few humans, unless 'soul-torturing sweat has been wrung out of their vitals'.

The most famous epitaph in history has traditionally been ascribed to Simonides. The speakers are the three hundred Spartan (Lakedaimonian) dead who fell with their leader Leonidas trying to hold the pass at Thermopylae against the invading Persians in 480 BC. Since their entire force was wiped out, they ask the reader of the inscription to take a message home for them:

> Tell them in Lakedaimon, passer-by,
> That here obedient to their word we lie.

Pindar of Thebes (522 or 518–432 or 438 BC) was likened by Horace to a surging force of nature (*Odes* 4.2) and was referred to by the Roman rhetorician Quintilian (first century AD) as 'by far the greatest of the nine lyric poets'. Of the nine, his are the largest number of complete works to survive – forty-four epinician odes written for the victors in the four major athletic games in four almost-intact books. Numerous

222

fragments of his lost thirteen books of verse in many other forms are also extant.

Pindar's odes celebrated the winners in the Olympian Games in honour of Zeus, the Pythian (Apollo), the Nemean (Zeus) and Isthmian (Poseidon) (see Question 23). He must have received handsome emoluments for these works, sometimes commissioned by rulers such as Hiero I or the King of Cyrene, at other times paid for by successful athletes themselves, their families or their native towns. These elaborate poems were then performed for the victor and his family – or as a public spectacle at court – by a choir of men or boys who danced while singing the words.

The odes, written in a Dorian literary dialect, are notoriously difficult because of their allusiveness, abrupt transitions, long syntactic units, complex stanzaic forms, severely condensed metaphors, and oblique approach to mythic and other subject-matter. Pindar usually begins his poems with the statement of his theme – the athlete and town he is to celebrate – sometimes preceded by a gnomic utterance such as 'Best of all things is water' ('*Ariston men hudor*'). He then connects the athlete, or his family, town, or site of victory, to a luminous moment in Greek myth, thus establishing a continuity between the present and the times when the gods manifested themselves to humans.

A deeply conservative and religious poet, Pindar seems to have had little interest in athletics, using the victories in the games as occasions for his profound probings into how the divine intersects with the human and how humans can attain something akin to godhead in their struggle to achieve. This formal, humourless, sublime and aristocratic poet, who firmly believed in his vatic, or sacred, function, sometimes found it difficult to end his poems after weaving their great mythic cores. Thus, his returns to the athlete and the present after his lofty imaginative flights occasionally result in crash – or at least emergency – landings. Alexander the Great spared Pindar's house when he destroyed Thebes in 335 BC, a century after the poet's death, probably because Pindar had lived at the court of Macedon's Alexander I and written an encomium of him.

Pindar's elaborate stanzas, built around strophe, antistrophe and epode, led to the development of the Pindaric (irregular) ode, as opposed to the Horatian (regular) ode. English poets who wrote Pindaric odes include Abraham Cowley, John Dryden, Alexander Pope, Thomas Gray, William Collins and William Wordsworth. Jonathan Swift's attempt to write one elicited his kinsman Dryden's remark, 'Cousin Swift, you will never be a poet.'

If we didn't have so many of Pindar's dazzling poems ('lords of the lyre', he called them), **Bacchylides** of Ceos (born c. 524 BC) might seem much more impressive than he does. He was Simonides' nephew and Pindar's rival in composing epinician odes for victors in the great athletic contests. Though polished and accomplished, he is conventional and predictable when compared with Pindar, the great 'Eagle of Thebes' who soars above all other Greek lyric poets. Bacchylides was rescued from oblivion when fifteen of his epinicians and six of his dithyrambs were dug out of the sands and rubbish heaps of Oxyrhynchus in Upper Egypt a little more than a century ago.

He composed a victory ode for the same occasion Pindar had written about in his first Olympian ode, the victory of the rider and horse of Hiero I in 476 BC. Bacchylides' 'Ode 5' is pleasant and skilful but full of fawning that is directed not only at Hiero but also at his racehorse Pherenikos. (Love me, love my horse.) The mythic section tells how Heracles descends into Hades to bring back Cerberus as one of his twelve labours (see Question 58); how he meets Meleager there, who bursts into tears and tells him about the Calydonian Boar Hunt and his cruel death at the hands of his own mother; how Heracles weeps for the only time in his life but is so impressed with Meleager's beauty that he asks him if he has an unmarried sister at home; and how Meleager suggests that Heracles check out Deianira. Then the wow finish: further praise of the Sicilian tyrant and his horse, a quotation from Hesiod, and a closing image of Zeus as 'the great gardener' preserving 'excellent plants' such as Hiero. Bacchylides is long on wind and short on metaphor – a 'talkative Siren', as that prolific Greek poet, Anonymous, called him.

The corresponding poem of Pindar, 'Olympian 1', with its powerful opening images of water being the best of all things, gold gleaming in the night, and the glorious sun, adopts a somewhat less sycophantic posture. The central myth refutes the common tale about the founder of the Olympian Games, the hero Pelops — that, as a boy, he was killed, cooked, and served up to the gods by his own father Tantalus; that Demeter unwittingly ate part of the shoulder before the horrific deed was discovered; that he thus received an ivory shoulder after being miraculously brought to life again — and substitutes for it a tale of the boy's being abducted by Poseidon to serve as his lover. In contrast to Bacchylides' treatment of myths as literary counters to be manipulated, Pindar's ode breathes an archaic fire by whose light the powerful old stories seem to unfold before our eyes as we read. Even while refuting the original myth of Pelops — with its child-murder, dismemberment and cannibalism — as a blasphemous affront to the gods, providing instead a tale of divine love (albeit pederastic), Pindar imparts a numinous glow to his poem that envelops both the beauty and the horror within a sacramental vision.

None the less, or perhaps for these very reasons, when Hiero finally won the prestigious chariot race at Olympia in 468 BC, he asked Bacchylides rather than Pindar to compose the victory ode. That poem turned out to be a bland and banal composition flimsily built around the story of Croesus' last-minute rescue from the pyre (see Question 37). At its close, Bacchylides refers to himself as 'the nightingale of Ceos', but Pindar, in his 'Pythian 2', likens his rival to an ape that is pretty only in the eyes of children.

Alcman (fl. c.630 BC), the earliest of the nine, was a composer of choral odes at Sparta who may have been born in easy-living Lydia in Asia Minor. His longest extant fragment is a parthenion, or ode to be recited by a chorus of maidens. The most interesting parts are the elaborate compliments paid by the chorus to its two leaders, who are extravagantly praised for their beauty and compared to dazzling racehorses. Some scholars have speculated on the lesbic nature of all this, but the fragment remains intriguingly opaque.

Stesichorus (c.632–c.552 BC) was probably born in southern Italy but lived at Himera in Sicily. His real name was said to be Teisias; Stesichorus, which means 'arranger of chorales', seems to have been a title or family name. His choral lyrics apparently influenced Pindar. Although we have only very short fragments of his work, we know that his lyrics retold many of the old myths from the Homeric and other heroic cycles, such as the Labours of Heracles.

The most famous story associated with him tells how he lost his sight for a poem in which he badmouthed Helen of Troy, who was often regarded as a goddess, for being the cause of the Trojan War. After retracting his words in his 'Palinode', he supposedly regained his sight. The palinode claimed that Helen never really abandoned her husband Menelaus and escaped to Troy with dashing Prince Paris, thus setting in motion the horrors of the war. No, it was only a very lifelike phantom of Helen created by Hera that did all this, while the real Helen was conveyed by Hermes to King Proteus of Egypt. Euripides later based his play *Helen* on this bizarre version of the events.

Ibycus (fl. mid-sixth century BC) was born in Rhegium in southern Italy, across the Straits of Messina from Sicily, where he went to live. Like Stesichorus, by whom he was influenced, Ibycus was a choral poet and also wrote erotic verse about young boys. One of his poems begins with the springtime ripening of grapes and 'Cydonian apples' (quinces, originally from Cydonia in Crete). In this season, he knows no respite from love as Aphrodite rocks his heart with storm blasts out of Thrace.

Ibycus supposedly died during a mugging in a grove while on his way to a musical competition. As the poet lay dying, his murderers heard him say to a flock of cranes overhead, 'May you avenge my death!' Later, while the literati thugs were enjoying a play, cranes flew over the amphitheatre during a scene in which the Furies were exacting their typically ghoulish vengeance (see Question 10). 'Look!' cried one of the muggers, pointing to the sky. 'The cranes of Ibycus!' At that, their heinous deed was discovered, and the murderers were duly executed. 'The cranes of Ibycus' came to mean 'unsuspected witnesses of a crime'.

Corinna of Tanagra, who was said to have instructed Pindar, was sometimes added to the list of the greatest Greek lyric poets. She is remembered today, if at all, not for her few remaining fragments, but for a criticism of Pindar's over-use of myth in one of his poems: 'One should sow by the handful, not by the sackful.' The quip became a proverb, but the story of her tutoring Pindar is probably apocryphal, since the language of Corinna's verse seems to place her in the third rather than the fifth century BC.

What are the 9 planets, and how long do they take to orbit the sun?

Mercury: 87.969 days	Saturn: 29.458 years
Venus: 224.701 days	Uranus: 84.013 years
Earth: 365.256 days	Neptune: 164.794 years
Mars: 686.98 days	Pluto: 248.54 years
Jupiter: 11.862 years	

THE WORD PLANET, from the Greek *planetes*, or wanderer, refers to any heavenly body, other than a comet, meteor or asteroid, that orbits a star like our sun. The wanderers in our solar system are hardly lonely, though, since (except for solitary Mercury and Venus) they are accompanied in their travels by at least seventy-eight moons. The whole system is probably the 4.5-billion-year-old progeny of a condensed nebula – a lot of dust and gas. And we now have evidence suggesting that other stars may also have planets.

The sun's gravitational pull on **Mercury** is so strong that the planet actually has 'tides' of solid rock on its surface. During its eighty-eight-day revolution about the sun, Mercury rotates on its axis every 58.7 days, making its year about 1.5 of its days long. The Romans, aware of its speedy transit, named it after the messenger of the gods. Like Pluto, Mercury is smaller than several moons in our solar system. Because the negligible atmosphere can't trap heat, day–night temperature differences are huge – it's about 750°F during the day and -300°F at night. Mercury's orbital motion differs a bit from that predicted by Sir Isaac Newton – an aberration that Albert Einstein used to prove the theory of relativity.

Venus is named after the Roman goddess of love and beauty. To ancient astronomers, the planet was known as the evening star (Hesperus or Vesper) and the morning star (Phosphorus or Lucifer). The romance ends there. Venus' clouds are composed of sulphuric acid. The greenhouse atmosphere is 96 per cent carbon dioxide and produces daytime temperatures of close to 900 °F. The atmospheric pressure on the surface is more than ninety times that at sea level on Earth. This combination of heat and pressure obliterated twelve 1960s-era Soviet satellites within an hour of landing. Each day on Venus (243 Earth days) is longer than one of its years (225 Earth days), and the sun rises in the west and sets in the east.

Bypassing **Earth** in our journey outward from the sun, we arrive at **Mars**, the Red Planet, named after the Roman war god. Mars has two tiny moons (probably former asteroids), Phobos (Greek, 'fear') and Deimos ('terror'), which are 13 and 7.5 miles across, respectively. The 1997 Pathfinder mission confirmed that the surface of Mars consists primarily of oxidised materials. The polar caps grow in winter and recede by summer. The thin atmosphere contains scant water, and morning clouds are typical. Rocks collected by Pathfinder and its rover suggest that flooding waters once ravaged at least parts of Mars.

Life on Mars has long been an Earthling preoccupation. American astronomer Percival Lowell, on seeing the surface canali first described by Italian astronomer Giovanni Schiaparelli, concluded that Martians had built canals to rival Venice's. Orson Welles panicked some Americans in 1938 by convincing them, during a radio performance of H. G. Wells's The War of the Worlds, that Martians had invaded. Laugh, but Mars is also the source of a tiny rock – ALH 84001 – that fell to Earth thousands of years ago and has raised speculations anew about the possibility of life on the Red Planet – not canal builders, but microscopic organisms. Maybe.

Named after the ruler of the Roman gods, **Jupiter** is an enormous gaseous planet. Although more than a thousand Earths could fit inside it, its mean density is only 24 per cent that of our planet. Scientists believe that Jupiter may be a kind of time capsule, closely reflecting the chemical composition of the nebula from which our solar system developed. It's gusty on Jupiter, with frequent cyclones and winds of up to four hundred miles per hour in various layers of the atmosphere.

The Red Spot is a fifteen-thousand-mile-wide everlasting storm. Four of Jupiter's sixteen known moons were discovered in 1610 by Galileo, who named them the 'Medicean Stars' after the Medici Grand Duke of Tuscany and his brothers. The moons were later renamed after four of Jupiter's lovers – Io, Europa, Ganymede and Callisto.

Saturn, the second-largest planet, named after the Roman god of agriculture, is best known for its rings (actually a hundred thousand ringlets), which were discovered by Galileo. He thought they were attached to the planet, however, and called them *ansae* (handles). The rings, labelled E, G, F, A, B, C and D as you approach the planet, are composed almost entirely of grains and boulders of ice with some muddy and rocky celestial detritus in the mix. The planetary probe *Voyager* showed that the Cassini division – the space between rings A and B discovered by Italian–French astronomer Giovanni Cassini in 1675 – actually contains five faint rings. Saturn has a dumpy look because it rotates so fast – a day lasting only ten hours, thirty-nine minutes – that its poles have become flattened. Like Jupiter, Saturn is still contracting after its formation from the primordial nebula. Less dense even than Jupiter, Saturn would float in water. The *Cassini* spacecraft, on a joint mission of NASA and the European and Italian space agencies, entered Saturn's orbit on 30 June 2004 for an extended close look at the planet, its ring system, and seven of its thirty-three known moons.

No one knows what knocked over **Uranus**. Its poles are where its equator should be and vice versa. When he discovered it in 1781, English astronomer William Herschel thought he'd found a comet and named it 'Georgium Sidus' ('Star of George', in honour of King George III). Then it was called Herschel for a while until a German astronomer, Johann Elert Bode, named it after the Greek god of the sky. Uranus has at least eleven rings and some partial rings, or arcs. The first of these weren't discovered until 1977, when *Voyager* investigated. *Voyager* also discovered ten of Uranus' seventeen moons, most of which are named after female characters in Shakespeare, such as Titania, Miranda, Rosalind, Portia, Juliet, Desdemona, Ophelia and Cordelia.

Voyager also first spotted six of the eight moons of **Neptune**. French astronomer and mathematician Urbain-Jean-Joseph Le Verrier predicted the planet's existence in 1846, based on irregularities in Uranus' orbit, and his hunch was confirmed within 1° almost immediately by German astronomer Johann Gottfried Galle. Neptune's Great Dark Spot is about as large as the Earth, and winds near it gust up to 1,200 mph. Named after the Roman sea god, Neptune has four rings, and the largest moon, Triton (also a sea god), may provide the fifth: it's being drawn slowly closer to the planet because of intense gravity and will fracture millions of years from now.

Percival Lowell predicted the existence of **Pluto** in 1905 because of disturbances in Uranus' orbit. It was sighted in 1930 after a meticulous visual search of the heavens by Clyde W. Tombaugh, a twenty-four-year-old self-taught American astronomer and telescope maker. During about 8 per cent of its orbital time (twenty years of its 248.5-year orbit), eccentric Pluto dips inside Neptune's orbit. Some consider frigid Pluto (named after the god of the underworld) and its sole, slightly smaller moon, Charon (another underworld deity), to be the largest bodies in the Kuiper belt, a group of small icy objects at the very edge of the solar system. Pluto and Charon are linked gravitationally so that the same hemispheres always face one another – like two touch-dancers whose gazes never waver.

In March 2004, a group of American astronomers announced the discovery of the largest object in the solar system since Tombaugh spotted Pluto. They named their new find Sedna after the Inuit goddess who lives at the bottom of the Arctic Ocean, and with good reason: Sedna, currently eight billion miles from the sun, has a surface temperature of about −400°F. Even more astounding, its elongated solar orbit, which requires 10,500 years for one revolution, will eventually carry it eighty-four billion miles away – about twenty-one times further from the sun than Pluto.

The diameter of Sedna is estimated to be only eight hundred to 1,100 miles. (By comparison, Pluto's diameter is about 1,400 miles, and Earth's is about eight thousand miles.) Is Sedna the tenth planet?

Astronomers don't agree because they haven't yet reached consensus on what a planet is. Some say that because of its diminutive size, even Pluto wouldn't be considered a planet if it were discovered today. Others object that size can't be the sole criterion for differentiating planets from other members of the solar system.

This argument won't be resolved soon, but most astronomers seem to agree that Sedna is part of the Oort cloud, a band of icy space material, including comets, that extends halfway to the nearest star. The biggest surprise is that the inner edge of the Oort cloud, which includes Sedna, is closer to the sun than previously thought. Furthermore, everyone involved in this debate expects that more objects like Sedna, perhaps even larger ones, will be found in the inner Oort cloud.

What are the 9 Circles of Dante's Inferno?

1. Limbo: the Virtuous Heathens
2. The Lustful
3. The Gluttons
4. The Avaricious and the Prodigal
5. The Wrathful and the Sullen
6. The Heretics
7. The Violent
8. The Fraudulent
9. The Treacherous

TO SPEAK OF THE 'NINE CIRCLES' of the *Inferno* (the first part of Dante's epic poem, *The Divine Comedy*) is a bit misleading, since the author crammed about four times that number of different kinds of sins and sinners into his Hell, which is shaped like a vast inverted hollow cone beneath the surface of the ground, with its vertex at the centre of the earth. But where did Dante get his main groupings from? In Canto 11 of the *Inferno*, the shade of the Roman poet Virgil, who guides Dante through Hell, explains its moral structure by referring to Aristotle's *Nicomachean Ethics*. In that work Dante had found a threefold division of wrongful behaviour that prompted his three major divisions of Hell into regions where the sins of incontinence, violence and fraud are punished (see Question 9).

Before visiting the First Circle, we have to mention 'Circle Zero', the eternal home of souls who remained neutral in life – the fence sitters, the lukewarm, who were neither good nor bad, but looked out only for themselves. Dante, the fierce political partisan and exile, heaps scorn on these pathetic cover-your-backside types who aren't even worthy enough to get into Hell proper. Instead, they suffer their paltry punishments outside the boundaries of Hell in a kind of antechamber or vestibule.

Circle 1, or Limbo, is the habitation of all the unbaptised who either lived virtuous lives or died too young to sin. Since baptism was viewed as a prerequisite for salvation, these Virtuous Heathens cannot enter Heaven, but neither are they physically punished. Their only pain is their perpetual deprivation of the sight of God. In an exclusive neighbourhood of Limbo, Dante has collected his heroes and heroines of the ancient and medieval world: great Greek, Roman and even Muslim warriors, scholars, poets and philosophers, culminating in a procession of the five greatest poets of antiquity who, naturally, invite Dante to join their select club.

In **Circle 2**, we find the first major grouping of the incontinent, the Lustful, including the star-crossed lovers Paolo Malatesta and Francesca da Rimini, forever thrashed about through the black sky of Hell by a tempest that represents their own tumultuous passions. It's interesting that Dante considers lust the least blameworthy sin (the sins and punishments get worse the further down you go). Taken as a group, lust and most of the other incontinent sins of **Circles 2 to 5** – gluttony, avarice, wrath and sullenness (which was often viewed as a form of sloth) – seem to suggest that Dante may have started his poem with the intention of covering only the seven deadly sins (see Question 38). If so, he changed his mind (saving the deadly sins as the organising principle for his *Purgatorio* instead) and embarked on a much-expanded version of the *Inferno*.

The boundary between the upper Hell of incontinence and the lower Hell of violence and fraud is the wall of the City of Dis (a name for Pluto, god of the underworld). After a confrontation with demons guarding the city walls, Dante and Virgil enter the gates and survey the fiery torments of the Heretics in **Circle 6**, who, though in lower Hell, remain outside its threefold moral division. The two poets then move on to **Circle 7**, which punishes the Violent, who are subdivided into the violent against others, against self (suicides and spendthrifts), and against God (blasphemers like Capaneus), nature (sodomites) and human industry (usurers).

To get to **Circle 8**, Dante and his guide have to fly down on the back of a monster named Geryon. The circle of fraud, named Malebolge ('evil pouches'), is shaped like a huge sloping circular arena divided into ten broad concentric trenches. In these, about fifteen kinds of fraudulent sinners are punished: pimps and seducers, flatterers, simoniacs (buyers and sellers of Church offices – we meet a few popes here), soothsayers and magicians, crooked politicians, hypocrites, thieves, false counsellors (like Ulysses), sowers of scandal and schism, and falsifiers or phoneys (alchemists, impersonators, counterfeiters and liars).

Finally, to reach **Circle 9**, the abode of treachery, which is fraud compounded by a shattered bond of trust, Dante and Virgil need the services of the giant Antaeus, who picks them up and sets them down on the frozen lake forming the floor of Hell. This last circle comprises four zones: Caina (traitors to family), Antenora (political traitors), Ptolomea (betrayers of guests) and Judecca (traitors to benefactors). At the very centre of Hell, the poets see the enormous three-faced figure of Lucifer (Satan), who chomps on Julius Caesar's assassins, Brutus and Cassius, with his side mouths, and Judas, the betrayer of Christ, with his central mouth. Lucifer is himself punished as the worst of all creatures for his revolt against the Benefactor who had made him brightest and mightiest of the angels (see Question 48).

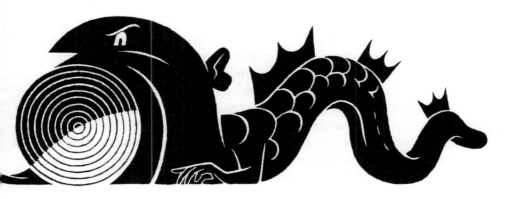

TEN

What are the 10 Commandments?

1. 'I am the Lord thy God, which have brought thee out of the land of Egypt, out of the house of bondage. Thou shalt have no other gods before me.'

2. 'Thou shalt not make unto thee any graven image, or any likeness of any thing that is in heaven above, or that is in the earth beneath, or that is in the water under the earth. Thou shalt not bow down thyself to them, nor serve them: for I the Lord thy God am a jealous God, visiting the iniquity of the fathers upon the children unto the third and fourth generation of them that hate me; and shewing mercy unto thousands of them that love me, and keep my commandments.'

3. 'Thou shalt not take the name of the Lord thy God in vain; for the Lord will not hold him guiltless that taketh his name in vain.'

4. 'Remember the sabbath day, to keep it holy. Six days shalt thou labour, and do all thy work. But the seventh day is the sabbath of the Lord thy God: in it thou shalt not do any work, thou, nor thy son, nor thy daughter, thy manservant, nor thy maidservant, nor thy cattle, nor thy stranger that is within thy gates. For in six days the Lord made heaven and earth, the sea, and all that in them is, and rested the seventh day: wherefore the Lord blessed the sabbath day, and hallowed it.'

5. 'Honour thy father and thy mother: that thy days may be long upon the land which the Lord thy God giveth thee.'
6. 'Thou shalt not kill.'
7. 'Thou shalt not commit adultery.'
8. 'Thou shalt not steal.'
9. 'Thou shalt not bear false witness against thy neighbour.'
10. 'Thou shalt not covet thy neighbour's house, thou shalt not covet thy neighbour's wife, nor his manservant, nor his maidservant, nor his ox, nor his ass, nor any thing that is thy neighbour's.'

(Exodus 20:2–17)

THE ISRAELITES COWERED at the foot of Sinai as Moses and Aaron ascended to meet Yahweh, who was obscured by a thick cloud of smoke, fire and lightning at the summit. Yahweh's voice could be heard over a din of thunder and trumpet blasts as he gave Moses his commandments, marking the establishment of the Mosaic Covenant between God and Israel.

The story of the Ten Commandments, also called the Decalogue (Greek, *deka logoi*, 'ten words'), occurs in two similar accounts, in Exodus 20 and Deuteronomy 5. In Deuteronomy, however, the scene takes place on Mount Horeb rather than Sinai, and Yahweh himself inscribes the covenant with his finger on stone tablets. In Exodus, Moses is the transcriber. It's also in the Deuteronomy account that we are told of 'the land of milk and honey' and are enjoined to 'stray neither to right nor to left' and to 'love the Lord, your God, with all your heart, and with all your soul, and with all your strength'. Both versions of the Ten Commandments were probably derived from a more ancient source that was less elaborate – more along the order of 'Thou shalt not kill'. Thus, the proposed 'date' of the Decalogue varies quite widely, from the sixteenth century BC to sometime after 750 BC.

The arrangement of the Ten Commandments differs in Judaism, Protestantism and Catholicism, partly because specific numbers are absent in both the Exodus and Deuteronomy texts. In the fifth century, St Augustine compounded the ambiguity by folding the second commandment into the first so that it read, 'I am the Lord thy God. Thou shalt not have strange gods before me; thou shalt not make to thyself any graven thing to adore it.' The third commandment then became the second, the fourth the third, and so on. To end up with the requisite ten, it became necessary to cleave the last commandment in two. Thus, the ninth became 'Thou shalt not covet thy neighbour's wife', and the tenth was reserved for all other situations in which endeavouring to keep up with the Joneses was deemed sinful. In the mid-sixteenth century, the Council of Trent adopted this arrangement – and also affirmed that the Ten Commandments applied to Christians, as they had to the Jews of the Old Testament.

The Roman Catholic and Lutheran churches still use Augustine's numbering system and justify it on the basis that the revised first commandment incorporates injunctions against false worship and the worship of false gods, which are clearly variations on the same heretical theme. This line of reasoning also facilitates the division of the original tenth commandment into two. Since the *acts* of adultery and theft are forbidden by two different commandments, it also made sense (at least in this schema) to separate the *desire* to commit these sins into two separate commandments. None the less, critics have suggested that Catholicism adhered to Augustine because burying the second commandment within the first de-emphasised it. This served to divert attention from the profusion of statues and religious images that – despite various iconoclastic rampages over the years – still enliven Catholic churches. Protestant denominations (other than Lutheranism), the Greek Orthodox Church and Judaism use the more conventional system of enumerating the commandments.

Whatever the arrangement, the Ten Commandments were, until recently, indelibly etched – one might almost say 'carved by the finger of God' – in the memory of most Jews, Catholics and Protestants. But when the host of a US late-night talk show took to the streets in the mid-1990s to ask people he met whether they could name any of the commandments, the only response of a shoulder-shrugging twenty-something was a diffident 'Free speech?'

What were the 10 plagues of Egypt?

1. The Nile and other waters of Egypt were turned to blood
2. Frogs
3. Lice (or maggots or mosquitoes or gnats)
4. Flies (or gadflies)
5. Death of livestock by pestilence
6. Boils
7. Hail
8. Locusts
9. Palpable darkness
10. Egyptian firstborn were slain

IN HIS PHILOSOPHICAL DICTIONARY, sceptical Voltaire claims that if Moses had really produced prodigies such as the plagues, he would have earned at least a passing mention in ancient Egyptian or Greek writings. None the less, for several thousand years, at the Seder meal inaugurating Passover, Jews all over the world have remembered the story of their ancestors' exodus from captivity in Egypt – and the ten plagues that afflicted the Egyptians before the Israelites were allowed to depart on their circuitous, forty-year trek back to a land 'flowing with milk and honey'.

The story of the plagues that led to the emancipation of the Jews is told in Exodus 7–12. With the aid of his brother, Aaron, the eighty-year-old Moses attempts to persuade Pharaoh to let the people go on a three-days' journey into the wilderness to perform sacrifices – a request that masks the ultimate goal of escape from an increasingly tyrannical 'house of bondage'. Why were ten plagues required to convince Pharaoh? God himself hardens Pharaoh's heart so that, after all the tribulations visited on them, 'the Egyptians may learn that I am the Lord' (Exodus 7:5).

At first, as proof of supernatural sanction, Aaron merely throws down his staff, which becomes a serpent, but Pharaoh's magicians match his feat. Although Aaron's serpent gobbles up all of theirs, Pharaoh is not impressed, so it's time for stronger medicine. When **the Nile and all the other waters of Egypt are turned to blood**, once again the crafty magicians are able to do as much. The Egyptians have to resort to digging for their drinking water, but Pharaoh sees no reason to change his mind. A week later, **a swarm of frogs** is made to emerge from the Nile and invade the Egyptians' houses, beds, ovens and kneading bowls. But the magicians cause even more frogs to swarm! Pharaoh promises to comply with Yahweh's resolutions but develops amnesia after Moses gets rid of the frogs. When **the lice** – or some other vexing insects – are formed of the dust of Egypt, the magicians are stymied and advise Pharaoh to relent.

But Pharaoh is still not convinced. He subjects himself and his people to successive plagues of **swarming flies**; **a pestilence that kills all the Egyptian livestock** (but spares the beasts of the Israelites); **an epidemic of boils** that torments man, animal and magician, caused by a handful of furnace soot that Moses flings into the air; **a fierce hailstorm** that destroys farmhands, trees, the flax and barley crop, and whatever livestock had survived the pestilence; and **a horde of locusts** that consumes the new shoots on the crops and infests the Egyptians' houses. The ninth plague is **palpable darkness lasting three days**, during which visibility is zero for the Egyptians (but not where the Israelites resided). Finally, on a grim midnight, **the Lord slays the firstborn of all the Egyptians**, from the firstborn of Pharaoh to those of the other Egyptians and even their animals. This devastating plague compels Pharaoh to let the people go. When he later pursues and tries to slaughter them, his armies meet with ignominious destruction at the Red Sea (or Sea of Reeds).

Most of the ten plagues have been interpreted as intensified forms of natural phenomena that did indeed plague Egypt. The changing of the water into blood, for example, has been associated with the periodic flow of red silt down the Nile from its headwaters. Locusts, described as winging in on the east wind, are sometimes swept over

Egypt by the hot sirocco from the Arabian Desert. The darkness so thick it can be felt has been linked with the khamsin, a hot southerly wind that blackens the skies of Egypt with dense sand and dust blown up from the Sahara.

An unknown editor has conflated three separate narrative strands in the account of the plagues in Exodus: that of J (the Yahwist, who calls God 'Yahweh'), E (the Elohist, who refers to God as 'Elohim') and P (the Priestly narrative). The J text is the main source for the plagues, mentioning six of them. In J, Moses speaks to Pharaoh directly and demands that the Israelites be allowed to depart. Pharaoh refuses, and Moses predicts the next plague. After each plague begins at the preannounced time, Pharaoh begs Moses to intervene with God to end it. Moses does so, but slippery Pharaoh fails to keep his end of the bargain. J claims the plagues do not affect the Israelites because they dwell in the province of Goshen, apart from the Egyptians.

The E strand of Exodus mentions four of the plagues, which are here caused by more directly miraculous intervention than in J, that is, by the actions of Moses, through whom God manifests his power. In E, the Israelites live together with the Egyptians and are spared the plague of darkness, but not of the water turning to blood, the hail or the locusts. In this text, the Israelites have time to despoil the Egyptians of gold and silver before they depart, whereas in J their hasty exodus – indeed, angry ejection by Pharaoh – is emphasised by their not having time to leaven their bread before baking it.

In P's text, four of the plagues become a kind of contest between the power of Aaron, acting for Moses, and Pharaoh's magicians, who reproduce some of them (the bloody Nile and the frogs) but can't quite manage the lice and are themselves covered with the boils.

The Seder (Hebrew, 'order') is a re-enactment of the meal on the night of the first Passover – in Hebrew, *pesach*, from a verb meaning 'to pass over, to spare'. The Aramaic form, *pascha*, gave rise to the Greek-derived English adjective 'paschal', which also gathered associations from the similar-sounding Greek verb *paschein*, 'to suffer'. Thus, when God struck down the firstborn of Egypt, he 'passed over' the houses of the Jews, whose doorposts and lintels had been sprinkled with the blood of the slaughtered paschal lamb.

The ritual text used at the Seder is the Haggadah, a story of the bondage in, and flight from, Egypt, recited by the head of the household. The text is interspersed with hymns, prayers, psalms and the youngest child's 'Four Questions'. As each of the ten plagues of Egypt is mentioned, a drop of wine is spilled from everyone's cup to avoid gloating over the misery of others, expressly forbidden in Proverbs 24:17: 'Rejoice not when your enemy falls, and when he stumbles, let not your heart exult.'

ELEVEN

Which were the 11 states of the Confederacy?

South Carolina	Texas
Mississippi	Virginia
Florida	Arkansas
Alabama	North Carolina
Georgia	Tennessee
Louisiana	

THE SEEDS OF THE CONFEDERACY were sown long before the bitter conflicts over states' rights and slavery tore through the United States in the mid-nineteenth century. They were present from the beginning, arising from geography, climate, culture, and major historical forces of the time such as the Industrial Revolution and the rise of the urban classes. The warm South's economy was agrarian and relied primarily on cotton. The less temperate Northern states rapidly became urbanised and industrialised as factories sprang up to manufacture goods ranging from hydraulic turbines to sewing machines, and their population swelled with the influx of European immigrants. What had seemed like a noble experiment – E pluribus unum – at the time the Union was formed gradually came to resemble two separate, and increasingly hostile, societies divided by the Mason–Dixon line.

Political tensions increased through the early decades of the nineteenth century as the country expanded westward and more states were admitted to the Union. North and South each wanted to maintain parity in the number of new slave and free states to avoid being out-voted in Congress. During those years inimitable orators and sectional leaders such as Daniel Webster of Massachusetts, Henry Clay of Kentucky and John C. Calhoun of South Carolina steered an increasingly acrimonious Congress and nation through a series of crises on tariffs, the extension of slavery, and nullification (on whether individual states had a constitutional right to nullify federal laws). The era was rife with attempts to keep a lid on the seething, conflicting demands of North and South, as evidenced by the very names of the Missouri Compromise (1820–1), the Compromise Tariff of 1833 and the Compromise of 1850 ('the Great Compromise'). Efforts at achieving a consensus grew steadily more futile until the boiling point was reached with the national elections of 1860.

The presidential election was a four-way contest between Democrats Stephen A. Douglas and John Breckinridge, Constitutional Union Party candidate John Bell and Republican Abraham Lincoln. State elections in Pennsylvania and Indiana held shortly before the national elections were swept by the Republicans – the first intimation of a Lincoln victory, which many Southerners believed would sound a death knell for their way of life. Before midnight of 6 November, Election Day, telegraphed returns confirmed that Lincoln had won.

Charleston, **South Carolina**, had been the epicentre of secession fever in the decades leading up to the Civil War. As soon as Lincoln's presidency was assured, the South Carolina legislature called for a secession convention, which assembled in December. At 1:15 p.m., on 20 December 1860, the 169 delegates voted unanimously to adopt the Ordinance of Secession: 'We, the people of the State of South Carolina, in Convention assembled, do declare and ordain . . . that the union now subsisting between South Carolina and other States under the name of "The United States of America" is hereby dissolved.'

South Carolina was soon followed by **Mississippi**, **Florida**, **Alabama**, **Georgia**, **Louisiana** and **Texas**. On 8 February 1861, the Confederate States of America was officially organised with a constitution similar to that of the United States, except that it ensured and protected 'the institution of Negro slavery', known among Southerners as 'our peculiar domestic institution'. Delegates from the seven states of the new polity convened in Montgomery, Alabama, and, on 11 March, unanimously ratified the new constitution and chose Mississippian Jefferson Davis as provisional President and Alexander Hamilton Stephens of Georgia as Vice President. Notice was posted that the federal forts and Navy installations in South Carolina and elsewhere were slated for takeover by the state authorities. President James Buchanan, a timid man at the end of a weak presidency, did not contest the secessions.

Lincoln was inaugurated on 4 March, and the two nations waited anxiously to see what response he would make to the gauntlet thrown down by the Southern states. Lincoln refused to order the evacuation of Union soldiers holed up in Fort Sumter, located in the harbour of Charleston, South Carolina. In the early morning of 12 April 1861, Confederate cannons began firing on the Union flag over the fort – an act of treason – and war between the Northern and Southern states began.

The seven original states of the Confederacy were joined by **Virginia** in April and **Arkansas**, **North Carolina** and **Tennessee** shortly thereafter. (Four other slave states remained in the Union – Delaware, Kentucky, Maryland and Missouri – and the state now known as West Virginia seceded from Virginia and later joined the Union in 1863.) In May 1861, the capital, originally Montgomery, Alabama, was moved to Richmond, Virginia. In November, when general elections were held, Jefferson Davis was reconfirmed as President. He was inaugurated in February 1862 for a six-year term.

During its brief existence the primary political activity of the Confederate government was planning for and prosecuting the war. The first Congress held four sessions and the second only two. Major concerns that plagued the fledgling Confederacy were shortages of goods, dependence on Europe, and escalating inflation that nearly destroyed what was left of the war-ravaged economy. Further disabled by internal controversies and dwindling morale, the Confederate Congress in Richmond adjourned for the last time on 18 March 1865.

The Confederate states considered the Civil War – the War between the States, as they called it – the second American Revolution, fought against the new tyranny of the North. But when the fashionable society of Charleston flocked to the waterfront to watch the thrilling display of the war's opening salvos on that April morning in 1861, few expected that during the next four years 620,000 American brothers, husbands, fathers and sons, both Northern and Southern, would die in the struggle between the Union and Dixie.

A footnote to the brief, bloody existence of the Confederate States of America was the Supreme Court decision in *Texas* v. *White* (1869) declaring secession to be an unconstitutional act.

TWELVE

What were the Latin names of the 12 months, and what did they mean?

Januarius: from Janus, the two-faced god of gates and door-ways

Februarius: from *februare*, 'to purify', because of a Roman purification feast celebrated on 15 February

Martius: named after Mars, the Roman god of agriculture and, later, war

Aprilis: from Latin *aperire* ('to open', as in the buds of spring), or perhaps 'the month of Venus', from the Etruscan *apru*, from Aphro, an abbreviated form of the Greek Aphrodite

Maius: from Maia, the Italic goddess of spring, daughter of Faunus and wife of Vulcan

Junius: from the name of the Roman Junius clan, related to the name of the goddess Juno, wife of Jupiter and protector of women

Julius: from Julius Caesar, born in this month

Augustus: from Augustus Caesar

September: from *septem*, 'seven' (when the Roman year began in March)

October: from *octo*, 'eight'

November: from *novem*, 'nine'

December: from *decem*, 'ten'

OUR WORD CALENDAR derives ultimately from Latin *kalendae*, the Romans' term for the day of the new moon and, thus, the first day of their months. The earliest Latin calendar, traditionally attributed to Romulus, had only ten months and 304 days – six months of thirty days and four of thirty-one. Apparently, the time after the end of December – what later became January and February – was not officially reckoned in this calendar because all agricultural activity came to a standstill with the gathering and storing of the last crops and did not resume until the first preparation of the ground for the next season's crop at the beginning of March.

A more rational calendar may have been introduced to the early Romans by their highly civilised overlords in Etruria in the person of Rome's fifth King, the Etruscan Tarquin the Elder (Tarquinius Priscus). It was also often attributed to their semi-legendary second King, the all-purpose savant and religious lawgiver Numa Pompilius.

In this lunar calendar of twelve months and 355 days, four months had thirty-one days, the new month of February had twenty-eight, and the other seven months, including the new month of January, had twenty-nine days. The Romans, who considered even numbers unlucky, thus made all their months contain an odd number of days, except February, which, since it featured a prominent festival in honour of the dead, was considered unlucky anyway. In an attempt to rectify the discrepancy between this lunar 355-day year and the solar year, an intercalary month called Mercedonius (or Mercedinus or Intercalaris) of twenty-two or twenty-three days was, perhaps later, inserted into the calendar between 23 and 24 February every two years.

The accumulating errors of this system, which was poorly worked out in practice, caused the year to be about three months out of sync with the true solar year by the time of Julius Caesar. During his dictatorship, Caesar decided to revamp the Roman calendar with the aid of the Alexandrian Greek astronomer Sosigenes. This involved making 46 BC a huge year of 445 days before embarking on a solar year, modelled on the Egyptian. The new Julian calendar of 365 days, which was instituted on 1 January 45 BC, lengthened the shorter months and inserted an intercalary day every four years between 23 and 24 February as a 'leap day', whereas we have tacked it to the end of the month as the 29th. This extra day was needed because the solar year is actually about six hours longer than 365 days.

This calendar served well enough until its small lack of precision – eleven minutes and forty seconds each year – added up over the centuries. In 1582 Pope Gregory XIII promulgated the adoption of a more accurate calendar (which Protestant England and its American colonies did not adopt until 1752, and which Russia only accepted in 1918). To square the calendar with the sun again, the Pope decreed that the day after 4 October 1582 should be 15 October. With some further fine-tuning – for example, century years such as 1600, 1700 and so forth, should not be leap years unless evenly divisible by four hundred – this Gregorian calendar is the one we use today.

January, affixed to the most ancient Roman calendar as the eleventh month, became the first month of the year only in 153 BC. A *janus* was an arch or gate in Latin, and *janua* was the word for 'door'. (Compare our word 'janitor'.) Janus, the god with two faces, guardian of all gates and doorways, was later considered to be the god of beginnings, especially of the year, but that was a derivative meaning.

His two-facedness probably arose from the fact that his role required him to be vigilant for thieves, evil spirits and other forms of intruders. He was subsequently thought to be looking back to the old year and forward to the new – as indicated by his image, which had an old face and a young one, in his small shrine in Rome's Forum, in front of the Senate House. The bronze doors of his shrine were thrown open in times of war and shut in peacetime. During the first seven hundred years of Rome's existence, they were closed on only three occasions. The feast of Janus that occurred during the ninth day of his month was presumably called Ianuar.

February was named after the appurtenances of a purification feast for the atonement for sins celebrated on 15 February. This Lupercalia was also a fertility festival that aimed to ensure abundant crops, flocks and human offspring during the following year. (Remember that February

249

started out as the last Roman month.) Priests called Lupercals ran semi-naked around the bounds of the old city with thongs cut from the hides of sacrificed goats, using them to strike women who stepped forward in the hope that the ritual would prevent sterility or guarantee a good delivery in those who were pregnant. The thongs were called februa, from februare, 'to purify'. In Shakespeare's Julius Caesar, based on Plutarch's Lives, the consul Mark Antony, a member of the Lupercal priesthood, is one of the runners. He makes use of the public spectacle to offer Caesar a royal diadem three times, which the dictator very reluctantly refuses.

March was named after Mars, originally a springtime deity of sprouting vegetation, who had several feasts during this month, including his birthday on 1 March. Later, Mars became god of war, probably since the war campaigns broken off during the cold winter months were resumed in March.

Because this month was named after Mars, Ovid (in his Fasti, an unfinished long poem, c. AD 8, on the Roman calendar) presumed that **April** was named after Venus – war followed by its opposite, love – especially since their counterparts in Greek mythology, Ares and Aphrodite, were lovers (see Question 57). In addition, Mars, as the father of the twins Romulus and Remus, was regarded as the progenitor of the Roman race. Venus, as the divine mother of the Trojan hero Aeneas (who came to Italy after the Trojan War and sired a line of proto-Roman kings), was also a remote ancestress of the Romans. In fact, some have thought the name of the month derives from an Etruscan form of the Greek goddess Aphrodite's name, but it may just come from Latin aperire, 'to open'.

May appears to have taken its name from Maia, an Italic goddess of growing plants. As daughter of Faunus – grandson of the great god Saturn – and wife of Vulcan, the god of volcanic fire, Maia was well connected.

In the Fasti, Ovid thought May took its name from maiores, the elders of the state, whereas he saw **June** as having been named after the young men, the juvenes. The latter month's name, however, is usually assumed to have been borrowed from the Etruscan form of Juno's name, Uni. Some say the name of the Junius clan, which no doubt traced its lineage back to the goddess, was the intermediate link between Juno and the month.

By order of Mark Antony immediately after Julius Caesar's assassination on 15 March 44 BC, the Senate decreed that Quintilis (the old-time 'fifth month'), the month of Caesar's birth, should assume his name, Julius, our **July**. Given Caesar's role in revising the calendar – not to speak of his titanic achievements in war, politics, statecraft, oratory, the writing of history, and amatory matters – this was only fair.

August, originally called Sextilis ('sixth month'), was renamed by a decree of the Senate in 27 BC to honour the first Roman Emperor, Augustus Caesar, who formally accepted the honour only in 8 BC. This, too, was only fair, since his great-uncle and adoptive father, Julius Caesar, had lent his name to July. The Senate urged Augustus to choose September, his birth month, but Augustus preferred Sextilis, during which he had first become consul, celebrated his three greatest triumphs, and secured the conquest of Egypt. The story goes that, because Sextilis had only thirty days, Augustus filched a day from February so that his month would be no less august in length than Uncle Julius'. Some scholars say Sextilis already had thirty-one days.

Although **September**, **October**, **November** and **December** haven't been the seventh, eighth, ninth and tenth months in more than 2,100 years, those numbers are still fossilised in their names. The highly conservative and traditional Romans would have liked that very much.

Who were the 12 Olympian gods and their Roman equivalents?

Zeus: Jupiter or Jove
Hera: Juno
Poseidon: Neptune
Hades: Pluto
Pallas Athene: Minerva
Apollo
Artemis: Diana

Aphrodite: Venus
Hermes: Mercury
Ares: Mars
Hephaestus: Vulcan or Mulciber
Hestia: Vesta (later
    supplanted by Dionysus
    or Bacchus)

THE STORY OF the twelve Olympian gods of Greece – epitomes of radiance, beauty and power – begins at a decidedly primitive state of affairs. At the beginning of time, Earth, or Gaea, who emerged out of Chaos, fell in love with the Sky (Uranus), who, according to very ancient sources, was her own son by the North Wind. She soon bore Uranus six sons, the Titans, who towered above the mountains, and six daughters, the Titanesses, who became their brothers' wives. Although Uranus took great pride in these twelve children (who included Hyperion the sun god, Phoebe the moon goddess, and Oceanus the god of the world-encircling waters), he was revolted by the other offspring Gaea bore him – the three one-eyed Cyclopes and three fifty-headed, hundred-armed sons, the Hecatoncheires. These six monsters Uranus hurled into Tartarus, in the very bowels of the underworld.

Deeply resentful, Gaea begged the Titans to kill their father and free their brothers from Tartarus, producing a flint sickle she had made for the occasion. Only Cronus, the youngest and strongest Titan, accepted the challenge, boldly seizing Uranus by the genitals and castrating him. When the blood spurting from the wound fell to earth, the Three Erinyes (Furies) sprang up from this sodden ground (see Question 10).

Cronus, who became Lord of the Universe after overthrowing his father, flung his monstrous brothers back into Tartarus almost immediately after he had freed them, enraging his mother. But Gaea knew of a prophecy that one of Cronus' children would be more powerful than his father. Cronus knew it, too, so he promptly gulped down each of the children whom his wife, the Titaness Rhea, bore him: Hestia, Demeter, Hera, Hades and Poseidon. Naturally, Rhea disapproved of her husband's eating habits. When expecting her sixth child, she conspired with Gaea to save it. Instead of an infant, she handed Cronus a rock wrapped in swaddling clothes, which he bolted down without suspecting any deceit.

The baby, named **Zeus**, was spirited away to a cave on a mountain in Crete to be raised in secret by the Goat-nymph Amalthea, who nursed him with her milk and fed him the nectar and ambrosia that flowed from her horns. His playmate was his foster brother, the Goat-Pan. Outside the cave, Gaea had placed the armed Curetes to clash their swords against their shields so that Cronus couldn't hear the baby cry. Zeus later expressed his gratitude to Amalthea by placing her in the heavens as the constellation Capricorn (see Question 61).

Zeus attained adulthood in one year and took the Titaness Metis as his first wife. Clever Metis counselled Zeus against trying to defeat his father Cronus on his own. Instead, she and Rhea (who still mourned her first five children) prepared an emetic, which they mixed with Cronus' favourite beverage. He vomited, and returned Hestia, Demeter, Hera, Hades, Poseidon and the rock-baby – all safe and sound – to their mother. Zeus later placed the rock at Delphi, where it was revered.

With his newly restored brothers and sisters, Zeus now warred on the Titans, who were led by mighty Atlas (for Cronus was getting on in years). Zeus killed Campe, the gaoleress of Tartarus, and set free his uncles, the Cyclopes and Hecatoncheires, once again. The Cyclopes, enlisted in the war against the Titans, forged a thunderbolt for Zeus, a trident for Poseidon, and a helmet of invisibility for Hades.

The three brothers made their move against Cronus, and Zeus struck him with his thunderbolt. At that, the Hecatoncheires barraged the rest of the Titans with rocks. When a loud cry from the Goat-Pan struck even further terror into the Titans (hence our word *panic*), they fled either to Tartarus or a British island, with the Hundred-Handed Ones as guards. No harm came to the Titanesses because their number included Zeus' mother, Rhea, and his wife Metis. Cronus fled to Italy, where, as the Latin god Saturn, he ushered in the Golden Age, when war was unknown, people fed on acorns and drank only water, and no one eviscerated the earth by planting crops or digging for gold, or furrowed the sea with ships in quest of riches.

After Zeus blasted the monster Typhon with his thunderbolt, he moved to form a government. When the three sons of Cronus drew lots, Poseidon became the god of the seas, Hades of the dead and the underworld, and Zeus of the heavens. The earth remained common to all three. Zeus now settled the gods in an otherworldly paradise on the summit of Mount Olympus in the northern Greek region of Thessaly.

The king of the newly established Olympian gods apparently ravished his own mother Rhea in the form of a serpent: he wasn't called 'Father Zeus' for nothing. He then went on to sire the Nine Muses on the Titaness Mnemosyne (see Question 47) and the Seasons and Three Fates (see Question 13) on Themis, the Titaness goddess of justice. Hermes was his son by Atlas' daughter Maia. Zeus and Leto, also a daughter of Titans, assumed the form of quails to make love when Apollo and Artemis were engendered.

Zeus was also the father of Dionysus. When Semele, daughter of King Cadmus of Thebes, was pregnant with this child, she was persuaded by jealous Hera to ask Zeus to reveal himself to her in his true glory. Zeus, who had given Semele any wish – and was angry because she refused him her bed unless he manifested his deity to her – complied with her foolish request. The mortal woman was immediately burned to a cinder amid thunder and lightning. None the less, Hermes managed to save the premature child by sewing him for an additional three months inside a curious incubator, Zeus' thigh. Dionysus, also known as Bacchus, went on to become the god of wine, intoxication, orgies and savage revelry, but also of Greek tragedy. He is sometimes called *digonos* ('twice-born').

The innumerable amours of Zeus resulted in the birth of heroes such as Perseus, Minos, Heracles (see Question 58), and many others, not to mention all the Olympian gods who weren't his siblings. The theme of Hera's jealousy over Zeus' philanderings is one of the great comic leitmotifs in Greek mythology, though things often ended tragically for his mortal lovers.

Zeus and his sister **Hera** were reunited after Cronus was banished. He seduced her by taking the form of a cuckoo; when she cuddled it, he resumed his own shape and took her by force. Gaea presented them with a tree filled with golden apples, and their wedding night lasted three hundred years. The children of Zeus and Hera included Ares, Hephaestus and Hebe, though some accounts claim Hephaestus was the offspring of Hera alone. Hebe, the goddess of youth, was cupbearer to the Olympians (until taking a revealing pratfall) and eventually married the deified Heracles.

Hera could renew her virginity each year by bathing in a sacred spring near her favourite city, Argos. Married women turned to this long-suffering First Lady of Olympus for help, and Eileithyia, goddess of childbirth, was sometimes thought to be her daughter (or Hera herself). Capricious and vengeful, Hera became a fierce enemy of Troy mainly because Trojan Paris had offended her pride by awarding the golden apple of beauty to Aphrodite.

The changeable face of the sea mirrors the changing moods of **Poseidon**, who became god of the sea at the same time as his brothers Zeus and Hades took possession of the sky and the underworld, respectively. Poseidon lives in a gold palace at the bottom of the sea, and storms abate at the approach of his chariot, which is drawn by brass-hoofed, golden-maned horses. With his trident he can stab the ground to create earthquakes, thus earning the epithet 'Earthshaker'. He invented horses, whose gallop is like the movement of waves.

Perhaps Poseidon's violent, mercurial nature made it difficult to find a mate. He decided on Amphitrite, a daughter of the old sea god, Nereus, but she fled. Only Delphinus ('dolphin') was able to persuade her to return to Poseidon. Thereafter, dolphins were Poseidon's favourite sea creatures, and in gratitude he placed Delphinus in the night sky as a constellation.

Once, after Poseidon and Apollo had offended Zeus, he compelled them to serve haughty Laomedon, King of Troy, for a year. Apollo tended Laomedon's flocks on Mount Ida, and Poseidon (with or without Apollo's help) built the walls of the city. But when the King refused to pay them for their work, Poseidon sent a sea monster to ravage Troy. Eventually, the King was forced to offer his daughter Hesione to the monster as a sacrifice to appease Poseidon, but she was rescued at the last minute by Heracles. Poseidon thus bore a grudge against Troy and enthusiastically helped the Greek army in the Trojan War.

After the war, the wily Greek hero Odysseus escaped death at the hands of the one-eyed Cyclops Polyphemus, a gigantic son of Poseidon, by blinding the monster with a red-hot stake. For this, the implacable god of the sea delayed Odysseus' return to his homeland of Ithaca by ten years and drowned the rest of his men.

Poseidon's sexual appetite was nearly as impressive as that of his brother Zeus, but some genetic defect caused him to sire mainly horses, monsters, or blue-green sea gods like Triton. (The great hunter, handsome Orion, was an exception.) In the form of a stallion, Poseidon impregnated his sister Demeter, who was unsuccessfully disguised as a mare. The result was the sacred wild horse, Arion. The winged horse Pegasus was said to be his son by the Gorgon Medusa. This loose behaviour infuriated Amphitrite, who turned one of her rivals, Scylla, into a voracious six-headed creature with twelve feet. (Odysseus encounters her, too, across from the whirlpool Charybdis.)

Apparently not content with lordship over the sea, Poseidon vied with other gods for the possession of several cities. His most famous dispute was with Athene for Athens. He staked his claim by flinging his trident into the ground near the Acropolis; she planted her new invention there – an olive tree. The arbitration held on Mount Olympus decided in favour of Athene, after whom the city was named.

With his brothers Zeus and Poseidon, **Hades** ('the unseen one') formed a triad of chief Greek gods. Although grim Hades spent almost no time above ground, he was, strictly speaking, an Olympian. He was also called Pluto, 'the rich one', because all the earth's mineral treasures belonged to him. Since his underworld realm was always ready for new residents, he was sometimes known as 'the hospitable one'.

Like his brothers, Hades had a troubled marital history. He pursued his niece Kore, 'the maiden', who was the daughter of Zeus and Demeter, goddess of agriculture. Perhaps sensing that the girl would not willingly go off to live in such a dead town as the underworld, Hades kidnapped her in his black chariot. In retaliation, Demeter ruined the harvest, causing mass starvation. Zeus finally told Hades he had to relinquish his bride, now called Persephone ('she who brings destruction'). This would be possible, however, only if she had eaten no food in the underworld, but she had already snacked on four pomegranate seeds. In a compromise between her husband and her distraught mother, Persephone spent six (or four) months of each year with Hades and the rest of the time on earth with Demeter during the growing season.

The strange birth of **Pallas Athene** brings us back to Zeus' first wife, Metis. Despite her help in defeating Cronus, Zeus ate her when she announced her first pregnancy. Like his father, he feared progeny more powerful than himself. After his meal, however, he got a terrible headache, and either Hephaestus or the Titan Prometheus was summoned to help him on the banks of Lake Tritonis in Libya. When his emergency medical technician relieved the pressure in Zeus' head with a blow of an axe blade, out popped Athene, a full-grown female warrior in battle regalia.

Grey-eyed Athene became her father's favourite. He soon let her brandish his thunderbolt and aegis, the shield or breastplate made of the goatskin of Amalthea embossed with Medusa's petrific head, which never failed to strike terror into the knees and hearts of all opponents in battle. Yet Athene's childhood was clouded by a tragic accident. While engaging in war-play with a human girl, she accidentally killed her. In tribute, she took the girl's name, Pallas, as her own first name.

As a battle goddess, Athene was a tireless defender of home and state from enemies and was inevitably accompanied by Nike, the spirit of victory. She was a fanatical partisan of the Greeks in the Trojan War, suggested to Odysseus the stratagem of the wooden horse, and protected that ever-resourceful hero on his long, dangerous odyssey home from Troy, delighting in his roguish lies and tall tales. Athene was also the goddess of wisdom and of the wise city of Athens, which erected the spectacular Parthenon ('temple of the virgin') on its Acropolis. A hopeless prude, Athene looked askance on any attempts on her chastity, such as a very clumsy one that Hephaestus once made.

Athene also had a domestic side, priding herself on the skill of her weaving and other womanly handicrafts. Usually mild-mannered, she lost her temper when a young princess, Arachne, challenged her to a weaving contest. After the angry goddess destroyed the girl's work, Arachne hanged herself, but Athene changed her into that greatest of weavers, the spider.

Apollo was often called Phoebus ('bright' or 'pure'). The birth of Apollo and his twin, Artemis, involved considerable travel because Hera, jealous of Zeus' union with Leto, set the serpent Python to pursue her until she was finally able to deliver on the island of Delos after a nine-day labour. Artemis, born first, served as midwife for Apollo. Both were devoted to their mother Leto – so much so that they killed all twelve or fourteen sons and daughters of Niobe and King Amphion of Thebes when Niobe boasted that she had many more children than Leto. ('Quality, not quantity', as Aesop would say.)

His brother Hephaestus presented Apollo with a bow and arrows when he was four days old. His first task was to slay Python, which had fled to Mother Earth's oracle at Delphi on Mount Parnassus. Apollo killed the serpent within the sacred precincts, and when Zeus heard of this sacrilege he ordered his son to purify himself at Tempe and, as further penance, preside over the athletic contests instituted in honour of Python, the Pythian Games. Apollo ignored Zeus and was purified elsewhere. Returning to Delphi, he seized the oracle there for himself. Delphi became the most sacred shrine of prophecy in the ancient world, though Apollo's oracular priestess was still known as the Pythoness.

A splendid musician, as well as a prophet and healer, Apollo taught the Muses to sing, accompanying them on his lyre. His art sometimes turned bloody, as in the case of the flute-playing satyr Marsyas, who challenged him to a musical contest. When the Muses, who were sitting as judges, decided in favour of Apollo, the god flayed Marsyas alive. He also once beat Pan in a musical contest. When King Midas, who had overheard the competition, spoke out in favour of Pan, Apollo conferred on him the insignia of all tone-deaf music critics – a pair of ass's ears.

Although Apollo never married, he fathered quite a few children, including the rowdy Corybantes on the Muse Thalia (see Question 47), and Asclepius, who was the first physician. He loved the nymph Daphne, but while in pursuit of her, he saw her take root and metamorphose into a laurel tree. Ever afterwards, the laurel remained his emblem and the symbol of the divine verse he inspired. Apollo also fell in love with a beautiful boy, Hyacinthus, with whom the West Wind Zephyrus was also smitten (see Question 16). One day, while Apollo showed the young man how to throw a discus or quoit, jealous Zephyrus gusted and blew it towards Hyacinthus, splitting his skull open. Sentimental Apollo caused the hyacinth flower to bloom from the dead boy's blood.

Apollo's twin, **Artemis**, was also called Cynthia and Delia in reference to Mount Cynthus on her native island of Delos. According to the Alexandrian poet Callimachus, three-year-old Artemis asked her father Zeus for these things: eternal virginity, as many names as Apollo, a bow and arrows, the ability to light the world, a city of her own, all the world's mountains, sixty ocean nymphs as her maids of honour, twenty more nymphs to care for her hounds, and a stylish hunting outfit. Zeus granted everything.

Artemis was a devoted huntress, aided by ten hounds given her by Pan and a silver bow and arrows forged for her by the Cyclopes. She held a pine torch aloft as she drove her chariot, which was pulled by horned does. Artemis is also goddess of the moon, perhaps in answer to her wish to bring light to the world.

Contradictions abound in the characters of the Greek gods, not least because their attributes and associated myths are an amalgam of numerous minor and foreign deities and a palimpsest of literary or cultic traditions. Artemis is no exception.

She is a virgin but also a goddess of childbirth. She visits the earth with plagues and kills impertinent humans instantly but is also the protector of children and wildlife. Agamemnon was constrained to sacrifice his daughter Iphigenia to Artemis before the Greek fleet could sail for Troy, a penalty for killing one of her stags. When King Oeneus of Calydon forgot to make a ritual sacrifice to Artemis, she sent a boar to ravage his kingdom. When the unlucky hunter Actaeon caught a glimpse of Artemis in the nude as she bathed in a stream, she turned him into a stag and watched him get ripped apart by his own dogs.

Aphrodite ('foam-born'), the goddess of love and desire, was said to have arisen from the foam surrounding the genitals of Uranus when Cronus severed them and flung them into the sea. After her birth, Aphrodite rode a large seashell to Cythera, a small island off the Peloponnesian coast, but then moved on to Paphos on Cyprus, which became a great centre of her worship. Hence her names of Cytherea or the Cyprian. In other accounts, she was the daughter of Zeus and Dione, the Titaness goddess of oak trees, where lusty doves nested. Indeed, Aphrodite was always accompanied by doves and lecherous sparrows. The story of her sea birth may be associated with Mediterranean beliefs about the aphrodisiac powers of seafood.

After Zeus arranged Aphrodite's marriage to the lame blacksmith god Hephaestus, she continued to wear an enchanted girdle that caused men and gods to fall in love with whoever wore it – though she hardly had need of beauty aids. She bore three children, Phobos, Deimos and Harmonia, who were ostensibly Hephaestus' but actually the fruit of her liaison with the scoundrelly war god Ares.

Informed of his wife's affair, Hephaestus trapped the lovers in his own bed with an invisible, unbreakable web. After summoning the gods to witness Aphrodite's infidelity (the goddesses modestly declined), he asked for a divorce and the return of the gifts he had given Zeus in return for her hand. An amusing scene developed, with Hermes, Apollo and Poseidon making facetious remarks while practically drooling at the sight of the naked 'golden Aphrodite'. After being released, the goddess restored her virginity by bathing in the sea near Paphos.

Her renewed virginity didn't last long. She bore the male/female Hermaphroditus to Hermes and a pair of boys to Poseidon. She presented randy Dionysus with a son, Priapus, whom disapproving Hera endowed with a comically outsized phallus.

Not content to mismanage her own love life, Aphrodite wreaked havoc on that of others. When the wife of the first King of Cyprus claimed that the beauty of her daughter Smyrna exceeded Aphrodite's, the miffed goddess arranged for the girl to fall in love with her father, Cinyras, and to trick him into lying with her. The product of this unholy union was the irresistibly beautiful Adonis, who was born when Aphrodite turned Smyrna into a myrrh tree to help her escape her father's wrath. By Adonis, Aphrodite later had two children, but he himself was gored to death by a wild boar. By Butes, one of the Argonauts, she became the mother of Eryx, a future king of Sicily. By the mortal Anchises, she became the mother of the Trojan hero Aeneas, who sailed to Italy after the destruction of Troy and established a dynasty that ultimately led to Romulus and Remus and the founding of Rome.

The rascal **Hermes** was son of Zeus and Maia. He began to look out for his own interests – and his mother's – the day he was born in a cave on Mount Cyllene in Arcadia. While Maia recuperated, Hermes made his way to the pasture where Apollo kept his prized white cows. He stole fifty of them, tying leaves or bark on their hooves and his own feet, to muddle any tracks, and a broom to each one's tail to brush them away. Some say Hermes also made the beasts walk backward to confuse Apollo further while leading them to pasture near his mother's cave. Alerted by an oracle to the theft, its perpetrator and his whereabouts, Apollo entered the cave and, despite Maia's protests that he was only a newborn, took the cattle rustler to Mount Olympus for arbitration. On the way, Hermes explained that Apollo could have all the cows back except for the two he had sacrificed to the twelve Olympian gods. 'Who is the twelfth?' asked Apollo. '*I* am,' replied the cocksure Hermes (who had also just been the first to offer animals in sacrifice).

When Apollo heard Hermes play the lyre he had invented out of a tortoise shell strung with seven sheep-gut strings, he offered his cows for it. When he heard the infant play on the reed pipes he also had devised, Apollo traded his golden herding staff for them and made Hermes god of shepherds.

Zeus was impressed with his tiny son's abilities. After gently reprimanding him about lying and stealing, he made Hermes his herald with the responsibility to safeguard treaties, commerce and unimpeded travel. Apollo's golden staff (later entwined with two snakes, topped with wings and known as the caduceus) became an emblem of Hermes' role as messenger, and it subsequently was made an icon of the medical profession.

Thereafter, Hermes travelled with his staff, a winged helmet and winged sandals, and Zeus admitted him to the Olympian family – a place he had already arrogated to himself. Furthermore, he made sure that his dear mother Maia moved to Olympus with him. Hermes rarely told the whole truth, but he never again lied outright. His ability to think on his feet qualified him as the god of messengers, orators, travellers and thieves.

Exemplifying Juvenal's dictum of *mens sana in corpore sano* ('a sound mind in a sound body'), Hermes learned how to tell the future and invented astronomy, the musical scale, numbers, weights and measures, and the alphabet (though some say that Cadmus introduced it into Greece), as well as boxing and gymnastics. When someone died, kindly Hermes escorted the soul to the banks of the infernal River Styx, where it embarked on a skiff that Charon ferried across to the realm of Hades (see Question 26). A common epithet of Hermes is Argeiphontes ('slayer of Argus'), referring to the hundred-eyed servant of Hera ordered to keep strict watch on Zeus' paramour Io, disguised as a heifer, to make sure Zeus couldn't get at her. Working for his father, Hermes started playing the flute so soporifically that all of Argus' eyes gradually closed. At that, Hermes cut off his head, but Hera enshrined all those eyes in the tail of her favourite bird, the peacock.

The name *Hermes* may mean 'pillar'. The earliest images of the god appear to have been the long, square marble or wooden pillars called *hermae*, or herms, that consisted of the god's head at the top and a phallus at the midsection. These were often set up in squares and main roads or as milestones, sometimes with travel directions or other inscriptions.

Ares, a war god and son of Zeus and Hera, was universally hated, even by his parents. He hailed from Thrace, a barely Greek region in the north inhabited by brutish, belligerent primitives. In contrast to Athene, a goddess of 'just wars', Ares was a brawler and bully, always on the prowl for armed conflict and bloodshed for their own sake. Much of this turmoil was instigated by his sister and constant companion Eris ('discord'). Other members of his battlefield entourage were the war goddess Enyo and his sons by Aphrodite, Phobos ('fear') and Deimos ('terror'). Whenever Athene opposed him on the battlefield, she trounced and humiliated him, as on the ringing plains of windy Troy, where Ares sided with the Trojans.

Always eager for battle in Homer's *Iliad*, but less than stoical when wounded, Ares tended to flee to Olympus in search of pharmaceutical cures. His relationship with Aphrodite was complex, since she loathed all his deeds except those conducted between the sheets. Their children may have included Eros (Cupid), the mischievous god of love. Ares was also the progenitor of the Amazons, the tribe of fierce female warriors.

Hephaestus, the god of fire and metalwork, was the son of Zeus and Hera (or, in some versions, of Hera alone by parthenogenesis). Because he was ugly and born with weak, spindly legs, Hera, in an access of unmotherly rage, flung him from Mount Olympus. Fortunately, he landed in the ocean and was raised by the sea nymphs Thetis and Eurynome, who decided that because of his disabilities he might be suited to life as a smith.

In this vocation, he excelled. The jewellery he crafted attracted the attention of none other than Hera, who greatly admired the brooch he had fashioned for Thetis. On visiting his forge, Hera was so taken with his other work that she had his shop moved to Mount Olympus and greatly expanded. There, Hephaestus branched out into general contracting, building the upscale mansions of the gods. He also cast Zeus' shield and sceptre, and the armour and shield of Achilles in the *Iliad*; of Heracles in the Hesiod-like poem *The Shield of Herakles*; and, as Vulcan, of Aeneas in the *Aeneid*. After a shaky start, Hephaestus became Hera's favourite, and it was she who arranged his ruinous marriage to Aphrodite – a Greek version of Beauty and the Beast.

Hephaestus was not, however, a favourite of Zeus. When Zeus punished Hera for her cheekiness by suspending her by the wrists, with anvils hanging from her ankles, Hephaestus remonstrated with him. His reward was yet another forcible ejection from Olympus. As John Milton tells it in *Paradise Lost* (1.741−6), he was

> . . . thrown by angry Jove
> Sheer o'er the Crystal Battlements: from Morn
> To Noon he fell, from Noon to dewy Eve,
> A Summer's day; and with the setting Sun
> Dropt from the Zenith like a falling Star,
> On Lemnos th' Aegaean Isle . . .

Hephaestus landed hard, breaking both his legs. After that, he always wore gold leg braces. Perhaps because of his estrangement from two-timing Aphrodite, Hephaestus created a pair of golden, silver-tongued and intelligent mechanical women to serve as his helpers in the forge.

Hestia, goddess of the hearth, eldest child of Cronus and Rhea, and sister of Zeus, was a genuine virgin, unlike the retread varieties so common on Olympus. Priapus of the megaphallus once tried to rape her as she slept, but when the braying of an ass (itself an emblem of lust) awoke her in time, she drove Priapus away howling.

Hestia's symbol, the hearth, was revered as the focal point of a Greek family's food preparation, warmth, illumination and spirituality. Prayers were dedicated to her at the beginning and end of every meal. Hestia was regarded as uniformly protective, kind and charitable. To mistreat a suppliant or guest was an offence against her (and Zeus, too). As a goddess of domesticity, she also invented the art of house-building.

Her public shrines consisted of large hearths with perpetual fires. When locals went on the road, they often took coals from these fires with them. Solemn oaths were sworn in Hestia's name. Yet the virtuous but staid Hestia was gradually supplanted as one of the twelve Olympian gods in post-Homeric myth by **Dionysus**, the divine inspirer of ecstatic frenzies. In religion, the appeal to emotion often outweighs that of simple piety. In Rome, however, the cult and perpetual flame of Hestia's counterpart, Vesta, were tended by the city's most prestigious priestesses, the vestal virgins.

What were the 12 labours of Heracles?

1. Kill and flay the Nemean lion
2. Kill the Lernaean Hydra
3. Capture the Arcadian stag
4. Capture the Erymanthian boar
5. Cleanse the Augean stables
6. Kill the Stymphalian birds
7. Capture the Cretan bull
8. Capture the man-eating mares of Diomedes
9. Fetch the Amazon queen Hippolyte's girdle
10. Fetch the oxen of the three-bodied monster Geryon
11. Bring back the golden apples of the Hesperides
12. Bring the three-headed dog Cerberus up from the underworld

THE ANCIENT GREEKS blamed on feminine wiles all the daunting labours that Heracles (Latin, Hercules) had to perform. It was the goddess Hera who duped her husband Zeus into taking an oath that made him subordinate his soon-to-be-born son Heracles to Eurystheus, who was also waiting to be born.

Zeus had impregnated Heracles' mother-to-be, Alcmene of Thebes, while her husband Amphitryon was away at war, disguising himself as her homecoming spouse and causing the night they spent together to last the length of three. Hera, ever resentful of Zeus' philanderings, decided to exact revenge by frustrating his grand designs for Heracles.

Zeus had boasted to Hera that his son would rule the royal House of Perseus, the great Greek hero, now dead, who was his son by yet another mortal woman, Danaë. Hera tricked him into swearing that the first prince born of the House of Perseus before nightfall would be the Greek King of Kings. When Zeus readily consented – knowing Heracles' birth was imminent and that of any other contender months away – Hera hastened the birth of Eurystheus, grandson of Perseus, so that this seven-months child was born an hour before Heracles, great-grandson of Perseus, whose birth she delayed. Thus Eurystheus grew up to become King of Mycenae, the Greek High King – and Zeus' son Heracles didn't.

Of course, Zeus flew into a rage when he discovered Hera's deceit, but he couldn't renege on his promise. He did, however, exact a compromise by which, although Eurystheus would reign, Heracles would be made a god after he had successfully completed his twelve labours.

Heracles, whose name means 'glory of Hera', was born for adventure, beginning with his strangling two huge snakes Hera sent against him while he was still in his cradle. He became the strongest and greatest Greek hero, delighting in using his wild-olive club and his bow and arrows to deal swift death to fierce animals, monsters, ogres, villains, centaurs, bandits, would-be rapists, bullies and other offenders against human decency. He had a bad temper, though, and drank far too much wine for the good of those around him. Once, when his music teacher Linus reprimanded him for not knowing his lesson, Heracles killed him with a single blow of the master's own lyre. But he had a good heart (and great appetites), often repenting of the manslaughters, homicides and other indiscretions he committed while enraged or drunk.

One time he went much too far, murdering his wife Megara and their three sons. Although this was the result of a fit of insanity that his implacable foe Hera had visited on him, Heracles was determined to be purified of the heinous deed. When he consulted the oracle of Apollo at Delphi, the priestess advised him to present himself to his kinsman – that's right, King Eurystheus of Mycenae in the Peloponnese, just the kind of guy for dishing out penances – and serve him for twelve years, after which he would become an immortal god. This arrangement was in keeping with the terms of the Zeus–Hera pact.

The labours (*athloi*, related to our word *athletics*) were all tough, beginning with the first task Eurystheus imposed on Heracles – **to kill and flay the Nemean lion**, a huge beast with an impermeable pelt. Some traditions say the lion fell from the moon, whereas others claim Hera vomited it up. Nemea, north-west of Mycenae, was being depopulated by the monster. After Heracles failed to kill it with his arrows, sword and club, he trapped the animal in its cave and strangled it to death, losing a finger in the process. He started back for Mycenae, carrying the dead lion on his shoulders, but not before rededicating the Nemean Games to Zeus. These games, along with the Olympian, Pythian and Isthmian, were the most famous athletic contests of ancient Greece. On shakier authority, Heracles is also said to have founded the Olympian Games (see Question 23).

But how was he going to skin the Nemean lion? It occurred to him that the beast's own deadly claws might have the best chance of piercing its pelt. From that time, Heracles wore the lion's skin as armour and its head as a helmet. Also from that time, whenever Heracles returned with one of his monsters, dead or alive – like something the cat brings home – Eurystheus would cower underground in a brazen urn.

Eurystheus now despatched Heracles **to kill the Lernaean Hydra**. Lerna, on the east coast of the Peloponnese, south-west of Mycenae, was being devastated by the Hydra, a gigantic venomous water snake with nine serpent heads, of which the middle one was immortal. The Hydra lived near the bottomless Lernaean swamp. When Heracles encountered it, he tried to club its heads, but as soon as he smashed one off, two new ones sprouted up to take its place – hence the expression 'a hydra-headed problem'. Heracles' nephew and charioteer Iolaus now ran up and cauterised the root of each smashed head with a fiery brand. Once the flow of blood was thus stanched, the heads could not regenerate themselves. But the remaining immortal head Heracles cut off and buried under a massive rock. After eviscerating the monster, he dipped his arrows in its gall, which rendered the slightest wound from them lethal.

To capture the Arcadian stag (sometimes called the Ceryneian hind) was the next labour. The stag, sacred to Artemis, had brass hooves and golden horns and roamed wild in Arcadia, at the heart of the Peloponnese. Heracles hunted it for a full year before capturing it with a precisely aimed bowshot that pinned its forelegs together. The arrow passed between bone and sinew so that it drew no blood – remember, these arrows are poisoned. He then hoisted the beast on to his shoulders and carried it alive all the way back to Eurystheus.

The fourth labour was **to capture the Erymanthian boar**, a savage beast that ran amok on the slopes of Mount Erymanthus in Achaia, the district north of Arcadia. Killing it would have been far easier than capturing it. None the less, Heracles shouted so loud that he drove it out of its covert and into a snowbank, pounced on its back, and chained it up or trapped it in a net. But after carrying it alive on his shoulders to Eurystheus, he decided to treat himself to a cruise – the first ever – by joining Jason's Argonaut expedition.

Refreshed from his sea voyage, Heracles was now sent by a sniggering Eurystheus **to cleanse the Augean stables**, by no means the easiest of his labours, since King Augeas of Elis in the western Peloponnese hadn't had the job done in thirty years and had three thousand head of cattle. Besides, Heracles had to do it all in one day. No wonder an Augean task is a formidably difficult and, often, distasteful one. The hero accomplished it, without so much as coming near any dung, by diverting the rivers Alpheus and Peneus through the stables and blasting the filth away. Because of a misunderstanding about the terms of his service, however, Heracles later found it necessary to slay Augeas and all his sons.

Heracles was afterwards sent off **to kill the Stymphalian birds** – not cute little feathered friends, but crane-sized man-eaters with brass wings, claws and beaks. These birds, sacred to the war god Ares, flocked around a marsh in Stymphalus, north-west of Mycenae, often taking to the air and killing their human and animal prey by strafing them with their brazen feathers. They also posed an environmental hazard by discharging their poisonous excrement over cultivated fields. Heracles realised there were too many of them to kill with his arrows, so he made a terrifying noise with a rattle that Athene gave him. When the birds all flocked into the air, he shot as many as he could, while the rest escaped to the Isle of Ares in the Black Sea.

Heracles' seventh labour was **to capture the Cretan bull**, a fire-breathing monster that was making life tough on the island of Crete. No one is quite sure whether this bull was the one that had fathered the Minotaur on the wife of King Minos, naughty Queen Pasiphaë, or the bull that bore Zeus' love Europa on its back from Tyre to Crete. Be that as it may, Heracles sailed to Crete and took care of business. Eurystheus must have remained hidden in his urn for quite a while after the bull arrived, but he eventually ordered it to be set free as a gift to Hera. Some say it was later slain by 'the Athenian Heracles', Theseus, near Marathon.

Next came the order **to capture the man-eating mares of Diomedes**. These four mares of the son of Ares, King Diomedes of Thrace, in the wild north-east of the Greek world, were bound to their bronze mangers with chains and fed on the flesh of the King's unpleasantly surprised guests. Heracles arrived with some followers, untethered the mares and drove them towards the sea. When the King and his men pursued, Heracles flooded the plain by cutting a channel. The men turned and ran while Heracles clubbed Diomedes to death and fed him to his own mares. After finishing their meal, the horses were easier to handle, so Heracles yoked them to Diomedes' chariot and drove them all the way back to Mycenae, where Eurystheus set them free.

To fetch the Amazon queen Hippolyte's girdle was the ninth labour. This was originally the golden girdle of the war god Ares, and Eurystheus wanted it as a gift for his daughter Admete. The Amazons, descendants of the war god, lived near the Black Sea coast. The women, who were the warriors and rulers, broke their infant males' arms and legs to make them unfit for war or travel but still capable of housework. Amazonian women, the first soldiers to use cavalry in war, were fierce fighters who captured Troy and conquered an empire for themselves. But the Amazon queen Hippolyte took a liking to Heracles, who had arrived with a shipful of men, and offered him her girdle as a love gift. Hera had meanwhile spread the rumour that Heracles planned to abduct the Queen, so her followers attacked the Greek force. Heracles thereupon killed Hippolyte, took her girdle and slaughtered huge numbers of Amazonian warriors.

Geryon was King of Tartessus in Spain, at the limits of the known world. Heracles was now sent **to fetch the oxen of Geryon**, who was supposed to be the strongest man alive, and no wonder, since 'he' was really Siamese triplets joined at the waist – with wings, no less. His beautiful red cattle were kept on the island of Erytheia in the western ocean and guarded by a huge herdsman and his two-headed dog. When Heracles got to Tartessus, he set up the so-called Pillars of Heracles on either side of the straits of Gibraltar. (The Romans later thought that 'Ne plus ultra' – 'No further!' – had been posted on them.) After sailing to the island, Heracles quickly despatched the herdsman and dog and drove off the cattle. When the King heard the news, he confronted Heracles, but the thrifty hero jumped to Geryon's flank and shot an arrow clean through all three of him. Hera, who had come to the King's assistance, was shot by Heracles through the right breast and sent howling to Olympus. His journey back across Europe with the cattle was jam-packed with adventures in Gaul, Liguria, Italy (including the future site of Rome, after he had taken a wrong right-turn down into the peninsula), Sicily, etc. These 'side-labours' (called *parerga*) were sometimes more interesting than the main event.

Now Eurystheus started getting creative. A really difficult assignment was the eleventh labour, **to bring back the golden apples of the Hesperides**. The precious tree that grew such fruits had been the wedding gift of Gaea, Mother Earth, to Hera, who had planted it in a garden on the slopes of Mount Atlas in Africa (or in the country of the Hyperboreans). Hera asked the three daughters of Atlas, the Hesperides, to guard the tree, but when she realised they were pilfering the fruit themselves, she made the hundred-headed dragon Ladon coil around the tree and remain on the lookout. Now, Heracles had been warned by a reliable source not to pick the apples himself but to let the Titan Atlas do it. The only problem was that Atlas had been sentenced by the victorious Olympian gods to hold up the encircling globe of the heavens on his shoulders. This task Heracles decided to take over while Atlas (actually, his daughters, who were good at it) picked three golden apples. After killing Ladon with a bowshot, Heracles shouldered the skies. But when Atlas regained his freedom, he was reluctant to surrender it, saying he would take the apples to Eurystheus himself. Heracles now employed the ruse of asking the dim-witted giant to hold up the sky again, just for a second, while Heracles put a pad on his head. So long, Atlas. Catch you later.

On his way back with the golden apples, Heracles was confronted by Antaeus, King of Libya, a lion-eating giant who forced all strangers to wrestle with him to the death. As a son of Mother Earth, Antaeus increased in strength as long as his feet or any other part of him remained in contact with her. When Heracles threw him, Antaeus just got stronger, so he did the only thing he could – heaving the giant off the ground, he bear-hugged him to death.

Heracles also stopped off in Egypt, where he killed King Busiris, brother of Antaeus, who wanted to make a human sacrifice of the Greek hero. After that, Heracles unshackled Prometheus from a mountainside in the Caucasus and shot the vulture that ate the Titan's liver, which grew back each day for the bird's next repast. It's clear that the *parerga* are distinctly in danger of stealing the eleventh labour's thunder.

Last, but certainly not least: **to bring the three-headed dog Cerberus up from the underworld**. Once Heracles had made his way into the nether regions, descending near Taenarum in Laconia in the southern Peloponnese, he was able to intimidate Charon, the ferryman of the infernal River Styx, to convey him across that waterway into Tartarus (see Question 26). This is where Heracles freed his friend Theseus from confinement in a magical chair, to which he had been sentenced for trying to carry off Persephone, wife of Hades, king of the underworld. But when Heracles ripped the Athenian hero from his Super-Glue seat, Theseus left half his backside on it. That's why Athenian men allegedly have such trim buttocks.

When Heracles demanded Cerberus from Hades, the gloomy god replied that he could have him if he was able to subdue him without using his club or arrows. Heracles gripped the monstrous dog by the throat and squeezed hard, just beneath the spot where the three heads, with their manes of hissing serpents, branched off. Cerberus went limp and let Heracles drag him off to the upper world, with the foam that slavered from his mouths turning into the poisonous herb aconite (wolfsbane or monkshood). When they got to Mycenae, Eurystheus was offering a sacrifice and had the temerity to give Heracles a slave's portion of the flesh. By this time totally fed up with Eurystheus, and having paid his full measure of penance, Heracles killed three of his cruel overlord's sons. He then took Cerberus back down to the underworld.

The earliest appearance of the labours as a group of twelve was probably in the metope carvings of the temple of Zeus at Olympia (c.560 BC). But besides the labours, Heracles had so many other adventures that to relate them all would take a night as long as the one in which he was conceived. Here are some highlights. He served as a slave and henpecked lover (spinning wool while dressed in women's clothes) to Queen Omphale of Lydia in Asia Minor. He sacked the city of Troy. He helped the gods fight off the Giants on the fields of Phlegra. He wrestled with Death to bring back Alcestis, who had willingly died in place of her husband, King Admetus. A full life by any standards.

He died as he had lived. When his new wife, Deianira, was on the brink of being raped by Nessus the centaur, who was carrying her on his back across the River Evenus, Heracles unleashed one of his poisoned arrows at long range and pierced the brute through the heart. The dying centaur told Deianira that if she mixed his blood into the wool that she used to weave a garment for Heracles, she would never again have to worry about his unfaithfulness to her. Of course, the shirt Deianira wove for her husband, after he had taken a mistress, was poisoned with the gall of the Hydra (see labour 2) via the blood of vengeful Nessus.

Heracles roared in excruciating pain, tried to rip off the shirt but only succeeded in tearing off his own flesh, plunged into a stream, which only exacerbated the searing torment, and uprooted trees in his agony. This was in fulfilment of a prophecy stating that no living man could ever kill Heracles but that a dead foe would. Heracles now bade his son Hyllus build a lofty funeral pyre for him. As soon as it was kindled, and Heracles lay down on its summit, Zeus struck the pyre with a thunderbolt and consumed his beloved son's mortal part while bringing his soul up to Olympus in a four-horse chariot. Hera now received him as a son and gave him her daughter Hebe, goddess of youth, in marriage.

It's said that after he sired Heracles, Zeus refrained from sex with mortal women because he could never hope to beget another such hero – and we'd have to agree. His first mortal love had been Niobe. Alcmene, the mother of Heracles, was sixteenth in descent from Niobe, so Zeus didn't exactly restrain himself unduly, with so many generations of beautiful women from which to choose his lovers.

Who were the 12 Apostles?

Peter	Thomas
Andrew	Simon the Zealot
James the Greater	Jude (or Thaddeus)
John	James the Less
Matthew	Judas Iscariot (replaced by
Philip	Matthias)
Bartholomew (or Nathanael)	

IN GREEK AN APOSTOLOS IS 'A PERSON SENT'. Christ sent the Twelve Apostles he had chosen on several missions of preaching and teaching and also enjoined them to spread the Gospel after he had ascended into Heaven. The selection of Twelve Apostles was an allusion to the twelve tribes of Israel, and the Apostles themselves appreciated the importance of maintaining a cadre of twelve when they replaced the traitorous suicide Judas Iscariot with Matthias. Except for Matthew the tax collector — and apparently Judas — they were all men who worked with their hands.

Peter, James the Greater and John constituted an inner circle within the Twelve. They were with Christ during his Transfiguration on Mount Tabor, at his raising from the dead of Jairus' daughter, and during the Agony in the Garden of Gethsemane.

Simon bar Jonah (son of John) was renamed Peter, the Greek name (Petros) that corresponds to the Aramaic Kepha, 'rock'. Simon Peter and his brother Andrew were fishermen and business partners of the brothers James and John in the coastal town of Capernaum on the Sea of Galilee. According to the Gospel of John, Christ identified Peter as 'the rock' at their first meeting, and, from the start, Peter — a bluff, gruff, impulsive man — emerged as the natural leader of the Twelve. He was the first Apostle to affirm the divinity of Christ and to witness the Resurrection. Christ says to him, 'You are Petros and on this petra [rock] I will build my Church' (Matthew 16:18). The papacy assumes its authority from this punning Petrine verse, which is emblazoned in huge gold capitals, in both Greek and Latin, in the interior of St Peter's Basilica in Rome. Other Christian denominations, however, do not interpret this verse as instituting a successive high priesthood.

Peter is a central figure in some of the more memorable stories in the Gospels. When he sees Christ walking on the surface of a lake towards his boat, he says, 'Lord, if it is you, command me to come to you on the water.' At Christ's bidding, Peter steps out of the boat and walks on the water towards his master. Suddenly realising what he is doing, and noticing the lashing of the winds and waves, he becomes frightened, begins to sink, and cries out, 'Lord, save me!' Christ stretches his hand out to him but says, 'O you of little faith, why did you doubt?' (Matthew 14:22–33).

The Gospel of John identifies Peter as the disciple who draws his sword and strikes off the ear of the high priest's servant Malchus during Christ's arrest in the Garden of Gethsemane (John 18:10). Yet, by dawn, Peter has three times denied even knowing Christ. This was precisely what he vowed never to do when Christ predicted his renunciation only hours earlier at the Last Supper.

After the Resurrection, Peter was the acknowledged leader of the Christians in Jerusalem for about fifteen years. According to tradition, he was martyred in Rome, where he had reportedly served as its first bishop, during the persecutions of Nero in 64 or 67. Legend says he asked to be crucified upside down because he felt unworthy to die in the same manner as Christ. Despite extensive excavations, the remains of Peter, said to rest in the catacombs of San Sebastiano on the Appian Way or beneath the high altar of St Peter's Basilica, have never been identified.

Peter's brother **Andrew** (Greek, 'manly') was referred to as *protokletos*, 'the first called', in Byzantine tradition, since he is the first Apostle named in John 1:40. According to fourth-century writings, Andrew was crucified on an X-shaped cross, or Andrew's cross. His supposed remains were removed from Patrai, Greece, to Constantinople in 357.

More than a millennium later, his skull was sent to Rome to function as a prop for whipping up enthusiasm for one final Crusade against the Turks. The concocter of this abortive scheme, Pope Pius II (reigned 1458–64), displayed the sacred skull before a crowd of the faithful from the steps of St Peter's. In 1964, Pope Paul VI was gracious enough to return Andrew's head to Patrai. Andrew is the patron saint of Scotland (whose flag bears the X-cross) and Russia.

Boanerges, or 'sons of thunder' (Grecianised Hebrew), is what Christ called the sons of Zebedee, **James** and **John**, apparently for asking him whether they should call down fire from Heaven on a Samaritan town for not having received him (Mark 3:17; Luke 9:51–6). At one point, the brothers make the presumptuous request (denied) to sit on either side of Christ's heavenly throne (Mark 10:35–40). The fourth Gospel was long credited to John, who is called John the Evangelist (see Question 21) or John the Divine. Tradition also ascribed to him three New Testament epistles and the book of Revelation (see Question 18). In depictions of the Last Supper, John is usually represented as the youngest Apostle, beardless, and with his head resting on Christ's shoulder as 'the disciple that Jesus loved'. He was the only Apostle not martyred and supposedly died at a very advanced age at Ephesus.

His brother James, in contrast, is the only Apostle whose martyrdom is described in the New Testament. To appease the Pharisaic Jews in their contention with Christian Jews, King Herod Agrippa I of Judaea (AD 41–4) had James killed 'by the sword' (Acts 12:1–2). (Peter was arrested at about the same time, but an angel appeared in his prison cell and freed him from his chains.) Since medieval times, a legend has maintained that after James was beheaded in Jerusalem, his body was miraculously transported to north-western Spain, where he had supposedly conducted a mission. Even today, pilgrims travel as much as a thousand miles by foot to the cathedral of Santiago ('St James') de Compostela, where his remains allegedly rest.

Matthew, in some passages referred to as Levi, was a tax collector, an occupation greatly scorned by the Jews. Christ, who was passing by as Matthew sat at his work table, said, 'Follow me' (Matthew 9:9). The tax

277

collector did, and shortly afterwards Christ dined at Matthew's house, much to the surprise of the Pharisees. Christ told them that he had come to save sinners, not the righteous. Matthew was reputed to be the author of the first Gospel. After Christ's Resurrection, Matthew is reported to have travelled to Ethiopia and Persia, although his remains are claimed by Salerno, Italy.

Philip, like Simon Peter and Andrew, came from Bethsaida, and, like Andrew, had been a follower of John the Baptist. It was Philip to whom Christ, surrounded by a teeming crowd at the Sea of Galilee, addressed the question, 'Where can we buy enough food for them to eat?' When Philip suggested that even two hundred days' wages would be insufficient, Christ multiplied the few available loaves and fishes. Little else is known of Philip, and various works attributed to him were probably written in the third or fourth century. He may have been crucified.

Bartholomew (Hebrew, 'son of Tolmai'), mentioned in the Gospels of Matthew, Mark and Luke, and a resident of Cana in Galilee, was probably the same person called Nathanael in the Gospel of John. Bartholomew is a family name, and Nathanael may have been his given name. When his friend Philip told him about Jesus, Nathanael asked, 'Can anything good come from Nazareth?' Philip brought him to Christ, who said upon seeing him, 'Here is a true Israelite. There is no duplicity in him' (John 1:46–7). Perhaps the best-travelled of the Apostles, Bartholomew is said to have preached in south-west Asia, India, Ethiopia, Persia and Turkey, and to have been skinned alive and beheaded in Armenia. His remains, like those of most of the Apostles, are said to be in Italy (in Rome). In Michelangelo's epic fresco in the Sistine Chapel, *The Last Judgement*, St Bartholomew holds in his hands his flayed skin – with the artist's doleful self-portrait for a face.

Thomas, called the Twin (Greek, *Didymos*) in John 21:2, is best known as 'Doubting Thomas'. He was not present with the other disciples at Christ's first few post-Resurrection appearances and, refusing to take these reports on faith, insisted on having more tangible proof. When at last Christ appeared to him and insisted that he put his fingers into the wounds of the crucifixion, Thomas exclaimed, 'My Lord and my God!' Christ responded, 'Blessed are those who have not yet seen and have believed' (John 20:29). Thomas subsequently preached in north-western Persia and is said to have been martyred in Madras, India. Several apocryphal writings, including a once-influential Gospel of Thomas, were attributed to him. His remains are of course reputed to be in Italy.

Simon and **Jude** may have been Zealots, members of a nationalistic Jewish group dedicated to violent overthrow of the Roman government in Judaea, though whether this movement existed in the time of Christ is controversial. Little is known of these two Apostles, and they apparently travelled and preached together in Persia after Christ's Ascension. Jude, mentioned in Luke 6 and Acts 1, was probably the same man as the Apostle called Thaddeus in Matthew 10 and Mark 3. Jude is the patron saint of desperate causes.

James the Less, identified as the son of Alphaeus in Matthew, Mark and Luke, was supposedly martyred in Persia. We don't know whether his remains made their way to Italy.

No one really knows what the second name of **Judas Iscariot** meant. Improbable is the derivation from Latin *sicarius*, 'assassin'; a more mundane but plausible explanation is 'the man from Kerioth' in the territory of Judah. Medieval legend endowed Judas with red hair, an evil portent in the Mediterranean world. He was probably the treasurer of the Apostles. His knack for monetary affairs destroyed his ministry, however, when he sold Christ to the chief priests and elders for thirty pieces of silver after the Last Supper, at which Christ predicted that one of the Twelve would betray him. That night, in the Garden of Gethsemane, Judas identified Christ for his captors with a kiss. Accounts of Judas' suicide vary (hanging or a gut-bursting fall), and Dante places him in the very deepest pit of his *Inferno* (see Question 52).

Two men were nominated to replace Judas: Joseph Barsabbas, who was also known as Justus, and Matthias (Acts 1:23–6). The Apostles prayed and drew lots, deciding on **Matthias**, who is said to have evangelised parts of Turkey. He, too, was martyred and, yes, his remains ended up in Rome.

Who were the 12 knights of the Round Table?

Lancelot	Lamorack
Galahad	Torre
Bors	Kay
Perceval	Gareth
Gawain	Bedivere
Tristan	Mordred

NO STORY OF BRITISH ORIGIN has inspired as much imaginative literature through the ages – in English, French, German and even medieval Hebrew – as that of King Arthur and his knights of the Round Table. Yet little is known of the historical Arthur, and the Round Table knights (with one possible exception) are purely fictional characters.

Ancient Latin documents in the British Museum relate that at the battle of Badon (AD 490 or 518), a military leader named Arthur 'carried the cross of Our Lord Jesus Christ on his shoulders for three days and three nights, and the Britons were victorious'. Scholars believe Arthur may have led the successful defence of south-west Britain, and its Romanised Celtic Britons, against advancing Saxon invaders from the Continent. He may have been an accomplished horseman trained in Roman cavalry techniques, and this may explain his success against the undisciplined hordes of Teutonic barbarians. The victory at Mount Badon was so decisive that it halted the Saxon advance for a half-century. But not a shred of evidence suggests that Arthur was a king, held court in Camelot or presided over a Round Table.

Large-scale embellishment of Arthur's story began, about six centuries after he lived, in the *History of the Kings of Britain* (c. 1136), written in Latin by the chronicler Geoffrey of Monmouth. In the interim, the tale was embroidered by the Welsh, who rallied to fight the Saxons and embraced the Arthurian legend, and by the Britons, some of whom migrated in the sixth and seventh centuries to what is today Brittany in France to escape the Saxons.

Over the ages, Arthur's reputation as a military commander who defended the Christian Britons from the Saxon invaders was inflated into that of Arthur, King of Britain, who conquered much of Europe and whose heroic reign incorporated magic, chivalry, British nationalism, Christian mysticism, courtly love and boundless romance.

In addition to his association with the Round Table and Camelot (sometimes identified with Caerleon, Monmouthshire, in south Wales), this Arthur of pure legend was said to be the son of the British King Uther Pendragon ('chief dragon'), who begot him on Igraine after the sorcerer Merlin changed the King's form into that of the lady's husband, the Duke of Tintagel in Cornwall. Merlin, son of the devil and a nun, became the boy's mentor. In some versions, Arthur extracted the magical sword Excalibur from a rock, thereby confirming his claim to the British throne at the age of fifteen; in others, he received it from the Lady of the Lake.

The first surviving mention of the Round Table occurs in the *Roman de Brut* (1155), a fanciful verse history of the Britons written by the Anglo-Norman poet Wace, probably on commission from Henry II of England. Wace tells how Arthur used a round banquet table so that none of his barons could claim precedence over the others — a notion that may have been borrowed from Celtic tradition.

Later writers elaborated the Round Table into the central organising symbol of Arthurian literature and the medieval chivalric code. To win a place at this table was the most any storybook knight could hope for, and the code of Christian knighthood it exemplified had a profound impact on the princely houses of Europe in the Middle Ages, in which the legend of Arthur was widely known. Fixed to the wall of a thirteenth-century hall in Winchester is a table eighteen feet in diameter reputed to be the Round Table itself. Like the hall, however, it dates from about seven centuries after Arthur supposedly lived.

The motif of the Round Table was powerfully energised when it merged with that of the quest for the Holy Grail (medieval Latin, *cratella*, 'bowl'), the silver cup or platter Christ was said to have used at the Last Supper. Because only the purest knight could approach the Grail, the quest for this ineffably sacred vessel became the ultimate trial of Arthur's Round Table paladins.

The notion of a table vessel imbued with magical powers to produce whatever food one desired stemmed from Celtic legend, but the hollow vessel was also an ancient fertility symbol. In French poet Chrétien de Troyes's unfinished Arthurian romance, *Perceval, ou le conte du Graal* (c. 1175), the Grail is a mystical hollow platter, now usually interpreted as a female sex symbol, which appears in connection with a phallic bleeding lance or spear (identified with the one used to wound Christ on the cross).

The first unequivocal association of the Grail cup with the one Christ used at the Last Supper occurs in Robert de Boron's French poem *Joseph d'Arimathie, ou le Roman de l'estoire dou Graal* (c. 1202). According to this story, Joseph of Arimathea, mentioned in the Gospels, constructed a table to commemorate the Last Supper, leaving one place empty, the Siege Perilous ('perilous seat'), to mark the betrayal of Judas. By this time, the French *Sangreal* ('Holy Grail') had been thoroughly confused with *Sang Real*, the 'royal blood' of Christ, some of which Joseph of Arimathea was supposed to have preserved in the Grail and brought to Wales.

Not only did Arthur come into possession of Joseph's table, but only the Round Table knight destined to succeed in the Grail quest could occupy the Siege Perilous. Other legends say Merlin constructed the Round Table for Uther Pendragon and that Arthur received it as part of his wife Guinevere's dowry from her father, King Leodegrance, who had received it from Arthur's father.

But who were the twelve knights of the Round Table? No easy answer suggests itself because, in the countless versions of the stories about Arthur, many dozens of knights are assigned a place at his table. Depending on the source, the Round Table seated anywhere from twelve (in remembrance of Christ's Apostles) to 150. The most comprehensive listing appears in Sir Thomas Malory's *Le Morte d'Arthur* (1470), edited and printed by the first English printer William Caxton in 1485, an epic recounting of nearly all the Arthurian tales. In this first book of magnificent English prose, well over a hundred Round Table knights are named. Although the twelve discussed here are among the most significant, they are by no means canonical.

Foremost is **Lancelot**, the greatest and most tragic of the Round Table knights. He first appears as an Arthurian knight in the twelfth-century poetic romances of Chrétien de Troyes, who narrates the story of his adulterous affair with Guinevere, King Arthur's Queen. He was the son of King Ban of Benwick (in Brittany) but was raised by the enchantress Vivien, the Lady of the Lake, who introduced him to Arthur's court (hence his name Lancelot du Lac). Although most writers considered Lancelot the apotheosis of chivalry, torn between his love for Guinevere and his loyalty to Arthur, he never succeeds in the Grail quest because of his adultery. Moreover, his illicit relationship ultimately causes the death of Arthur and the destruction of the brotherhood of the Round Table. In the end, Guinevere becomes a nun, and Lancelot dies a hermit.

Success in the mystical quest is reserved for Lancelot's son, **Galahad**, 'the Grail Knight'. Galahad first figures in thirteenth-century French stories about the Grail as the son of Lancelot and Elaine, daughter of King Pelles. When Galahad appears at Arthur's court, a mysterious old man declares him the only one pure enough to sit in the Siege Perilous. Arthur immediately knights the young man, who has inherited his father's fighting mettle but is chaste, pure-hearted and piously austere. Galahad sees the Grail in the castle of King Pelles, where he also has a vision of Christ.

At the time, Galahad is accompanied by Perceval and **Bors**, who also see the Grail. These three knights of the Round Table are the only ones to accomplish the great quest. Bors later becomes a hermit at Glastonbury and buries the other two Grail knights at the Spiritual Palace at Sarras.

But before the invention of Galahad, **Perceval** was the only knight to win the Grail, the best-known account being in Chrétien de Troyes's *Perceval*. Most versions agree that he was a simple but immensely strong

boy raised in the woods by his mother. He encounters knights riding –
'glittering hauberks, their bright helmets, lances and shields' – and
thinks they must be angels. When he learns they are Arthur's knights, he
leaves his protesting mother to reveal his strength and join the fellow-
ship of the Round Table, in due course transforming himself from
country bumpkin into Grail hero.

In the castle of the wounded Fisher King, Perceval sees the Grail
and is awed by the vessel's gold and precious stones, 'richer and more
varied than might be found in earth or sea; no gem could compare
with those in the Grail'. By remaining speechless before it, however,
he misses the opportunity to heal the Fisher King, who is, unbe-
knownst to Perceval, his uncle. The most celebrated version of Perceval's
story is *Parzival* (c. 1210), an epic poem by Wolfram von Eschenbach,
a masterpiece of medieval German literature. This poem inspired
Richard Wagner's final opera, the mystical *Parsifal* (1882) that Nietzsche
so heartily loathed.

Gawain failed in the Grail quest because of placing his trust in the
knightly code rather than in the spiritual realm. He is known as
Arthur's loyal nephew (or cousin). Scholars trace his literary heritage
back to Celtic mythology, in particular the solar god Gwalchmei, whose
strength, like Gawain's in some accounts, increased and decreased with
the daily waxing and waning of the sun.

Gawain is the hero of a Middle English poetic gem of unknown
authorship, *Sir Gawayne and the Grene Knight* (c. 1370). In this narrative
poem of superb craftsmanship, Gawain is an honourable and courteous
Christian knight who faces a terrifying supernatural challenge. He must
withstand the return axe-blow, in one year's time, of a brawny green
knight whom he has already beheaded – but to no avail. He must also
fend off an apparent seduction by the beautiful wife of his host, Sir
Bercilak. It all ends happily, though the young hero learns that his
former exalted opinion of his chivalric honour was a little overblown.

In the romances of Chrétien de Troyes, Gawain was a notch below
the likes of Lancelot and Galahad, with a tendency to womanise and
to fight for the sake of fighting. In Malory's *Le Morte d'Arthur*, Lancelot

unwittingly kills two of Gawain's brothers – Gareth and Gaheris – while rescuing Guinevere from being burned at the stake for her adultery. Gawain swears revenge and, with Arthur and his army, pursues Lancelot to France, where he is fatally wounded by that hero. He dies on his return to Britain.

The tragic love story of **Tristan** (or Tristram) and Iseult the Fair, grafted on to the Arthurian cycle in the early thirteenth century, parallels the adulterous tale of Lancelot and Guinevere, both involving treason to liege lords. Tristan's uncle, King Mark of Cornwall, is to marry Iseult, a young Irish princess. Tristan – irresistibly handsome, valiant, and a wonderful harpist and poet – fetches the bride-to-be, who falls in love with him. Aboard ship on the way to Cornwall, Tristan and Iseult unknowingly drink a love potion, and an overwhelming passion grips them, sweeping aside every other consideration. Iseult is married to Mark, but the two lovers continue their affair, are discovered, and die.

Gottfried von Strassburg's long German poem *Tristan* (c. 1210) inspired Wagner's opera *Tristan und Isolde* (1865), which extolled passionate love as the highest human value. Isolde sings the heart-wrenching 'Liebestod' ('love-death') in farewell to the dead Tristan in her arms, begging for death as a release just before falling lifeless over his body.

In Malory's account, **Lamorack** of Wales was the son of King Pellinore and the brother of Perceval and Torre. After Lancelot and Tristan he was the bravest Round Table knight. Because of a grudge, he revealed the adulterous relationship of Tristan and Iseult. He himself (like Arthur) was the adulterous lover of Queen Morgawse, who was beheaded by her son Gaheris after he caught them in bed. Another son, Gawain, sent Lamorack to his eternal reward for debauching his mother.

Torre, whom King Pellinore fathered on a milkmaid, was the first to be made a Round Table knight. The fact that he was knighted before Gawain caused consternation in Arthur's court because his father had killed Gawain's father, King Lot.

Arthur's royal seneschal, or steward, **Kay**, was raised with Arthur because Merlin had presented the royal infant to Kay's father, Sir Ector, and his mother. Kay became a churlish, sarcastic name-caller, a rude and boastful but lousy warrior in some accounts. Yet Arthur never set him straight, perhaps because of their early bond. His rough speech was said to have resulted from being raised by a crude wet-nurse, since Arthur had usurped Kay's place at his mother's breast.

Gareth of Orkney was the youngest son of King Lot and Queen Morgawse and the brother of Gawain. He agreed to serve as a scullion for a year under Kay, who dubbed him 'Beaumains' because of his big hands. Gareth was then knighted and became Lancelot's favourite. After rescuing Lady Lyonesse from Sir Ironsyde in the Castle Perilous, he married her. While Lancelot rescued Guinevere from a fiery death at the stake, he unwittingly killed Gareth, thus earning Gawain's enmity.

At Arthur's bidding, **Bedivere** (or Bedevere), called the Bold, flung Excalibur out over the water so that the Lady of the Lake could retrieve it, raising only her white-robed arm above the surface. One of the few to survive Arthur's last apocalyptic battle against Mordred, Bedivere was with the King on the occasion of his strange removal from the world.

Some sources say **Mordred** was Arthur's bastard son, and others his nephew. The confusion probably arises from Mordred's parentage: he is the product of Arthur's unwitting sexual escapade with his half-sister Morgawse (his aunt, according to Malory), and this would make Mordred both Arthur's son and nephew. In any event, he is the darkest figure in Arthurian lore, the embodiment of Arthur's sin, a kind of Freudian 'return of the repressed' who ends up destroying the King and the Round Table knights.

In Malory's account, Mordred reveals to Arthur the affair between Lancelot and Guinevere, forces a conflict between the two men, and then seizes the throne and tries to marry Guinevere while Arthur is fighting Lancelot in France. Arthur and his army rush back to England to face the usurper, but in the ensuing battles almost all the Round Table knights meet their death. In a final conflict on Salisbury Plain, amid countless dead, Arthur runs Mordred through with a spear, just as Mordred deals him a savage blow to the head. So massive was the wound Arthur inflicted on the traitor that the sunlight shone clear through

Mordred's body before he fell dead. The wounded Arthur was borne away on a barge by lovely ladies in mourning to the Isle of Avalon, presided over by the enchantress Queen Morgan le Fay, his half-sister.

Some evidence suggests Mordred, too, may have been a historical figure. The same documents in the British Museum that contain the first mention of Arthur and his victory at Badon also note that (in 511 or 539) there occurred 'the battle of Camlann, in which Arthur and Mordred perished'.

Fascination with Arthur and his Round Table knights survived well into the nineteenth and twentieth centuries. Here are only a few of many examples: William Morris's 'The Defence of Guenevere' (1858); Alfred, Lord Tennyson's series of long poems, Idylls of the King (1859–85), a sanitised, bowdlerised, Protestantised version of Malory's uninhibited tales; Mark Twain's irreverent A Connecticut Yankee in King Arthur's Court (1889); T. H. White's tetralogy, The Once and Future King (1939–58); Lerner and Loewe's musical Camelot (1960), which became a leitmotif of President John F. Kennedy's administration (1961–3); and Marion Zimmer Bradley's bestseller, The Mists of Avalon (1982).

Legend says King Arthur, magically healed of his wounds, lies asleep in a cave and will return to defend his beloved England when it is next invaded. This may help explain why the English royal family avoids naming any foreseeable heir to the throne 'Arthur' – Henry VIII's elder brother may have been the last – besides the sheer presumptuousness of the gesture. But although Malory assures us Arthur is really dead and buried in Glastonbury, he cannot resist reporting the prophetic epitaph: HIC IACET ARTHURUS, REX QUONDAM REXQUE FUTURUS – 'Here lies Arthur, the once and future King.'

What are the 12 signs of the zodiac and the sources of their names?

Aries: the Ram whose golden fleece was sought by Jason and the Argonauts

Taurus: the Bull whose shape Zeus assumed to carry off Europa

Gemini: the Twins, usually identified with Castor and Polydeuces

Cancer: the Crab that attacked Heracles while he fought with the Nemean Lion

Leo: the Nemean Lion killed by Heracles

Virgo: the Virgin goddess of justice, Astraea, daughter of Zeus

Libra: the Balance (scales of justice) of Astraea

Scorpio: a Scorpion sent to kill Orion the hunter

Sagittarius: the Archer, usually thought of as the bow-wielding centaur Chiron

Capricorn: the Goat that nurtured the infant Zeus

Aquarius: the Water-bearer Ganymede, cupbearer of the gods

Pisces: the two Fishes that helped Aphrodite and her son Eros escape from the monster Typhon

EARLY SKYWATCHERS IN BABYLONIA are thought to have first proposed that the movements of certain celestial bodies might be used to forecast earthly events. Similar astrological beliefs sprang up in ancient peoples as disparate as the Chinese and the Mayans, but they acquired particular sophistication in Ptolemaic Egypt (305–30 BC). There, in line with the Aristotelian principle that earth, the centre of the universe, was orbited at regular intervals by the sun, moon, planets and stars, Greek mathematicians mapped the sun's apparent yearly path.

They divided this celestial circle, the ecliptic, into twelve sections, each thirty degrees wide. Each division was considered to be the residence, or house, of a 'planet' known to the ancients (Mercury, Venus, Mars, Jupiter and Saturn, each assigned to two houses, and the sun and moon to one each). The twelve divisions were each also associated with a zodiacal sign, or constellation.

The constellations were simple groupings of bright stars that suggested to fertile ancient imaginations the outlines of various mythological characters. More important, the complex interplay of the celestial bodies in the macrocosm – their changing relative positions as they rose and set throughout the night and moved across the sky throughout the year – was used to predict events affecting the individual human being (the microcosm). For this purpose, a person was said to have been born under the sign of the constellation that the sun occupied at the time of his or her birth.

The precepts of astrology exerted a significant influence well beyond the Middle Ages, with many Renaissance courts featuring professional astrologers, until the rise of modern astronomy discredited the geocentric worldview and much of its associated baggage. Yet, despite the outdated claims of astrology, fascination with the mysterious zodiac persists, as attested by the horoscope columns of many daily newspapers (not to mention the short-lived 'Age of Aquarius' in the 1960s).

The constellations still have powerful tales to tell. The remainder of this essay deals with the Greek mythological sources of the zodiacal signs (whose names are all from Latin, though), rather than with their supposed astrological characteristics, which are best left to the noted philosophers and raconteurs of the 'So, what's your sign?' school.

The story of **Aries** ('the Ram') begins with Phrixus, a young Aeolian man in a bind. When he failed to respond to his aunt's sexual advances, she accused him of rape. This coincided with a plot against him by his evil stepmother, and he was doomed to be sacrificed to Zeus. As his weeping father was about to cut the young man's throat, Heracles, who was just passing by, wrenched the blade from him and told him that Zeus abhorred human sacrifice. At the same time, one of the gods sent a ram with a golden fleece to rescue Phrixus and his sister Helle.

The two climbed aboard, and the magical ram flew. Helle fell off, splashing down into the strait between Europe and Asia, thereafter called the Hellespont ('Helle's sea'). Phrixus and the ram touched down safely in Colchis on the Black Sea coast. There, the ram instructed Phrixus to sacrifice him to Zeus and take his fleece to the King, Aeëtes, who would become foster father to Phrixus. Many years later, Jason and the Argonauts sailed on the famous expedition to retrieve the golden fleece. To commemorate the ram's accomplishments and laudable self-effacement, Zeus placed him in the sky as a constellation.

The story of **Taurus** ('the Bull') concerns, as do innumerable Greek myths, the amorous adventures of Zeus. This time, he fell in love with gentle Europa. Since she spent her time with friends walking among the herds in Tyre, a city on the Phoenician coast, Zeus assumed the form of a white bull. Europa was enchanted with the lovely creature, who let her drape him with flowers. She trusted him so much that one day she climbed on his back and rode him along the beach. When he suddenly jumped in the water and started swimming out rapidly, she had no choice but to cling to his neck.

Zeus swam to the island of Crete, transformed himself into an eagle, and had his way with her. The result was three sons: Minos (later King of Crete), Rhadamanthys and Sarpedon. Zeus was so fond of Europa that he named Europe after her, since he had brought her from the shores of Asia to Crete. To remind himself of his dalliance, he made a constellation of his *alter-ego* bull.

Like many stories about the liaisons of Zeus, that of **Gemini** ('the Twins') is complicated. Zeus impregnated Leda, wife of King Tyndareus of Sparta, in the form of a swan. Since she had also slept with her husband that same night, she conceived his children, too. According to one version, Leda eventually laid two eggs. One contained her immortal children by Zeus: Polydeuces (or Pollux) and his sister Helen, whose face later launched a thousand ships against Troy (actually 1,186). The other egg held Leda's mortal children by Tyndareus: Castor and his sister Clytemnestra, who became the wife and murderer of Agamemnon (see Question 10).

Castor and Polydeuces, often called the Dioscuri ('sons of Zeus'), were a fine team with complementary skills. Castor the equestrian and Polydeuces the boxer were noted victors at the Olympian Games (see Question 23). They rescued their prepubescent sister Helen from the lecherous hands of middle-aged Theseus, sailed with the Argonauts, and participated in the Calydonian Boar Hunt. When mortal Castor was killed in a dispute over women with two other brothers, Polydeuces begged Zeus to let him remain with his beloved Castor. Zeus arranged matters so that the twins could spend alternate days together in the underworld and on Mount Olympus. He also set them in the heavens as the constellation Gemini because of their brotherly devotion. They are the patrons of sailors and are said to manifest themselves as the bright electrical discharges that sometimes appear on the masts and rigging of ships during storms — usually called St Elmo's fire.

The constellation of **Cancer** ('the Crab') is the handiwork of Hera. The area south-west of Mycenae called Lerna was held hostage by the Hydra, a water snake with nine heads, one of which was immortal. As one of his twelve labours, Heracles was despatched to kill it (see Question 58). With the help of his nephew, Iolaus, Heracles vanquished the hideous thing, but not before the Hydra's ally, Hera, sent a gigantic crab. When it pinched Heracles on the heel, he smashed its shell with his foot. In appreciation of the crab's valiant effort, Hera immortalised the pathetic creature in the heavens.

Another feat of Heracles is commemorated in the constellation **Leo** ('the Lion'). As the first of his twelve labours, Heracles was ordered to kill a supernatural lion that was ravaging the countryside on the outskirts of Nemea. Because the creature had an impenetrable hide, Heracles had to strangle it and use its own claws to skin it. Zeus, rightly proud of his awesome son, made a constellation of the vanquished lion.

The constellation **Virgo** represents Astraea, virgin goddess of justice, innocence and purity. She was the last deity to leave the earth during the Iron Age, which was characterised by crime, war and depravity. But this daughter of Zeus and Themis will come back when a brighter tomorrow dawns, as Virgil (70–19 BC) claimed in his Fourth Eclogue: 'Now the Virgin returns, too; now Saturn's Golden Age returns.' In the Middle Ages, this was seen as a prophecy of Christ's birth.

Libra ('the Balance'), usually thought of as the figure of a woman holding the scales of justice, or as the scales alone, is often said to refer to Astraea again. This is a boring constellation.

The legend of **Scorpio** is closely connected with that of the gigantic hunter Orion, son of the sea god Poseidon. Several stories associate the scorpion with Orion's death via the agency of Artemis, goddess of the hunt. In one, Orion boasted that he had killed every wild beast in Crete – unaware that Artemis was also a wildlife conservationist. In retaliation, she raised a giant scorpion from the earth, which stung Orion to death. The two of them, Orion and the scorpion, were set in heaven as a warning against hubris.

A variant of this story has Artemis discovering that Orion had been lustfully hunting her girlfriends, the seven Pleiades. She conjured up the scorpion to take him out, but then also set Orion and the Pleiades in heaven. In yet another version, Artemis' brother Apollo feared gorgeous Orion might prove irresistible to his virgin sister. He thus tricked her into shooting Orion dead with an arrow while the latter tried to elude the huge scorpion Apollo had set on him. On realising what she had done, Artemis summoned Apollo's son, the physician Asclepius, to restore Orion to life. Before he could do so, however, Zeus zapped Asclepius with a thunderbolt. Artemis then set Orion in the sky as a constellation, forever pursued by the Scorpion.

Sagittarius ('the Archer') is generally assumed to represent Chiron, chief of the centaurs, who taught Asclepius everything he knew about medicine. His demise is linked to the fourth labour of Heracles, who, during his pursuit of the Erymanthian boar, had a violent confrontation with several centaurs. As they fled to his friend, the archer Chiron, for safety, one of his poisoned arrows accidently struck Chiron in the knee.

Although in agony from his wound, immortal Chiron was denied the relief of death. Some stories claim Prometheus accepted the transfer of Chiron's perpetuity to himself so that the learned and kindly old centaur could die. Others say Zeus placed Chiron in the heavens as a constellation, thereby putting him out of his misery.

Capricorn ('the Goat', literally 'goat horn') is a stellar representation of the Goat-nymph Amalthea ('tender'), who breast-fed infant Zeus in Crete and gave him nutritional snacks of nectar and ambrosia from her horns while he was hidden from his father, the neonate-eating Cronus (see Question 57). She is associated with the cornucopia, or horn of plenty, either as presenting it to Zeus or receiving it from him. As a full-fledged Olympian, Zeus expressed his gratitude to his wet-nurse by placing her in the sky as the constellation Capricorn.

Aquarius ('the Water-bearer') represents Ganymede, the son of Tros, King of Troy. Ganymede, who became cupbearer to the gods on Olympus, was wildly attractive to women everywhere – and to Zeus, too. It's said that the first Olympian cupbearer, Hebe, Zeus' daughter by Hera, slipped and fell while serving at table and was disgraced when her dishevelled clothing revealed her finer assets. Zeus capitalised on this mishap to dismiss Hebe. He then assumed the shape of an eagle to abduct young Ganymede from a field near Troy, take him up to Olympus, and make him his catamite (a word derived from Ganymede's name). The cupbearer job was a cover, a stratagem since employed in executive mansions worldwide. Hermes later made a condolence visit to King Tros to assure him that his son was happy and well and that Zeus had conferred on him the gift of immortality – and a constellation in his likeness.

The story of **Pisces** ('the Fishes') involves Aphrodite, goddess of love, and her son Eros (Cupid). They were being pursued by Typhon (or Typhoeus), the most wicked and formidable monster that ever lived, who had a hundred serpent heads and quantities of serpent hands and feet to match. While trying to confiscate Mount Olympus from the gods, Typhon cornered Aphrodite and Eros on a beach, where they expected the worst. Just in the nick of time, two dolphins arrived, and the erotic pair stepped on their backs and were wafted to safety. The monster was ultimately blasted by Zeus' thunderbolt and buried in Tartarus beneath Sicily's Mount Etna, whose volcanic eruptions are Typhon's fiery eructations. The helpful dolphins – who were not fish at all – were rewarded with quite a misnomer of a constellation, Pisces.

INDEX